The Limits of Forgiveness

The Limits of Forgiveness

Case Studies in the Distortion of a Biblical Ideal

Maria Mayo

Fortress Press
Minneapolis

THE LIMITS OF FORGIVENESS

Case Studies in the Distortion of a Biblical Ideal

Cover design: Ivy Palmer Skrade

Cover image: Abstract art vintage background ©iStock / Thinkstock

Library of Congress Cataloging-in-Publication Data is available

Paperback ISBN: 978-1-4514-9308-5

eBook ISBN: 978-1-5064-0037-2

The paper used in this publication meets the minimum requirements of American National Standard for Information Sciences — Permanence of Paper for Printed Library Materials, ANSI Z329.48-1984.

Manufactured in the U.S.A.

This book was produced using PressBooks.com, and PDF rendering was done by PrinceXML.

For Walter Gabriel
et vitam venturi saeculi

The world in which pardon is all-powerful becomes inhuman.
—Emmanuel Lévinas

Contents

Foreword   xi

Acknowledgements   xvii

Abbreviations   xxi

1. Introduction: Mapping the Forgiveness Territory   1

2. Repentance and Repair, or "Ethical Bungee   47
    Jumping"? Forgiveness in the
    "Seventy-Times-Seven" Instructions and
    Victim-Offender Mediation

3. Community Cohesion, or a Hegemony of   97
    Harmony? Forgiveness in the Lord's Prayer and
    in Post-apartheid South Africa

4. Passionate Prayer, or Pastoral Pressure?   159
    Forgiveness in Luke 23:34a and the Pastoral Care
    of Victims of Domestic Violence

    Conclusion: The Future of Forgiveness   207

    Bibliography   215

    Index of Authors   247

    Index of Scripture References   251

Foreword

Our values, even our emotions, have a history: people in other times and places did not feel the same way we do. This is one of the reasons why I find my own profession as a classical scholar endlessly fascinating. On close inspection, a Greek or Latin word that is normally translated as "anger" or "pity" turns out not quite to fit my preconceptions of these ideas, and I start wondering what the ancients might have meant. When Aristotle says, for example, that we cannot be angry at people we fear, I ask myself: What does he mean by "anger"—or, more properly, by the Greek word that we, perhaps too casually, translate that way.

I had the same rather disorienting experience when I began investigating the ancient Greek and Roman notion of forgiveness. I thought I knew the meaning of the terms in question, but when I found Aristotle insisting that forgiveness is only for involuntary acts, something seemed amiss: if I have hurt someone unintentionally, I may try to excuse my action and explain how it came about, but surely we forgive people for deliberate offenses, not for those for which we are not personally responsible. Aristotle's word must, I thought, mean something else—"pardon" or "exoneration," for example, which applies precisely to involuntary acts, or perhaps he meant something like "understanding" or "sympathy." But if this was the case, and Greek usage in general indicated that it was, then how did the ancient Greeks speak about forgiveness as we understand the word? Or might it be the case that they did not think in terms of forgiveness at all, with all the baggage that the idea carries today—apologies, sincere remorse, signs of repentance, change of heart, the whole panoply of concepts and activities that are part and parcel of what we mean by forgiving?

I came to the conclusion that in fact the Greeks and Romans in the classical era did not regard "forgiveness" (in our sense of the word) as a fundamental precondition for reconciliation. There are, after all, other ways of resolving conflicts and healing injured sensibilities. But then there arose the question: when did our notion of forgiveness come into being? A likely candidate, of course, was the Bible—both the Hebrew Bible and the Greek New Testament. And indeed I did find forgiveness there, but there was, nevertheless, a catch: for the most part, it is God who forgives in the Bible, and what is more, he demands repentance (there is less concern with sincerity, since it is impossible to fool God). There are cases of human beings forgiving one another, but they turn out to be rare and subject to diverse interpretations. For example, when we are asked to forgive our debtors, we all recognize that "forgive" in this sense means something like "remit" or "cancel" the debt, and does not imply the moral dimension that we associate with the forgiveness of wrongdoing (as for sins, only God can forgive those). A debt is not a crime, and I can cancel it if I please, without demanding an apology or even an excuse on the part of my debtor.

Recently, forgiveness has acquired yet another aspect, which we may call its therapeutic value. Instead of focusing on the offender's attitude toward the harm that he or she has done and the need for remorse and—it is fair to say—even a spiritual conversion, there is a tendency today to look to the benefits that forgiveness confers on the injured party and the psychological need that we as victims have to "get over it" or "get past it," to cease being plagued by feelings of resentment and fantasies of revenge and to get on with our lives in a healthy and constructive way. This is all well and good, but it threatens to denature the moral dimension of forgiveness, turning it into a purely individual (I had almost said egotistical) matter. Surely forgiveness should involve two agents who are morally responsible, not just one. If forgiveness is unconditional, in the sense of imposing no conditions at all upon the wrongdoer, it would seem to undercut or diminish the offender's humanity: how can I atone for a wrong I have committed if you do not even care what I think or feel? Is getting over my guilt also merely a matter of getting on with it?

Tracing the history of forgiveness can help make us aware of some of the complexities associated with the modern idea, and even invite us to reconsider the premises of our ethical convictions. But given the role that forgiveness plays in the Bible, and the continuing authority of the Bible in matters of conscience for Jews and Christians and even for many who are neither, a historical approach to forgiveness assumes yet another aspect. It is not just a question of noticing that forgiveness, as it is popularly conceived today, may differ from ancient views; we may also want to know whether what we think of as Christian forgiveness really corresponds to what the Bible reveals about the idea. Does the Bible authorize a "therapeutic" conception of forgiveness, in which we are called upon simply to forgive, irrespective of repentance on the part of the offender? Or is biblical forgiveness in fact conditional upon repentance and remorse, and does it so oblige us to consider the moral responsibility of the wrongdoer?

In the brilliant and passionate book that is in your hands, Maria Mayo makes a powerful case for the necessity of repentance as a condition for forgiveness in the Gospels and the Bible generally. But that is not all: she also illustrates the harm that a purely therapeutic conception of forgiveness can do and has done, both on the private level, for example in cases of domestic violence and abuse, and on the larger stage, as in the work of the Truth and Reconciliation Commission in South Africa. Demanding forgiveness when there has been no moral transformation on the part of the offender can serve to encourage battered women to accept their condition and even to blame themselves for the abuse that they suffer, as though they had not found it in their hearts to forgive fully (and by the way, by remaining with their unrepentant husbands they offer them new opportunities to sin). Indeed, even where the offender does apologize, there is the possibility of a cycle of mistreatment and ostensible remorse that leaves the victim perpetually vulnerable. On the world level, those who have been unable to forgive their oppressors are sometimes made to feel guilty for their lack of Christian compassion, as though their stubborn resentment were somehow a sign of moral failure. Again, the legal movement known as restorative justice places a huge value on the process of forgiveness between the offender and the victim, which can sometimes result in a diminished sentence for a crime. This may be to the good of society, or it may not, especially if forgiving is perceived as morally obligatory and hence acquires a coercive power. Thus, how we read and interpret the biblical examples of forgiveness is of urgent importance today.

Maria Mayo writes as a biblical scholar, as a moral philosopher, and as a woman who has suffered the kind of injury that puts the requirement of forgiveness into question. She takes on the really tricky problems in social justice and pastoral care and reveals the danger of a facile attitude toward universal and unreflecting forgiveness. This book will make you think hard about what forgiveness means, when and where it is deserved or has been earned, and how it is represented in the Bible, which is so often taken as the fountainhead of forgiveness as a virtue. It is simultaneously a work of profound scholarship and practical ethics, and it offers both a challenge and a hope.

David Konstan
New York University

Acknowledgements

Forgiveness may have its limits, but the enormous intellectual generosity I have received in writing this book has none. Developed first as a dissertation in History and Critical Theories of Religion at Vanderbilt University, this project has been a communal effort, and I am grateful beyond measure to everyone who has supported me and worked with me along the way.

For their financial support, I thank Vanderbilt University's Center for the Study of Religion and Culture as well as the College of Arts and Science for generous grants in support of my research on forgiveness and conflict transformation in Israel and South Africa. The Auschwitz Jewish Center Foundation provided funding for summer research in Poland and allowed me to make valuable connections with Holocaust survivors and others thinking about life in the aftermath of atrocity. Vanderbilt University also awarded several Graduate Student Travel Grants that allowed me to present my work at academic conferences and collaborate with other scholars.

To the members of my dissertation committee who persevered with me, I thank you. Barbara McClure pressed me to think more deeply about the pastoral implications of my arguments. With Erin O'Hara O'Connor I shared long walks and vivacious talks about forgiveness in legal contexts. Jay Geller provided tough questions, tough love, and enduring support. David Konstan turned my e-mail fan letter into the start of a lovely friendship, and I have benefited so much from his sincere engagement with my work. Finally, I give my enormous and endless thanks to Amy-Jill Levine for listening to me, championing my ideas, feeding kangaroos with me, and providing an exquisite model for what it means to be a great scholar and teacher in the world. I am grateful to my entire committee for their patience, optimism, and faith in me and my work.

The strength of this book is a result of the contributions of a broad community of scholars. Annalise Acorn read and contributed to my critical work on restorative justice with much good humor and encouragement. Colleen Murphy reviewed my South Africa material and provided helpful questions about the role of forgiveness in conflict transformation. I am also indebted to Thomas Brudholm, Howard Zehr, Jennifer Llewellyn, Susan Szmania, Arthur Boers, Susan J. Brison, Charles Griswold, L. Gregory Jones, Alice MacLachlan, Evon Flesberg, Jim Harrison, and Peter Horsfield for generously sharing articles, connections, kind words, and good advice. I am lucky to have so many friends and colleagues who challenged my ideas, edited my writing, answered questions, talked through arguments, and inspired me over the course of writing this book: Diane Segroves, John Mogabgab, James Barker, John Kutsko, Philip Eubanks, Debbie Kirk Lewis, Courtney Brkic, Nick Ketter, Dahron Johnson, Trudy Stringer, Kaye Murphey, Dale Johnson, Markus Eberl, Kelsey King, Marie McEntire, Viki Matson.

I have also benefited greatly from all the churches and other communities that have invited me to speak and teach about forgiveness, thus allowing the valuable experiences and opinions of laypeople to inform my writing. Ginn Fourie and the Lyndi Fourie Foundation welcomed me in Cape Town, engaged my questions, and helped shape my research in South Africa. To Hans Tiefel, my very first religion professor at the College of William & Mary, I offer overflowing thanks for teaching me how to think critically and setting me on this course long ago.

Dr. Samuel O. Okpaku read my chapters, rooted for me, and kept me humble and sane throughout my years at Vanderbilt University. I am so very thankful for my parents, Lynda and Jerry Mayo, who helped me start a new life in Nashville and encouraged me throughout this educational extravaganza. And to my little boy, Walter Gabriel: I wrote every word of this book while I was waiting for you. May you and your big heart fill the whole world with love.

Maria Mayo
Nashville, Tennessee

Abbreviations

ABD   *Anchor Bible Dictionary*. Edited by David Noel Freedman. 6 vols. New York: Doubleday, 1992

ABRL   Anchor Bible Reference Library

ANF   *Ante-Nicene Fathers*

BAGD   Bauer, Walter, William F. Arndt, F. Wilbur Gingrich, and Frederick W. Danker. *Greek-English Lexicon of the New Testament and Other Early Christian Literature*. 2nd ed. Chicago: University of Chicago Press, 1979

BETL   Bibliotheca Ephemeridum Theologicarum Lovaniensium

BibInt   *Biblical Interpretation*

CBQ   *Catholic Biblical Quarterly*

FF   Foundations and Facets

IBC   Interpretation: A Bible Commentary for Teaching and Preaching

ICC   International Critical Commentary

JBL   *Journal of Biblical Literature*

JTISup   Journal for Theological Interpretation, Supplements

LHBOTS   The Library of Hebrew Bible/Old Testament Studies

NAC   New American Commentary

NIB   *The New Interpreter's Bible*. Edited by Leander E. Keck. 12 vols. Nashville: Abingdon, 1994–2004

NICNT   New International Commentary on the New Testament

NIGTC	New International Greek Testament Commentary
NovTSup	Supplements to Novum Testamentum
NPNF[1]	*Nicene and Post-Nicene Fathers*, Series 1
NPNF[2]	*Nicene and Post-Nicene Fathers*, Series 2
NTS	*New Testament Studies*
SBL	Society of Biblical Literature
SNTSMS	Society for New Testament Studies Monograph Series
SP	Sacra Pagina
TNTC	Tyndale New Testament Commentaries
ZNW	*Zeitschrift für die neutestamentliche Wissenschaft und die Kunde der älteren Kirche*

1

Introduction: Mapping the Forgiveness Territory

Forgiveness has a history. As far back as the biblical record, authors have depicted forgiveness as a way to repair relationships and heal communities. In Christian accounts forgiveness serves as an antidote to revenge, a mechanism for staying in right relationship with God, and a way to hold communities together. In the modern age, it becomes the psychological power of the individual to supersede negative emotions in the aftermath of violence. Celebrated by therapists and talk-show hosts, forgiveness emerges as both a sparkling moral ideal and the amazing accomplishment of magnanimous victims. *So miraculous,* onlookers whisper. *So Christlike!*

The particular story of forgiveness told in these pages claims less expansive beginnings. As a young woman, I was nearly killed by an intruder who broke into my home early one Sunday morning. The attacker was never caught. When I woke from a coma, the difficult work of recovering from my injuries spread out before me. In the hospital, I listened to well-meaning visitors issue a series of religious platitudes: *This is all part of God's plan. The Lord works in mysterious ways. God saved you for a reason.*

I collected these words in lieu of responding to them. I just listened and blinked my eyes, which for weeks remained bright red with hemorrhage.

You will never be fully healed until you forgive the man who did this.

I added this one to my mental list. I lingered on the words: *until you forgive.*

The God invoked in those bedside platitudes seemed overwhelming and abusive. Part of God's plan? Saved for a reason? Saved at all, and by the same God who watched it all unfold until that last moment of saving?

And by implication, this was also a God who would watch to see if I forgave my attacker and then judge me by my act of charity toward the stranger who nearly beat me to death. If I believed in God as I lay in that hospital bed for all those weeks, it was not this God.

You will never be fully healed until you forgive the man who did this.

I knew with everything in me that this was wrong.

This book seeks to examine and provide alternatives to Christian forgiveness imperatives that are presented to victims of wrongdoing in general and violence in particular. Advocates of forgiveness often promote it as a religious and moral obligation and cite the New Testament as support. Three texts appear frequently in arguments for forgiveness: Jesus's "seventy times seven" instructions (Matt. 18:21–22; Luke 17:3–4), in which Jesus instructs his disciples to forgive boundlessly ("seventy times seven times" in Matthew [18:21], and "seven times seven times" in Luke [17:4]); the Lord's Prayer (Matt. 6:9–13; Luke 11:1–4), in which God's forgiveness is intertwined with human willingness to forgive; and Jesus's cry from the cross, "Father, forgive them" (Luke 23:34a). Close readings of these texts, however, open to interpretations other than the simplistic, "you must forgive."

Advocates of forgiveness conflate certain biblical understandings, such as that forgiveness is an absolute requirement, with contemporary, psychological notions of the term, like forgiveness as unconditional and unilateral. This sometimes reflects an overinterpretation of the biblical material; while Jesus's instructions often appear absolute, closer readings suggest that his account of forgiveness contains ambiguities and conditions. Forgiveness in the teachings of Jesus appears to be closely tied to reconciliation (i.e., restoring relationships), is used as a means of strengthening the nascent Christian community, and requires repentance from the offender. In contemporary contexts, though, a different vision of forgiveness emerges, one that is focused primarily on the individual victim and defined as an emotional or psychological change that is unilateral (involving only the person forgiving) and unconditional (requiring nothing from the offender, especially repentance). The danger arises when this idea of forgiveness is read back into the biblical instructions, and unilateral, unconditional forgiveness is presented to victims as a moral imperative. As David Konstan observes, "Forgiveness, in the modern acceptation of the word, did not exist in classical antiquity or in the early Judeo–Christian tradition … The modern conception, which involves a moral transformation in the offender and a corresponding change of heart in the forgiver, is of relatively recent vintage as a moral idea."[1]

When such conflation occurs, victims are sometimes pressured to forgive by pastors, psychologists, legal representatives, family

---

1. David Konstan, *Before Forgiveness: The Origins of a Moral Idea* (New York: Cambridge University Press, 2010), 165–66.

members, or friends. Such pressure can be both physically and psychologically harmful.[2] In her work on trauma and recovery, Judith Lewis Herman describes the "cruel torture" of forgiveness that appears to be out of reach to most victims.[3] In some cases, victims succumb to pressure, forgive unrepentant offenders (who are potentially still dangerous), and make themselves vulnerable to future injury.[4]

I explore the problem of pressuring victims to forgive across three contexts. First, I examine the growing restorative justice movement that views responding to crime as a question of restoring relationships among the victim, the offender, and the community rather than—or sometimes in addition to—punishing offenders. In the process, forgiveness becomes a catchword for "healing" and victims are pressed, both explicitly and tacitly, to forgive offenders and repair

2. On the negative effects of pressuring victims to forgive, see Kerrie James, "The Interactional Process of Forgiveness and Responsibility: A Critical Assessment of the Family Therapy Literature," in *Hope and Despair in Narrative and Family Therapy: Adversity, Forgiveness, and Reconciliation*, ed. Carmel Flaskas, Imelda McCarthy, and Jim Sheehan (New York: Routledge, 2007), 127–38 (135–36); Sharon Lamb, "Women, Abuse, and Forgiveness: A Special Case," in *Before Forgiving: Cautionary Views of Forgiveness in Psychotherapy*, ed. Sharon Lamb and Jeffrie G. Murphy (Oxford and New York: Oxford University Press, 2002), 155–71 (esp. 156–61); Benjamin E. Sanders and Mary B. Meinig, "Immediate Issues Affecting Long-term Family Resolution in Cases of Parent-Child Sexual Abuse," in *Treatment of Child Abuse: Common Ground for Mental Health, Medical, and Legal Practitioners*, ed. Robert M. Reece (Baltimore, MD: The Johns Hopkins University Press, 2000), 36–53 (46); Kathryn Norlock, *Forgiveness from a Feminist Perspective* (Lanham, MD: Lexington Books, 2009), 28.

3. Judith Lewis Herman, *Trauma and Recovery: The Aftermath of Violence—From Domestic Abuse to Political Terror* (New York: Basic Books, 1992), 190.

4. Carol J. Adams, *Woman-Battering*, Creative Pastoral Care and Counseling Series (Minneapolis, MN: Augsburg Fortress, 1994), 49; James Leehan, *Pastoral Care for Survivors of Family Abuse* (Louisville, KY: Westminster/John Knox Press, 1989), 104; James Newton Poling, "Preaching to Perpetrators of Violence," in *Telling the Truth: Preaching about Sexual and Domestic Violence*, ed. John S. McClure and Nancy J. Ramsay (Cleveland, OH: United Church Press, 1998), 71–82 (80). On the dangers of premature forgiveness, see Margaret R. Holmgren, *Forgiveness and Retribution: Responding to Wrongdoing* (New York: Cambridge University Press, 2012), 53, 63–64. On forgiveness as a lack of self-respect, see Jeffrie G. Murphy, "Forgiveness and Resentment," in *Forgiveness and Mercy*, ed. Jeffrie G. Murphy and Jean Hampton, Cambridge Studies in Philosophy and Law (Cambridge, UK: Cambridge University Press, 1998), 14–34 (18).

the broken relationship, even when the offender was a stranger and no relationship preceded the crime. Restorative justice advocates frequently combine biblical instructions and contemporary psychological notions in promoting a unilateral, unconditional version of forgiveness. Furthermore, they present forgiveness as the good half of a dichotomy in which being consumed by negative emotions such as anger, resentment, indignation, and rage is the only alternative.

Second, I consider forgiveness in the context of the South African Truth and Reconciliation Commission (TRC), focusing specifically on the writings and speeches of Archbishop Desmond Tutu. Here again, victims of apartheid and anti-apartheid violence are presented with a unilateral, unconditional task of forgiveness that claims its warrant from New Testament teachings. Because of the public nature of the Human Rights Violations Committee (HRVC) hearings, the celebrity of Desmond Tutu, and the religious ideas he imported into the process, the rhetoric of forgiveness was publicly known. Victims were under enormous pressure to forgive and reconcile with former combatants for the sake of the "New South Africa." The TRC and Bishop Tutu presented anger and resentment as forgiveness's "demonic other,"[5] and gave victims no choice but to forgive if they wanted to claim a place in the new, reconciled state.

Finally, I look at language of forgiveness in the pastoral care of victims of domestic violence. Again, some pastoral-care practitioners predicate their contemporary notions of unilateral and unconditional forgiveness on biblical texts; the result is a religious imperative to forgive even when the offender is unrepentant or still a threat to the victim. As in the first two cases, a dichotomy emerges in the pastoral-care literature that positions forgiveness against corrosive negative

---

5. Thomas Brudholm, *Resentment's Virtue: Jean Améry and the Refusal to Forgive* (Philadelphia, PA: Temple University Press, 2008), 29.

emotions. Victims must forgive regardless of the disposition of the offender in order to save themselves from being consumed by anger and to remain right with God.

Alongside each of the three case studies, I consider a particular Gospel text that provides both the basis for the discussion in context as well as a lens for reconsidering forgiveness in that setting. Because these biblical passages are so important in these contexts, I seek to understand not only what forgiveness is and how it works, but what the Bible has to say about it and whether that has been understood in the most helpful way possible.

I examine forgiveness in the restorative justice movement alongside Jesus's seventy-times-seven instructions (Matt. 18:21–22; Luke 17:3–4) in order to demonstrate that the biblical material contains a call for offender repentance (Luke 17:4 and Matt. 18:15–17) that would serve victims well in this alternative justice process. The Lord's Prayer (Matt. 6:9–13; Luke 11:2–4) provides a way of thinking about forgiveness in post-apartheid South Africa, also by way of illuminating the role of repentance as seen in the plea for forgiveness, "forgive us our trespasses/sins/debts." Finally, I consider Jesus's cry from the cross, "Father, forgive them" (Luke 23:34a), in the context of pastoral care for victims of domestic violence. Here I demonstrate how calls to imitate Christ through patient suffering or unconditional forgiveness misinterpret the biblical text. On the cross, Jesus *prays* for the forgiveness of his attackers and does not forgive them himself. This recognition provides an alternative path for faithful imitation.

Jesus's teachings on forgiveness

Understandings of forgiveness have shifted from the biblical account to the present-day emphasis on unconditional forgiveness requiring only the victim's participation. First I show how forgiveness in the teachings of Jesus is active, relational, and conditional. Next I present the work of several key thinkers from the fields of philosophy, theology, and psychology who draw on the biblical material but demonstrate the shift toward more emotional, individual understandings of the concept.

A full summary of research and analysis of the three primary texts in this study appear in the chapters to follow. Here I present the major themes and implications of these texts as well as other mentions of forgiveness in the Gospel texts. Throughout this book, I use the New Revised Standard Version of the Bible unless otherwise noted.

The forgiveness material in the Gospels can be divided into four categories:

	Matthew	Mark	Luke	John
1. Direct instructions to forgive	6:9–13 (the Lord's Prayer)		11:2–4	
	6:14–15 (forgive others in order to be forgiven by God)	11:25	6:37–38	20:22–23
	18:21–22 (forgive seventy-seven times)		17:3–4 (if there is repentance you must forgive; forgive seven times)	
	18:23–35 (parable of the unforgiving servant)			
2. Pronouncements of forgiveness	9:2–8 (the healing of the paralyzed man)	2:2–12	5:17–26	
			7:36–50 (a woman's sins have been forgiven)	

3. Warnings about the	12:32		3:29	12:10
unforgivable sin				
4. The prayer for				23:34a
forgiveness from the cross				

These citations represent the totality of Jesus's discussions of forgiveness in the Gospels.[6] For the purposes of this project, I focus most closely on Jesus's instructions about interpersonal forgiveness as opposed to his words on divine forgiveness. In this category, there are three results of forgiveness: restoration of relationship (Matt. 18:21–22 and Luke 17:3–4), reciprocal responsibility to God (Matt. 6:14–15; Mark 11:25; Luke 6:37–38; and John 20:22–23), and cancellation of a debt (Matt. 6:9–13 and Luke 11:2–4; Matt. 18:23–35). The discussions of debt cancellation may be understood metaphorically as referring to the release from the moral debt incurred by sinning against one's neighbor, and thus they may be folded into the categories of restoration of relationship and reciprocal responsibility to God.

The purpose of this taxonomy is to distill Jesus's teachings on forgiveness to their core and then to draw a contrast with contemporary understandings of forgiveness that claim Gospel antecedents. For example, nowhere in these texts does Jesus suggest that forgiveness should be unconditional. On the contrary, in the seventy-times-seven instructions in Matthew and Luke, Jesus details measures for offender repentance before the victim is obligated to forgive:

---

6. While some interpreters also include as examples of forgiveness Luke 6:27–28 and Matt. 5:44–45 (love your enemies); Luke 15:11–32 (the prodigal son); and John 8:1–11 (the woman caught in adultery), these texts do not mention forgiveness by name and I do not include them in my account.

Matt. 18:15–17, 21–22	Luke 17:3–4

"If another member of the church sins against you, go and point out the fault when the two of you are alone. *If the member listens to you,* you have regained that one. But if you are not listened to, take one or two others along with you, so that every word may be confirmed by the evidence of two or three witnesses. If the member refuses to listen to them, tell it to the church; and if the offender refuses to listen even to the church, let such a one be to you as a Gentile and a tax-collector." … Then Peter came and said to him, "Lord, if another member of the church sins against me, how often should I forgive? As many as seven times?" Jesus said to him, "Not seven times, but, I tell you, seventy-seven times."

Be on your guard! If another disciple sins, you must rebuke the offender, and *if there is repentance,* you must forgive. And if the same person sins against you seven times a day, and turns back to you seven times and says, "I repent," you must forgive.

With regard to the text in Matthew, I interpret the discussion of community discipline that precedes the seventy-times-seven instruction as a call for repentance or, at the very least, for acknowledgment of wrongdoing: "*If the member listens to you,* you have regained that one." In the absence of being receptive to rebuke, the offending member is cast out of the community, although not without the possibility of reinclusion; gentiles and tax collectors are frequent subjects of evangelism.[7] The point here is that the offender has a responsibility to respond to first the individual's and then the community's concern. I interpret this as a call for repentance. Only when that condition has been met are Jesus's listeners required to forgive boundlessly. Note also that this forgiveness instruction concerns "a member of the church" (Matt. 18:15); that is, there is a

---

7. For examples, see John 4:5–26 (Samaritan woman); Luke 19:1–10 (staying at Zaccheus's house); Matt. 10:3 and Luke 5:27 (calling of Matthew); Matt. 8:5–13 (healing of the centurion's servant); Mark 2:13–17 (dinner with the tax collectors).

previous relationship that has been damaged and must be repaired for the sake of the community.

The Lord's Prayer offers both a model for repentance and an imperative to forgive:

Matt. 6:12	Luke 11:4
And forgive us our debts, as we also have forgiven our debtors.	And forgive us our sins, for we ourselves forgive everyone indebted to us.

In its expression of hope for reciprocal forgiveness, the prayerful voice first requests forgiveness. I interpret this initial plea as an expression of acknowledging sin, repentance, and of the need for forgiveness. The prayer, so understood, contains not only a statement about the relationship between divine and human forgiveness (we forgive others so God will forgive us), but also an acknowledgment of wrongdoing (we acknowledge that we have sinned and we repent). The fact that the prayer is recited regularly speaks to the importance of forgiveness in strengthening the nascent community.[8]

Immediately following Matthew's seventy-times-seven instructions comes the parable of the unforgiving servant, which is often read as an imperative for unconditional forgiveness:

> For this reason the kingdom of heaven may be compared to a king who wished to settle accounts with his slaves. When he began the reckoning, one who owed him ten thousand talents was brought to him; and, as he could not pay, his lord ordered him to be sold, together with his wife and children and all his possessions, and payment to be made. So the slave fell on his knees before him, saying, "Have patience with me, and I will pay you everything." And out of pity for him, the lord of that slave released him and forgave him the debt. But that same slave, as he went out, came upon one of his fellow slaves who owed him a hundred denarii; and seizing him by the throat, he said, "Pay what you owe."

---

8. The Didache instructs, "Pray this three times each day" (8:3). On the thrice-daily gatherings of the early community, see Aaron Milavec, *The Didache: Text, Translation, Analysis, and Commentary* (Collegeville, MN: Liturgical Press, 2003), 65.

Then his fellow slave fell down and pleaded with him, "Have patience with me, and I will pay you." But he refused; then he went and threw him into prison until he would pay the debt. When his fellow slaves saw what had happened, they were greatly distressed, and they went and reported to their lord all that had taken place. Then his lord summoned him and said to him, "You wicked slave! I forgave you all that debt because you pleaded with me. Should you not have had mercy on your fellow slave, as I had mercy on you?" And in anger his lord handed him over to be tortured until he would pay his entire debt. So my heavenly Father will also do to every one of you, if you do not forgive your brother or sister from your heart. (Matt. 18:23–35)

In this illustration, one's status as forgiven obligates one to approach others with a forgiving disposition. While it is clear that the parable's language of debt stands as a metaphor for sin, as it does in the Lord's Prayer, the story does not consider the moral implications that might accompany a spiteful or violent offense. David Konstan writes, "Remitting a debt does not imply any wrongdoing on the part of the debtor: it is simply an act of generosity on the part of the lender, equivalent to a gift. The liberated debtor makes no apologies, feels no remorse, and undergoes no change of heart in respect to the benefactor, for there has been no offense at all, whether voluntary or involuntary."[9] Without a consideration of wrongdoing, the parable is of limited use for understanding interpersonal forgiveness. Moreover, in the parable the consequence for not "paying it forward" is having one's own forgiveness rescinded and replaced with torture and imprisonment. Clearly this part of the parable does not serve as a model for how forgiveness and repentance should be handled. The story means to say something about interpersonal forgiveness beyond the literal context of monetary debt, but the message is not clear.

In his work on debt metaphors for sin and forgiveness in the Bible, Gary Anderson offers an interpretation of this parable: "We are in

9. Konstan, *Before Forgiveness*, 118.

danger of becoming debt-slaves when we sin. Should the act go uncorrected, then one will have to 'pay' for the 'cost' of the misdeed through the 'currency' of physical punishment. Fortunately God is merciful and will remit the debt we owe if we humbly beseech him."[10] Here Anderson lets humble beseeching stand in the place of repentance, but the analogy doesn't follow. As Konstan observes, there is no need for a person in debt to repent or show remorse. In any case, begging for mercy is quite a different thing from offering an apology.

In this parable, the metaphor of sin as debt creates a transactional relationship both between the human and the divine and among fellow human beings. Debts may be accrued and forgiven, or they may be offset by credits such as those gained in almsgiving.[11] Anderson explains, "How we talk about sin influences what we will *do* about it."[12] Talking about sin as debt allows for sin to be erased in the way debts can be erased, either by loan forgiveness or debtor repayment. In the parable, one's potential for debt forgiveness is linked to one's willingness to forgive others their debts. The same holds true for the petition in Matthew's version of the Lord's Prayer: first comes the plea for forgiveness ("forgive us our debts"; 6:12), followed by the condition for that forgiveness ("as we also have forgiven our debtors"; 6:12).

As with sin, how we talk about forgiveness also influences what we will do about it. Envisioning forgiveness as release from debt demonstrates that the effects of forgiveness may be visible and concrete; that is, forgiving a debt involves adjusting accounts so that the burden of the debt no longer weighs on the debtor. The sin-as-debt metaphor shows that forgiveness was something to be *done*,

10. Gary A. Anderson, *Sin: A History* (New Haven, CT: Yale University Press, 2009), 32–33.
11. Ibid., 14.
12. Ibid.

not something only to be thought or felt. While it is difficult to draw a one-to-one relationship between the forgiveness depicted in this parable and interpersonal forgiveness for things like betrayal, assault, or oppression, the metaphor is instructive about the impact of human forgiveness on divine forgiveness. According to Anderson, the parable illustrates that people are at risk for accruing debt when they sin, and the way out is through physical punishment. The hope is that God will be merciful and forgive the figurative debt just as human beings forgive the "debts" of one another.[13] There is no model for the debtor to follow other than to beseech God and to forgive others from the outset.

However, not all sin can be conceived as debt, or be as easily resolved by the victim's release of that debt. A victim's pain, physical injury, and fear of future harm may not be wiped away in one forgiving motion, or even if they are, they might reappear. The complexity and lability of such injuries makes conceiving of interpersonal sin as debt an insufficient analogy in the realm of human wrongdoing.[14] Crimes of physical violence, for example, often leave wounds that are not easily wiped away. Talking about forgiveness as the cancellation of a debt, then, has limits when it comes to more serious interpersonal offenses.

Finally, Jesus's stern words about the unforgivable sin (Mark 3:29//Matt. 12:32//Luke 12:10) provide the clearest evidence that forgiveness is neither an absolute good nor an unquestioned moral obligation. In these cases, Jesus explains that there is one sin that will not be forgiven (the agent is not named but is assumed to be God[15]):

---

13. Ibid., 32–33.
14. Linda Radzik, *Making Amends: Atonement in Morality, Law, and Politics* (Oxford and New York: Oxford University Press, 2009), 119.
15. Janet Meyer Everts, "Unforgivable Sin," in *ABD* 6:745; L. Gregory Jones, *Embodying Forgiveness: A Theological Analysis* (Grand Rapids, MI: Eerdmans, 1995), 194–95; John S. Nolland, *The Gospel of Matthew: A Commentary on the Greek Text*, NIGCT (Grand Rapids, MI: Eerdmans, 2005), 505–6; W. D. Davies and Dale C. Allison, eds., *Matthew: A Shorter*

blasphemy against the Holy Spirit. These cases, coupled with the image of the unforgiving king in the above parable, raise the question of whether forgiveness can be named a moral or religious obligation when even God does not behave accordingly. In all three Synoptic Gospels, unforgiveness—the withholding of forgiveness—is a distinct possibility.

However, unforgiveness as a fact of life also presents a serious threat to human beings whose salvation, according to the Gospel account, is utterly dependent on divine forgiveness. Even though the exact nature of God's forgiveness is not made explicit in the text, there is no doubt that humans need it and they must forgive each other in order to receive it. Matthew adds this coda to the Lord's Prayer: "For if you forgive others their trespasses, your heavenly Father will also forgive you; but if you do not forgive others, neither will your Father forgive your trespasses" (6:14–15), and Luke writes, "Do not judge, and you will not be judged; do not condemn, and you will not be condemned. Forgive, and you will be forgiven; give, and it will be given to you" (6:37–38).[16] For most Christian interpreters, forgiveness forms a triangular relationship among the victim, the offender, and God. Where the message of the parable is that being forgiven (by God or by others) should inspire further forgiveness, these verses suggest that human forgiveness inspires divine forgiveness. In Luke and Acts, forgiveness of sins becomes a synonym

---

Commentary (London and New York: T & T Clark, 2004), 201; Lamar Williamson, *Mark*, IBC (Louisville, KY: John Knox Press, 1983), 86.

16. This verse marks the only time in the Gospels in which the verb ἀπολύω is translated in the NRSV as "forgive." Elsewhere in the Gospels, ἀπολύω is taken to mean "send away" (Matt. 14:15, 22, 23; 15:23, 32, 39; Mark 6:36, 45; 8:3, 9; Luke 8:38; 9:12), "depart" (Luke 2:29), "divorce" (Matt. 1:19; 5:31, 32; 19:3, 7, 8, 9; Mark 10:2, 4, 11, 12; Luke 16:18), or "release" (Matt. 27:15, 17, 21, 26; Mark 15:6, 9, 11, 15; Luke 13:12; 14:4; 22:68; 23:16, 17, 18, 20, 22, 25; John 18:39; 19:10, 12).

for salvation.[17] The imperative to forgive is not just a moral issue; it is a soteriological necessity.

The Greek word most commonly translated as "forgive" in these texts is ἀφίημι, a verb whose semantic range includes "let go," "send away," "cancel," "remit," "pardon," "leave," "give up," "divorce," and "abandon," in addition to "forgive (debts)" and "forgive (sins)."[18] These meanings suggest that interpersonal forgiveness in the time of the composition of the Gospels had an active or outward character and was not only a matter of changing one's mind or feelings (an inward action). This verb appears a total of 146 times in the New Testament, but it is translated in the NRSV as "forgive" only thirty-eight of those times. Elsewhere it appears primarily as a transitive verb with a direct object: They *left* their nets (οἱ δὲ εὐθέως ἀφέντες τὰ δίκτυα, Matt. 4:20); *Leaving* the crowd *behind* (καὶ ἀφέντες τὸν ὄχλον, Mark 4:36); *Let* the children come to me (ἄφετε τὰ παιδία ἔρχεσθαι πρός με, Luke 18:16); *Let it alone* for one more year (ἄφες αὐτὴν καὶ τοῦτο τὸ ἔτος, Luke 13:8). In the Pauline literature, ἀφίημι also has the connotation of "divorce" (the husband should not *divorce* his wife [ἄνδρα γυναῖκα μὴ ἀφιέναι], 1 Cor. 7:11). In most cases, the verb depicts a concrete action, usually taken toward another person. Given this semantic range for ἀφίημι, first-century hearers would have understood forgiveness to have an active character. In other words, it is something one does (words spoken, action taken, physical things altered) rather than something one feels.

17. Gary S. Shogren, "Forgiveness (NT)," in *ABD* 2:836; Luke 1:77; 24:47; Acts 2:38; 5:31; 10:43; 13:38; 26:18.
18. Walter Bauer, William F. Arndt, F. Wilbur Gingrich, and Frederick W. Danker, eds., *Greek English Lexicon of the New Testament and Other Early Christian Literature*, 3rd ed. (Chicago, IL: University of Chicago Press, 1999), 125 (ἀφίημι) (hereafter BAGD); see also Rudolf Bultmann, "ἀφίημι," in *Theological Dictionary of the New Testament*, ed. G. Kittel and G. Friedrich, 10 vols. (Grand Rapids, MI: Eerdmans, 1964), 1:509.

Interpretations of forgiveness

The biblical forgiveness material has been interpreted in a variety of ways.[19] In contemporary literature, these instructions and forgiveness in general get developed in three main ways: forgiveness as strengthening the community, forgiveness as controlling negative emotions, and forgiveness as a therapeutic strategy that benefits the individual forgiver's health. In what follows I present some of the primary voices representing these three interpretations.

Forgiveness as strengthening community

According to Jesus's teachings, the offender's repentance and the relationship between victim and offender play important roles in forgiveness. In the Gospel texts, forgiveness is bilateral: the process involves action from the offender toward the victim with a tangible outcome such as a restored relationship or a strengthened community. When repentance is not forthcoming, forgiveness fails. For example, just prior to Jesus's instruction in Matthew to forgive boundlessly (18:21–22), community members who are not receptive to correction are cast out of the community. Luke's presentation of the boundless-forgiveness instruction contains the qualifier, "if there is repentance" (17:3–4). And when Jesus is on the cross, he offers a prayer for forgiveness rather than forgiving his executioners directly; one reason for this may be that they do not repent of their actions. Furthermore, God's forgiveness may be granted or removed for specific reasons (Mark 3:29//Matt. 12:32//Luke 12:10 [unforgivable sin]; Matt. 18:23–35 [unforgiving servant]; Matt. 6:14–15 [if you forgive, God will forgive you; if you don't forgive, God will not forgive you]). Forgiveness in the teachings of Jesus lacks explicit definition, but it is undoubtedly a relational or bilateral

---

19. See the individual chapters for histories of interpretation of the texts in question.

process that happens under certain conditions with tangible outcomes, such as strengthening the community.

A number of modern biblical interpreters retain this emphasis on community cohesion and repair of relationship. Here I discuss two examples, one secular and one religious: Hannah Arendt, who discusses the political implications of forgiveness, and L. Gregory Jones, who argues that forgiveness is crucial in the maintenance of the body of Christ. Both Arendt and Jones call for forgiveness as a necessity in repairing community relationships. This is a key theme for Jesus, and it undergirds the forgiveness emphases of both Desmond Tutu and advocates of restorative justice.

Hannah Arendt, theorizing forgiveness by way of New Testament sources, famously asserts, "The discoverer of the role of forgiveness in the realm of human affairs was Jesus of Nazareth."[20] Key for Arendt is Jesus's message that human forgiveness is not only possible but necessary for divine forgiveness and—more important—the survival of human community. She writes, "Trespassing is an everyday occurrence which is in the very nature of action's constant establishment of new relationships within a web of relations, and it needs forgiving, dismissing, in order to make it possible for life to go on."[21] "Forgiving" and "dismissing" are closely related here; Arendt envisions forgiveness as "the possible redemption from the predicament of irreversibility—of being unable to undo what one has done."[22] Reversed by forgiveness, the wrongdoing is effectively erased.

---

20. Hannah Arendt, *The Human Condition* (1958; Chicago, IL: University of Chicago Press, 1998), 238.
21. Ibid., 240. In her analysis, Arendt cites the healing of the paralytic in Luke (5:21–24), the Lord's Prayer and its addendum in Matthew (6:9–15), and Luke's instruction to forgive seven times seven times *if there is repentance* (Lk. 17:3–4; emphasis mine).
22. Arendt, *Human Condition*, 237.

For Arendt, forgiveness is an act of will that involves the forswearing of both resentment and revenge in response to wrongdoing. But this forgiveness is not just an absence of negative action, such as withholding anger or resentment. Forgiveness is a social act that reflects a commitment to renewed trust and preservation of community. Arendt calls this idea *amor mundi* (love of the world), and L. Gregory Jones uses the phrase "the body of Christ"[23] to refer to the same kind of community concern. Arendt's understanding of the value of forgiveness emphasizes the collective over the individual and emphasizes the ability of forgiveness to prevent destruction and repair communal relations. She pulls the basic theme of forgiveness as redemption and renewal from the New Testament and cites Jesus as its author,[24] but her model of political (or social) forgiveness lacks the divine reciprocity that characterizes discussions of forgiveness in the Gospels. Arendt thus transforms the divine imperative into a primarily communal one.

Pointing out that "crime and willed evil are rare," Arendt interprets Jesus's forgiveness instructions as applying mainly to mundane, everyday missteps, with forgiveness as a way to balance and correct wrongdoing in a community. She writes, "Only through this constant mutual release from what they do can men remain free agents, only by constant willingness to change their minds and start again can they be trusted with so great a power as that to begin something new."[25] Arendt's account of forgiveness does not include

---

23. Margaret Betz Hull, *The Hidden Philosophy of Hannah Arendt* (London: RoutledgeCurzon, 2002), 75; James Bernauer, S.J., "The Faith of Hannah Arendt: *Amor Mundi* and its Critique—Assimilation of Religious Experience," in *Amor Mundi: Explorations in the Faith and Thought of Hannah Arendt*, ed. J. W. Bernauer (Martinus Nijhoff Philosophy Library 26; Boston College Studies in Philosophy VII; Dordrecht, Netherlands: Martinus Nijhoff Publishers, 1987), 1–28. Jones, *Embodying Forgiveness*, 4, 16, 32–33, 46, 53, 131, 195, 207, 268. See also Joseph Butler, "Sermon IX: Upon Forgiveness of Injuries," in *The Works of Bishop Butler*, ed. David E. White (Rochester, NY: University of Rochester Press, 2006), 99.

24. Arendt, *Human Condition*, 240. She cites the reciprocal formulas offered in Matt. 6:14–15, 18:35, and Mark 11:25, along with the "seven times seven times" teaching in Luke (17:3–4).

more serious crimes, or "radical evil."[26] For such criminals, she offers another biblical prescription: "Where the deed itself dispossesses us of all power [to forgive or punish], we can indeed only repeat with Jesus: 'It were better for him that a millstone were hanged about his neck, and he cast into the sea'" (quoting Matt. 18:6).[27] Where the biblical text refers to a specific crime punishable by drowning, that is, putting a stumbling block in front of anyone who believes in Jesus, Arendt recontextualizes this to apply to crimes of impossible enormity.

In her report on the trial of Nazi criminal Adolf Eichmann, Arendt faces a man whose crimes during the Holocaust constitute such "radical evil." She explains why his crimes put him beyond the reach of the "mundane" forgiveness she describes earlier:

> Just as you supported and carried out a policy of not wanting to share the earth with the Jewish people and the people of a number of other nations—as though you and your superiors had any right to determine who should and should not inhabit the world—we find that no one, that is, no member of the human race, can be expected to want to share the earth with you. This is the reason, and the only reason, you must hang.[28]

In this case, *not* forgiving Eichmann (i.e., sentencing him to death) repairs the community. She writes, "The reparation effected in criminal cases is of an altogether different nature; it is the body politic itself that stands in need of being 'repaired,' and it is the general public order that has been thrown out of gear and must be restored, as it were."[29] Thus, not forgiving the most egregious crimes serves the

25. Arendt, *Human Condition*, 240.
26. Ibid., 241.
27. Ibid.
28. Hannah Arendt, *Eichmann in Jerusalem: A Report on the Banality of Evil* (1963; New York: Penguin Books, 2006), 279.
29. Ibid., 261.

same purpose as the mundane or trivial forgiveness Arendt describes: it repairs the community (or the body politic, or *amor mundi*).

L. Gregory Jones argues for an "embodied"—or, lived out in practice—understanding of forgiveness based on the teachings of Jesus.[30] He writes, "Humans are called to become holy by embodying [God's] forgiveness through specific habits and practices that seek to remember the past truthfully, to repair the brokenness, to heal divisions, and to reconcile and renew relationships."[31] Jones defines forgiveness as "not so much a word spoken, an action performed, or a feeling felt as it is an embodied way of life in an ever-deepening friendship with the Triune God and with others."[32] In Jones's account, forgiveness and reconciliation (figured as the repair of a broken relationship) are deeply intertwined. One does not occur without the other, and reconciliation is a necessary reflection of the forgiveness embodied by Jesus.[33] The "craft of forgiveness"[34] (or, forgiveness as an "embodied way of life")[35] means that forgiveness and reconciliation are inseparable. For Jones, forgiveness is meaningless without the repair of the relationship that was broken by the offense.

Jones goes to great lengths to define forgiveness not as a simple concept, but a way of life. In this way he follows Arendt by locating the significance of forgiveness in the social sphere. This relational nature of forgiveness leads Jones to criticize contemporary psychological approaches (see below) that allow for internal,

---

30. Jones, *Embodying Forgiveness,* xii, passim. He cites Luke 7:36–50 (sinful woman forgiven), Matt. 18 (community discipline, seventy times seven, the parable of the unforgiving servant), Matt. 5:44 (love your enemies), and John 20:23 (forgiving and retaining).
31. Jones, *Embodying Forgiveness,* xii.
32. Ibid.
33. Jones does acknowledge that sometimes "hope against hope" for reconciliation is as close as some might get to actual communion, but that hope is a key element of forgiveness (*Embodying Forgiveness,* 232).
34. Jones, *Embodying Forgiveness,* 207–25.
35. Jones, *Embodying Forgiveness,* xii, 88–89, 154, 218.

unilateral expressions of forgiveness and do not take the next step of communal action. However, Jones so thoroughly rejects the idea of forgiveness as a thought or action (he prefers to talk about "the craft of forgiveness" as a general way of life) that in the end he does not ever offer a clear definition of the term. Instead, there is nothing to separate Jones's "craft of forgiveness" from, say, a "craft of compassion" or "craft of charity." Furthermore, Jones's conflation of forgiveness and reconciliation negates the possibility of forgiveness in cases where reconciliation is impossible, undesirable, or both. Even so, his insistence on the communal and relational nature of forgiveness is helpful for the consideration of the difficult kinds of forgiveness presented in the case studies to follow.

Both Arendt and Jones preserve the active character of forgiveness and cite its importance for preserving communities and repairing relationships. Both draw on New Testament sources to demonstrate that forgiveness must be a way of life, whether secular or religious, and that it involves more than simply a change of mind or heart. They thereby offer more complex accounts than do advocates who embrace unilateral, unconditional forgiveness as the biblical imperative.

Forgiveness as controlling negative emotions

Nowhere does Jesus suggest that forgiveness involves only the control of a victim's anger or resentment toward the offender. However, this understanding of forgiveness is not uncommon among both religious and secular interpreters. The Anglican bishop Joseph Butler (1692–1752) advances a theory of forgiveness that, although grounded in the Gospels, defines forgiveness primarily as the act of controlling negative emotions. A number of later thinkers adopt this approach.

In his 1726 sermon "Upon Forgiveness of Injuries," Butler defines forgiveness as the forswearing of active resentment.[36] This marks the beginning of a trend in a number of disciplines toward apophatic definitions of forgiveness: defining forgiveness by what it is not. According to Butler, forgiveness prevents excessive resentment from damaging the body of Christ on earth[37] (L. Gregory Jones follows this line of thinking) and protects human salvation in the hereafter. Butler regards resentment itself as a "natural" emotion[38] and to be expected. However, "when this resentment entirely destroys our natural benevolence towards [our neighbor], it is excessive, and becomes malice or revenge," he explains. "The command to *prevent* its having this effect, i.e. to forgive injuries, is the same as to love our enemies."[39] Forgiveness, then, is defined as an antidote to excessive negative reactions that threaten love of neighbor. Rather than reacting positively to an offense, forgiveness primarily reacts against the possibility of anger or resentment.

Like Butler, Miroslav Volf locates the essence of forgiveness in the willingness to forgo a negative reaction to an offense. "Forgiveness cuts the tie of equivalence between the offense and the way we treat the offender," he writes. "I forgo all retribution. In forgiving, I absorb the injury—the way I may absorb, say, the financial impact of a bad business transaction."[40] Volf draws a direct equivalence between financial loss and other injury. The metaphorical language of "absorbing the injury" would be inappropriate counsel for victims of domestic violence, for example, for whom the injury is far from metaphorical. But as discussed above, such a transactional

---

36. Butler, "Upon Forgiveness," 96.
37. Ibid., 98.
38. Ibid., 96.
39. Ibid., 99 (emphasis mine). To forgive is to "prevent" resentment from having ill effects.
40. Miroslav Volf, *Free of Charge: Giving and Forgiving in a Culture Stripped of Grace* (Grand Rapids, MI: Zondervan, 2005), 170.

understanding of forgiveness leaves out the possibility for (or necessity of) repentance on the part of the offender. Any robust view of biblical forgiveness must address the role of repentance.

Psychologist Robert D. Enright also depends on the absence of negative emotions to capture the essence of forgiveness. He writes,

> The forgiveness process, properly understood and used, can free those bound by anger and resentment. It does not require accepting injustice or remaining in an abusive situation. It opens the door to reconciliation, but it does not require trusting someone who has proven untrustworthy. Even if the offender remains unrepentant, you can forgive and restore a sense of peace and well-being to your life.[41]

Like many other psychologists,[42] Enright pits forgiveness against a seemingly necessary negative opposite, in this case, being "bound by anger and resentment," or not just *feeling* anger, but being *controlled* by it. Enright defines forgiveness as "a willingness to abandon one's right to resentment, negative judgment, and indifferent behavior toward one who unjustly injured us, while fostering the undeserved qualities of compassion, generosity, and even love toward him or her."[43] He sees the father in the parable of the prodigal son (Luke 15:11–32) as a prime example of forgiveness-as-withholding-resentment when he welcomes his errant son home.[44] Forgiveness,

41. Robert D. Enright, *Forgiveness Is a Choice: A Step-by-Step Process for Resolving Anger and Restoring Hope* (Washington, DC: American Psychological Association, 2001), 43.

42. See, for example, Roy F. Baumeister, Julie Juola Exline, and Kristin L. Sommer, "The Victim Role, Grudge Theory, and Two Dimensions of Forgiveness," in *Dimensions of Forgiveness: A Research Approach*, ed. Everett L. Worthington (Radnor, PA: Temple Foundation Press, 1998), 79–80; Everett L. Worthington, "Initial Questions about the Art and Science of Forgiving," in *Handbook of Forgiveness*, ed. Everett L. Worthington (New York: Routledge, 2005), 1; Liz Gulliford, "Intrapersonal Forgiveness," in *Forgiveness in Context: Theology and Psychology in Creative Dialogue*, ed. Fraser Watts and Liz Gulliford (London: T&T Clark International, 2004), 84; Lewis B. Smedes, *Forgive and Forget: Healing the Hurts We Don't Deserve* (New York: HarperCollins, 1984), 2.

43. Robert D. Enright, Suzanne Freedman, and Julio Rique, "The Psychology of Interpersonal Forgiveness," in *Exploring Forgiveness*, ed. Robert D. Enright and Joanna North (Madison: University of Wisconsin Press, 1998), 46–47.

44. Enright, *Forgiveness Is a Choice*, 24–25.

again, is mainly a question of controlling or eradicating negative emotions.

Here, Enright joins philosopher Joanna North in defining forgiveness this way: "If we are to forgive, our resentment is to be overcome not by denying ourselves the right to that resentment, but by endeavoring to view the wrongdoer with compassion, benevolence and love while recognizing that he has willfully abandoned his right to them."[45] North often collaborates with Enright in developing materials advancing this emotional understanding of forgiveness. She writes, "Forgiveness, through such active mental and emotional endeavor, is therefore possible even in the absence of repentance and retribution. It is essentially an internal change of heart ... a *willed* change of heart—the successful result of an active endeavor to replace bad thoughts with good, bitterness and anger with compassion and affection."[46] North also cites the parable of the prodigal son (Luke 15:11–32) as an example of forgiveness that takes the form of (the father) withholding a negative reaction (to the son).[47] North also positions forgiveness as the good half of a dichotomy that presents anger, resentment, and other negative emotions as its necessary opposites. Forgiveness thus defined becomes primarily the state of *not* being angry, bitter, or resentful. Clearing away these negative emotions makes way for compassion, affection, and good thoughts. Forgiveness emerges here primarily as an exercise in thought control, as though no positive or constructive action can take place in the presence of anger and resentment.

Charles L. Griswold expands the apophatic definition of forgiveness to include refraining from negative actions as well as feelings.[48] Griswold points out that Butler defines forgiveness only

45. Joanna North, "Wrongdoing and Forgiveness," *Philosophy* 62 (1987): 502.
46. Ibid., 506.
47. Ibid., 501.

as forswearing *revenge* (an action), not *resentment* (a feeling). Then Griswold sets forth his own definition that fills the gap he sees in Butler: "Forgiveness does however mean overcoming negative *feelings* that embody and perpetuate the key features of resentment, feelings that very often accompany resentment—such as contempt and scorn—*insofar as* they are modulations of the moral hatred in question."[49] Thus Griswold defines forgiveness as an emotional state. He briefly considers the semantic range of ἀφίημι in the biblical texts and opts to merge the term with the Classical Greek term συγγνώμη in arriving at his own definition. He finds that when συγγνώμη is used to mean "forgiveness," the term carries more cognitive and emotional associations than does ἀφίημι (whose semantic range includes, in addition to "forgive," simple action verbs such as "leave" or "dismiss").[50] "Forswearing *the emotion* is indeed the ultimate goal," he writes. [51] However, defining forgiveness only as the absence of negative emotions disregards the constructive potential of forgiveness offered in the biblical account, as well as its bilateral character. While Butler and others draw—to varying degrees—from the teachings of Jesus to inform their definitions, their tendency to locate the action of forgiveness only in the mind or heart of the victim neglects the corporate and tangible nature of forgiveness presented in the Gospels.

Therapeutic forgiveness

This emphasis on forgiveness as a matter of forswearing resentment leads to a third trend in forgiveness research: defining forgiveness as needing only the participation of the victim. This understanding

---

48. Charles Griswold, *Forgiveness: A Philosophical Exploration* (New York: Cambridge University Press, 2007), 19–37.
49. Ibid., 41 (emphasis in original).
50. Ibid., 3. See n. 3 for his discussion of ἀφίημι. The term συγγνώμη appears once in the New Testament: "This I say by way of concession (συγγνώμη), not of command" (1 Cor. 7:6).
51. Griswold, *Forgiveness*, 42 (emphasis mine).

suggests that victims can and should overcome injury or wrongdoing by adjusting their thoughts and emotions in a positive way with regard to the offender, regardless of the offender's disposition or presence. Advocates of this brand of forgiveness often claim biblical warrant, but there is no indication in the teachings of Jesus that forgiveness requires only an emotional or mental exercise. Even so, psychologists, pastoral counselors, legal representatives, and others may pressure victims to forgive even when the offender is unknown, unrepentant, or still a threat. Victims may then be judged according to their willingness or ability to demonstrate forgiving thoughts toward the offender.

This unilateral, unconditional, emotional view of forgiveness appears most often in the work of psychologists and pastoral counselors. The "therapeutic"[52] understanding of forgiveness assumes not only that victims may transform their experience by changing how they think and feel about it, but also that such forgiveness is necessary for healing. The pressure on victims to forgive can be enormous.

Psychologists began to embrace forgiveness as a therapeutic strategy in the 1980s, and many credit Lewis B. Smedes and his 1984 book, *Forgive and Forget: Healing the Hurts We Don't Deserve*, as foundational for starting the "forgiveness movement." Smedes first defines forgiveness as "God's invention [and gift to humanity] for

52. Psychologists and pastoral caregivers use this term both to recommend psychological approaches to forgiveness and to criticize them; see, for example, Terry D. Hargrave, "Families and Forgiveness: A Theoretical and Therapeutic Framework," *The Family Journal* 2, no. 4 (1994): 339–48; and Cynthia Ransley and Terri Spy, *Forgiveness and the Healing Process: A Central Therapeutic Concern* (New York: Routledge, 2004), 31–50 (forgiveness as an effective therapeutic strategy); Chris Brauns, *Unpacking Forgiveness: Biblical Answers for Complex Questions and Deep Wounds* (Wheaton, IL: Crossway Books, 2008), 65 (therapeutic forgiveness as distinct from "biblical forgiveness"); Jones, *Embodying Forgiveness*, 35–70 (therapeutic forgiveness as "the Church's psychological captivity in Western culture"). I use the term to describe how forgiveness (often unconditional and unilateral) is promoted in therapeutic contexts (such as counseling) as an emotionally and psychologically curative approach to wrongdoing.

coming to terms with a world in which, despite their best intentions, people are unfair to each other and hurt each other deeply."[53] However, he downplays the importance of forgiveness in relationship or community repair. Forgiveness, he argues, is primarily something we do "*for our own sakes.*"[54]

In this slim volume, Smedes unleashes a cacophony of metaphors[55] that portray forgiveness in a positive, almost magical light and that suggest that forgiveness can be accomplished by any individual simply as an act of will:

> The only way to heal the pain that will not heal itself is to forgive the person who hurt you. Forgiving stops the reruns of pain. Forgiving heals your memory as you change your memory's vision. When you release the wrongdoer from the wrong, you cut a malignant tumor out of your inner life. You set a prisoner free, but you discover that the real prisoner was yourself.[56]

While Smedes often cites the New Testament as a source—he references the parable of the unforgiving servant (Matt. 18:23–35), the woman caught in adultery (John 8:1–11), and the parable of the prodigal son (Luke 15:11–32), among others[57]—his theories of forgiveness have very little grounding in the biblical text. The parable of the prodigal and the story of the woman caught in adultery

---

53. Smedes, *Forgive and Forget*, xi–xii.
54. Ibid., 30 (emphasis in original).
55. For example, see ibid., 94: "Forgiving is love's revolution against life's unfairness. When we forgive, we ignore the normal laws that strap us to the natural law of getting even and, by the alchemy of love, we release ourselves from our own painful pasts. We fly over a dues-paying morality in order to create a new future out of the past's unfairness. We free ourselves from the wrong that is locked in our private histories; we unshackle our spirits from malice; and, maybe, if we are lucky, we also restore a relationship that would otherwise be lost forever." Absent among these images is the metaphor of debt forgiveness.
56. Ibid., 133.
57. Smedes references the following texts in *Forgive and Forget*: the parable of the unforgiving servant (150), the story of the woman caught in adultery (48), the cry of dereliction (87), Judas's betrayal (16), Peter's denial (16, 108), the healing of the paralyzed man (94), the parable of the prodigal son (68), and the cry from the cross, "Father, forgive them" (11).

nowhere use the term "forgiveness." Nowhere does Jesus suggest that forgiveness stops pain or repairs memory. Nowhere is nonforgiveness described as if it were a tumor or disease, or forgiveness as psychic healing. And certainly, nowhere does Jesus advocate forgiveness as a form of self-care or self-improvement. These are modern ideas. Forgiveness as a way of making oneself feel better is more a product of the contemporary self-help movement than it is a biblical precept. Smedes conflates these emotional understandings of forgiveness with biblical examples and presents them as religious imperatives.

Such psychological formulations of forgiveness conflated with biblical imperatives can result in pressure on victims to change their thinking about an offense without necessarily holding offenders accountable. Here the problem is that these emotional formulations of forgiveness are written back into the biblical account. For example, Smedes cites the cry of dereliction ("My God, my God, why have you forsaken me?"; Matt. 27:46) as an instance where human beings who suffer and feel abandoned by God can choose even to forgive God.[58] In response to the seventy-times-seven instructions, Smedes emphasizes the endlessness of the numbers, but offers an emotional purpose. He writes, "Jesus was talking [in the seventy-times-seven instructions] about healing our memories of a wound that someone's wrong etched in our cemented past. Once we have stopped the abuse, we can forgive however many times that it might take us to finish our healing."[59] Here the beneficiary of the forgiveness is the individual who forgives, not the community. The only person involved in forgiving is the victim, and the hoped-for outcome is the healing of memories. This obscures the fact that the forgiveness Jesus called for required the participation of the offender and the

58. Ibid., 87–88.
59. Smedes, *The Art of Forgiving: When You Need to Forgive and Don't Know How* (New York: Random House, 1996), 161.

community, not just the victim. The role of the offender's repentance is lost in Smedes's analysis. Further, according to his reading of the seventy-times-seven texts, victims can be stuck in an indefinite limbo of suffering from an injury until they have forgiven enough.[60]

L. Gregory Jones critiques Smedes's work on this point. According to Jones, any definition of forgiveness that does not regard community as central is detached from the biblical tradition: "On Smedes's account . . . therapeutic forgiveness is divorced from Christian practices and doctrine; an individual's psychic health replaces the goal of substantive Christian community lived in faithfulness to the Triune God."[61] Although Smedes imagines that "when we forgive we ride the crest of love's cosmic wave; we walk in stride with God,"[62] Jones places this cosmic wave squarely outside the biblical tradition.

In spite of its religious underpinnings, Smedes's account has broad appeal among secular psychologists and pastoral caregivers alike. Everett L. Worthington cites Smedes for his understanding of forgiveness as benefiting a person's mental health.[63] Psychologists mostly proceed without appealing to biblical themes and images as Smedes does; thus forgiveness becomes a kind of psychological intervention that addresses only the emotional state of an individual.

Most psychological definitions of forgiveness share the following ideas with Smedes: forgiveness is good for the forgiver, forgiveness is the best response to wrongdoing (and the only other response is negative and harmful), and forgiveness may be unilateral or unconditional in nature (that is, not involving the wrongdoer in any way). As a result, forgiveness is often touted for its supposed health benefits, and victims of crime or other offenses are often pressed by

60. Ibid.
61. Jones, *Embodying Forgiveness*, 52.
62. Smedes, *Forgive and Forget*, 152.
63. Worthington, "Initial Questions," 1.

counselors to forgive in order to free themselves from suffering (both mental and physical) relating to the offense.[64]

As these psychological understandings permeate discussions of forgiveness in theology, law, philosophy, and pastoral care, professionals in these areas conflate them with their own understandings of the select biblical passages. The result is a moral and religious imperative on victims to forgive as a matter of controlling their thoughts and feelings.

Forgiveness and repentance

Jesus links his forgiveness instructions to the concept of repentance. Here I consider how the repentance requirement informs the process of forgiveness throughout the Gospels. In the New Testament, the primary term translated as "repentance" is μετάνοια (the verbal form, "to repent," is μετανοέω). This term appears throughout the Synoptic Gospels (but is absent in the Gospel of John). The relationship between repentance and forgiveness calls into question interpretations of Jesus's teachings that portray forgiveness as unilateral or unconditional.

---

64. For examples of these approaches, see Jennie C. Noll, "Forgiveness in People Experiencing Trauma," in Worthington, *Handbook of Forgiveness*, 363–75; Alex H. S. Harris and Carl E. Thoreson, "Forgiveness, Unforgiveness, Health, and Disease," in Worthington, *Handbook of Forgiveness*, 321–33; Loren Toussaint and Jon R. Webb, "Theoretical and Empirical Connections between Forgiveness, Mental Health, and Well-Being," in Worthington, *Handbook of Forgiveness*, 349–62; Jennifer P. Friedberg, Sonia Suchday, and Danielle V. Shelov, "The Impact of Forgiveness on Cardiovascular Reactivity and Recovery," *International Journal of Psychophysiology* 65, no. 2 (2007): 87–94; Martina Antonia Waltman, "The Psychological and Physiological Effects of Forgiveness Education in Male Patients with Coronary Artery Disease" (PhD diss., University of Wisconsin-Madison, 2002); Charlotte Vanoyen Witvliet, "Forgiveness and Health: Review and Reflections on a Matter of Faith, Feelings, and Physiology," *Journal of Psychology and Theology* 29 (2001): 212–24; Michael E. McCullough, Kenneth I. Pargament, and Carl E. Thoresen, "The Psychology of Forgiveness: History, Conceptual Issues, and Overview," in *Forgiveness: Theory, Research, and Practice*, ed. Michael E. McCullough, Kenneth I. Pargament, and Carl E. Thoresen (New York: Guilford Press, 2000), 1–14.

The basic meaning of μετάνοια is a "change of mind" and is closely linked with "turning" to faith in the gospel message.[65] In Luke, when the scribes and Pharisees question Jesus's disciples about his association with "tax collectors and sinners" (5:30), Jesus responds, "Those who are well have no need of a physician, but those who are sick; I have come to call not the righteous but sinners to repentance" (5:31–32). Here, repentance involves a change of mind (i.e., toward faith in the gospel) and a turn away from sinful behavior. Later in the Gospel, Jesus announces the great value of a repentant sinner's turn to righteousness: "There will be more joy in heaven over one sinner who repents than over ninety-nine righteous persons who need no repentance" (15:7). In his resurrection appearance, Jesus commissions the disciples to deliver this message: "repentance and forgiveness of sins is to be proclaimed in [my] name to all nations" (24:47). Here, repentance precedes forgiveness of sins.

The Gospel of Luke contains the only explicit mention in the Gospels of repentance in the context of interpersonal sin. Jesus warns his disciples, "Be on your guard! If another disciple [lit. "your brother"] sins, you must rebuke the offender, and if there is repentance, you must forgive. And if the same person sins against you seven times a day, and turns back to you seven times and says, 'I repent,' you must forgive" (17:3–4). The familial language indicates that forgiveness is a community matter. It is a multipart exercise: First the sinner must be rebuked, and if he repents, the victim is obligated to forgive him. If the person sins again, and repents again, forgiveness must follow "seven times" or ad infinitum. Jesus presumably expects that the one sinned against will be able to judge whether there has been sincere repentance. The "brother" language indicates that this instruction is meant for relationships within a specific community.

---

65. A. Boyd Luter, "Repentance (New Testament)," in *ABD* 5:672–73. See also discussions of repentance in the Hebrew literature, in which *teshuva* also carries the connotation of "turning."

In Luke's Gospel, the action of repentance is not restricted to an intellectual or emotional change. Early in the narrative, John the Baptist instructs, "Bear fruits worthy of repentance" (3:8). Thus the inward change must be outwardly enacted. According to John the Baptist, those fruits include sharing clothing and food with the poor, not overcharging for taxes, and not extorting money (3:10–14).[66] Such actions may or may not indicate regret or a sorrowful disposition toward the past, but they do demonstrate a change in action in the future.

Repentance in the Gospels is a prerequisite for forgiveness from both God and other human beings. Other than the actions described to sinners and tax collectors above, however, the Gospels offer no instruction on how to gauge the sincerity of any expression of repentance; this is left to the victim's judgment. For my purposes, I include apology ("I'm sorry," "Forgive me," "Pardon me") as an acknowledgment of wrongdoing and gesture of repentance, as in the petition for forgiveness in the Lord's Prayer: "Forgive us our debts/sins" (Matt. 6:12//Luke 11:4).[67] The spoken word has currency as repentance in the Lukan instruction: "[If the same brother] turns back to you seven times and says, 'I repent,' you must forgive" (17:4). Repentance in the Gospels has visible manifestations, whether in the form of changed behavior (tax collectors and sinners improving their practices) or spoken apology ("Forgive me," "I repent"). In Matthew's community-discipline instructions (18:15–20), repentance takes the form of being receptive to the rebuke of another member of the community or the community at large; since uncooperative members

---

66. This elaboration on the meaning of repentance occurs only in Luke; there is no corresponding instruction in Matthew or Mark. See Guy D. Nave, *The Role and Function of Repentance in Luke-Acts* (Atlanta, GA: Society of Biblical Literature, 2002), 132.

67. On the varieties of spoken apologies as requests for forgiveness, see Radzik, *Making Amends,* 56; on "forgive me" as an example of an apology, see Nick Smith, *I Was Wrong: The Meanings of Apologies* (New York: Cambridge University Press, 2008), vi, 263n17.

are cast out of the community (at least temporarily), the ensuing forgiveness instructions apply to those who listen and change their behavior. In Luke, the right response to such rebuke is repentance (17:3). In each of these cases, the victim (or the representative community, as in Matthew) must determine whether the repentance is sincere.

Repentance and obligatory forgiveness

To this point, I have argued that according to the Gospels' forgiveness instructions, a victim is not obligated to forgive when repentance is absent. The Gospel material portrays forgiveness as a bilateral exercise (i.e., involving effort from both victim and offender), and nothing in the Gospels suggests that victims should be pressured to forgive unrepentant, absent, or unknown offenders. I point this out in order to counter contemporary calls for unconditional and unilateral forgiveness that claim biblical precedent. However, this emphasis on repentance raises the question: What happens when the offender *is* repentant? Is a victim obligated to forgive when there is sincere repentance on the part of the offender?

According to the Gospel instructions, it appears that the answer is yes. Both Matthew and Luke indicate that boundless forgiveness is the appropriate response to a repentant offender: the seventy-times-seven instructions in Matt. 18:21–22 follow the section on community discipline and offender rebuke; in Luke 17:3–4, Jesus emphasizes unlimited forgiveness "if there is repentance." The Lord's Prayer (Matt. 6:12/Luke 11:4) and the parable of the unforgiving servant (Matt. 18:23–35) make plain that divine forgiveness is contingent on human willingness to forgive.

Even such straightforward instructions seem to allow room for individual discernment, however. The biblical requirement for outward manifestation of inward repentance introduces an element of time and judgment to repentance. For example, a victim cannot rely on words of apology alone. The offender's behavior must change over time to show that the repentance (both words and actions) is sincere; assessing this change becomes a matter of the victim's judgment.

In the Gospel of John, the risen Jesus commissions the disciples, standing in for the entire community, to do exactly this: use their own judgment in deciding whom and what sins to forgive. John describes, "He breathed on them and said to them, 'Receive the Holy Spirit. If you forgive the sins of any, they are forgiven them; if you retain the sins of any, they are retained'" (John 20:22–23). James W. Barker argues that John reformulates the Matthean instruction on binding and loosing (18:18) as a correction to offset the harsh consequences for nonforgiveness given in Matthew's parable of the unforgiving servant (those who do not forgive will be handed over for torture by God; 18:34–35).[68] Barker observes, "John emphasizes the disciples' authority to withhold forgiveness, concerning which Matthew had cautioned."[69]

Jesus grants this authority to forgive or retain sins to each disciple present, and to every member of the community by extension. While some argue that this applies only to the disciples functioning as a community,[70] I hold that Jesus means to grant this authority—along with the guiding wisdom of the Holy Spirit—to all members of the community for all time.[71]

---

68. James W. Barker, "John's Use of Matthew" (PhD diss., Vanderbilt University, 2011), 83–103; John shifts the language from "loosing" (λύω) to "forgiving" (ἀφίημι), thus matching the ἀφίημι language in Matt. 18:21–22 (seventy times seven) and 18:23–35 (parable of the unforgiving servant).

69. Barker, "John's Use of Matthew," 103.

70. Tobias Hägerland, *Jesus and the Forgiveness of Sins: An Aspect of His Prophetic Mission* (Cambridge, UK: Cambridge University Press, 2011), 75–76; Raymond E. Brown, "The Kerygma of the Gospel according to John," *Interpretation* 21 (1967): 391.

71. The fact that Jesus makes this announcement to an incomplete group of disciples (at least Thomas is missing; those in attendance are not named) indicates that he means his words to

This means that even in cases where the offender repents, the victim may opt not to forgive. Perhaps a crime is too enormous, the injuries too severe, or the ongoing fear is too great to warrant forgiveness. As each of the Synoptic Gospels attests, there is at least one sin that is beyond the province of God's forgiveness (see Jesus's warning about the sin that "will not be forgiven"; Mark 3:29//Matt. 12:32//Luke 12:10).

The instruction in John 20:22–23 does not contradict the forgiveness instructions in Matthew and Luke; instead, it provides a complement as it commissions the disciples (who represent the entire community) to judge carefully when deciding whether to forgive. The implication in these verses is that the Holy Spirit (which Jesus breathes onto the disciples just prior to the instruction) will guide such decisions. And regardless of whether a victim forgives or retains the sins of another, God will follow suit.[72]

With this intertextual reading, the forgiveness instructions in Matthew and Luke are tempered by Jesus's authorizing the disciples (and the community) to make their own decisions about forgiveness. From Matthew and Luke, it is clear that forgiveness plays an important role in community cohesion and individual salvation (i.e.,

apply to a broader audience. Craig S. Keener writes, "Although the promise is given directly to those present at the time, it will no more exclude later generations of Christians (such as John's audience) than it would Thomas once he believes" (*The Gospel of John: A Commentary* [Peabody, MA: Hendrickson Publishers, 2003], 2:1206). Just as Matthew's Great Commission (28:19–20) is taken to apply to all Christians at all times, so this "commission" also extends to all Christians. See Francis J. Moloney, *The Gospel of John*, Sacra Pagina (Collegeville, MN: Liturgical Press, 1998), 534; David Aune, *The Cultic Setting of Realized Eschatology in Early Christianity*, Supplements to Novum Testamentum 28 (Leiden: Brill, 1972), 83; Keener, *Gospel of John*, 2:1206; Leon Morris, *The Gospel According to John*, The New International Critical Commentary on the New Testament (Grand Rapids, MI: Eerdmans, 1995), 748–49; Frederick Dale Bruner, *The Gospel of John: A Commentary* (Grand Rapids, MI: Eerdmans, 2012), 1165; Steve E. Hansen, "Forgiving and Retaining Sin: A Study of the Text and Context of John 20:23," *Horizons in Biblical Theology* 19 (1997):27; Barker, "John's Use of Matthew," 103 (see his diagram for Jesus's words applying to individual acts of forgiveness).

72. This assumes the divine passive in John 20:23 ("they are forgiven them . . . they are retained"); see Barker, "John's Use of Matthew," 90. See n. 15 for further examples of the divine-passive construction.

forgiveness by God), but John's Jesus adds that forgiveness is not an absolute obligation. Rather, victims must discern whether forgiveness is appropriate, with the knowledge that God will act accordingly.

Forgiveness that inspires repentance

In contrast to the forgoing observations that Jesus's teaching presumes that repentance precedes forgiveness, there is a strain in Christian theology that views repentance as a response to—rather than a prerequisite for—divine forgiveness. Miroslav Volf likens forgiveness to a gift that must be received. He writes, "Forgivers' forgiving is not conditioned by repentance. The offenders' *being forgiven*, however, is conditioned by repentance. Without repentance the forgivers will keep forgiving but the offenders will remain unforgiven, in that they are untouched by that forgiveness."[73] With regard to divine forgiveness, first there is forgiveness, then the response of repentance, then the grabbing hold of forgiven-ness. It is only by responding with repentance that one may truly accept the gift of forgiveness, but it is the initial forgiveness that inspires the repentant response.[74] Volf's view is apparently a contemporary expression of Augustine's concept of prevenient grace as God's grace (and forgiveness) that occurs prior to any human action (including repentance).[75] In this view, Jesus's prayer from the cross, "Father, forgive them" (Luke 23:34a), becomes an example of grace (forgiveness) that precedes and then prompts human action (repentance).

---

73. Volf, *Free of Charge,* 183.
74. On Jesus's forgiveness on the cross as inspiring repentance, see Karin Scheiber, *Vergebung: Eine systematisch-theologische Untersuchung,* Religion in Philosophy and Theology 21 (Tübingen: Mohr Siebeck, 2006), 67.
75. Phillip Cary, *Inner Grace: Augustine in the Traditions of Plato and Paul* (Oxford: Oxford University Press, 2008), 26.

This line of thinking has made its way into psychological circles as a way to promote unconditional and unilateral forgiveness. In the realm of interpersonal forgiveness, "[g]enuine forgiveness can lead the sinner to understand their wrongdoing and repent," write Cynthia Ransley and Terri Spy.[76] In this view, forgiveness becomes a mode by which the victim could positively influence the wrongdoer. "If the expression of forgiveness is viewed as sincere," write Julie Juola Exline and Roy F. Baumeister, "the perpetrator could note the victim's admirable behavior and feel inspired (or perhaps shamed) toward repentance."[77] Such an understanding of the relationship between forgiveness and repentance becomes simply a way to heap a double burden on victims. Not only must they forgive unconditionally, but they must do so for the good of the perpetrator (i.e., to inspire his repentance).

Forgiveness and restorative justice

I turn now to summarize the chapters that follow. In the first case study, I provide a brief history of interpretation of Jesus's seventy-times-seven instructions (Matt. 18:21–22 and Luke 17:3–4). I demonstrate how the church fathers and the Reformers focus on the role of repentance in these instructions and how contemporary interpretations nevertheless abandon the emphasis on repentance that is clear in both Matthew's and Luke's versions. As a result of these more recent interpretations, victims who participate in restorative justice encounters are often presented with biblical imperatives for unlimited forgiveness that is also unilateral and unconditional (i.e.,

---

76. Ransley and Spy, *Forgiveness and the Healing Process*, 14.
77. Julie Juola Exline and Roy F. Baumeister, "Expressing Forgiveness and Repentance: Benefits and Barriers," in McCullough, Pargament, and Thoresen, *Forgiveness: Theory, Research, and Practice*, 137.

not requiring offender repentance), when the biblical material presents quite a different picture.

Restorative justice advocates idealize and heavily promote forgiveness while often claiming a biblical mandate. I call for a reexamination of the seventy-times-seven material and a reinstitution of a bilateral process of forgiveness that can and must include offender repentance. I am critical of the restorative justice movement's lavish praise of unconditional forgiveness both because it misappropriates the biblical teaching and because it threatens to revictimize the victim.

Claiming biblical foundations, restorative justice advocates emphasize forgiveness and reconciliation as the primary response to crime. A major facet of this movement is the practice of victim-offender mediation (VOM), where, together with a mediator, victims face offenders to talk about the effects of the crime. While pressure to forgive is taboo in this process, restorative justice advocates heavily promote forgiveness in other contexts and the tacit pressure to forgive is strong.

Since many restorative justice advocates cite biblical foundations for their work,[78] this case study examines how they import biblical

---

78. See, for example: Mark Umbreit and Marilyn Peterson Armour, *Restorative Justice Dialogue: An Essential Guide for Research and Practice* (New York: Springer Publishing Company, 2011), 69–70; Pierre Allard and Wayne Northey, "Christianity: The Rediscovery of Restorative Justice," in *The Spiritual Roots of Restorative Justice*, ed. Michael L. Hadley (Albany, NY: SUNY Press, 2001), 133–35; Christopher D. Marshall, *Beyond Retribution: A New Testament Vision for Justice, Crime, and Punishment*, Studies in Peace and Scripture (Grand Rapids, MI: Eerdmans, 2001), 268–69, 284; B. Bruce Cook, "Justice that Reconciles and Heals: Developing a Ministry for Crime Victims with a Restorative Justice Perspective" (DMin diss., Drew University, 2002), 24–25; Marc Forget, "Crime as Interpersonal Conflict: Reconciliation between Victim and Offender," in *Dilemmas of Reconciliation: Cases and Concepts*, ed. Carol Prager and Trudy Govier (Waterloo, ON: Wilfrid Laurier University Press, 2003), 111–36; and especially Howard Zehr, "Restoring Justice," in *God and the Victim: Theological Reflections on Evil, Victimization, Justice, and Forgiveness*, ed. Lisa Barnes Lampman and Michelle D. Shattuck (Grand Rapids, MI: Eerdmans, 1999), 131–59; and Zehr, *Changing Lenses: A New Focus for Crime and Justice*, Christian Peace Shelf (Scottdale, PA: Herald Press, 1990), 45–47, 51, 174, 185–86, 190, 228, and passim.

forgiveness instructions into a quasi-legal process and bring them to bear on victims in the context of mediation. The seventy-times-seven instructions in Matthew and Luke are especially prevalent in restorative justice literature. I show that only the "unlimited" character of forgiveness is preserved and celebrated, while the emphasis on offender repentance is usually downplayed and sometimes lost. I show how the trend in biblical studies also leans toward emphasizing the command for unlimited forgiveness.

In the context of restorative justice, VOM practices both enact and contradict the biblical instructions. While the process is presented as a dialogue—with roles for both the offender (to apologize) and the victim (to forgive)—such expectations render the encounter artificial and scripted. Further, there is much more discussion and praise of "forgiving" victims in the movement's literature than there is about repentant offenders. Victims are expected to forgive regardless of the offender's disposition, and this expectation is based largely on the supposed therapeutic benefits of forgiveness. Such forgiveness is presented as biblical, and so victims face not just a moral imperative, but also a theological one.

The goal of this case-study analysis is not to discount or reject the role of forgiveness in the aftermath of crime. Rather, I argue that a more thorough application of the bilateral model of forgiveness presented in the Gospels provides a more balanced and emotionally safer approach to VOM than the current idealized version of forgiveness. In the bilateral model, victims are not required to forgive offenders who are not repentant, and repentance must be judged to be sincere and reflected in concrete actions such as restitution where possible (also a key concept in restorative justice). In the absence of such repentance, victims may withhold forgiveness and reconciliation. This is exactly the process described in the seventy-times-seven material. When applied to restorative justice encounters, it stands to create a richer experience for victims.

Forgiveness and post-apartheid South Africa

In the context of post-apartheid South Africa, forgiveness language dominates the national discourse of reconciliation. During the Human Rights Violations Committee hearings of the Truth and Reconciliation Commission (1996–98 [original mandate], extended to 2002), victims of apartheid violence were sometimes implored to forgive even by the TRC chairperson himself, Archbishop Desmond Tutu. Forgiveness was touted both for its healing potential (mainly psychological, mainly for individuals) and its religious importance. Tutu's memoir of the period, *No Future without Forgiveness*,[79] reflects this imperative. Tutu repeatedly asserts that the future of the "new South Africa" is dependent on the unconditional forgiveness of the victims of apartheid and anti-apartheid violence.

Alongside this rhetoric of forgiveness, I consider the Lord's Prayer (Matt. 6:9–13; Luke 11:2–4). While Tutu does not frequently cite the prayer in his writings, he does mention its forgiveness imperative;[80] and its presence is implied with its daily recitation at the openings of the TRC hearings.[81] First I review the history of interpretation of these verses and note how the prayer functions as a tool for ensuring community cohesion. In the Gospel context, the Lord's Prayer unites voices toward common hopes and commitments: enough food,

79. Desmond Tutu, *No Future without Forgiveness* (New York: Doubleday, 1999).
80. Desmond Tutu, *God Is Not a Christian: And Other Provocations* (New York: HarperOne, 2011), 31 (citing Tutu's words with the South African Council of Churches in Mogopa in 1983); Desmond Tutu, *The Rainbow People of God: The Making of a Peaceful Revolution*, ed. John Allen (New York: Doubleday, 1994), 224.
81. Allan Aubrey Boesak, "'Just Another Jew in the Ditch': Incarnated Reconciliation," in *Radical Reconciliation: Beyond Political Pietism and Christian Quietism*, ed. Allan Aubrey Boesak and Curtiss Paul DeYoung (Maryknoll, NY: Orbis Books, 2012), 63.

mutual forgiveness, protection from evil, and the emergence of the kingdom of God on earth.[82] The prayer is a community prayer.

The Lord's Prayer is consistent with other accounts of forgiveness in the Gospels in that it emphasizes the bilateral character of forgiveness. The prayer contains both a plea and a promise: *forgive us as we forgive*. The plea contains an admission of guilt, a sense of repentance (i.e., asking for forgiveness), and a hope for divine pardon. The promise looks to enact that forgiveness in order to preserve and strengthen the early Christian community. The plea for forgiveness, which I interpret as an expression of repentance, is inseparable from the promise to forgive. The community repeats each of these pleas and promises when they pray together.

This interpretation of the Lord's Prayer is instructive in the context of the TRC and post-apartheid South Africa in that the promotion of forgiveness by Tutu and others often dismisses the need for repentance. Indeed, while victims in the HRVC hearings were often pressed to forgive, offenders appearing before the Amnesty Committee were not urged to apologize or otherwise show remorse. While the TRC has roles for both victims and offenders—the Human Rights Violations Committee and the Amnesty Committee hearings, respectively—the two are kept separate and there is no opportunity for dialogue. The rhetoric of victim forgiveness is not matched by a similar call for offender repentance or remorse, although coming before the Amnesty Committee with no guarantee of a positive outcome is a step in that direction.

---

82. Some interpret it as an eschatological prayer, with "daily bread" referring to the "heavenly manna of the latter days" and "Forgive us our debts" pointing to the coming time of judgment (Dale C. Allison, "Matthew," in *The Oxford Bible Commentary*, ed. John Barton and John Muddiman [New York: Oxford University Press, 2001], 856; see also W. D. Davies and D. C. Allison, *Matthew 1–7*, International Critical Commentary [London: T&T Clark International, 1988], 594). I interpret the prayer as having to do with everyday concerns, including acts of interpersonal forgiveness.

Together with his promotion of forgiveness, Tutu also frequently warned of the ill effects of negative emotions such as anger or resentment. Victims, then, were presented with an imperative to forgive based not on offender repentance but rather on promises of psychological or emotional healing. While he advocated forgiveness based on Christian imperatives, Tutu conflated that forgiveness with an idealized model of unconditional, unilateral forgiveness that would give birth to a new, reconciled South Africa.

In this chapter I also demonstrate that Tutu's repudiation of the negative emotions discounts the role played by anger and resentment in the years of protest leading up to the end of apartheid. Moving forward to a consideration of Tutu's thought during and after the TRC, I show that forgiveness alone is insufficient as a national ethic. In many ways, forgiveness and the reconciliation it often precedes may serve as powerful catalysts for conflict transformation. But forgiveness alone did not end apartheid; protest and anger and righteous indignation paved the way to the TRC. The biblical account does not preclude anger even as it calls for bilateral forgiveness. The TRC and Tutu would better serve victims with a reexamination of a process that calls for unconditional forgiveness. I propose the Lord's Prayer as a countervailing example of community cohesion that involves both repentance and forgiveness. Tutu's boosterism of unconditional, unilateral forgiveness may provide emotional catharsis in the short term, but pressuring victims toward this kind of forgiveness creates a weak version of reconciliation that is based on the emotional sacrifice of victims rather than mutual effort and respect.

Forgiveness and the pastoral care of victims of domestic violence

According to the National Institutes of Justice and the Centers for Disease Control, approximately 1.5 million women are victims of domestic abuse—that is, abuse by intimate partners—in the United States every year.[83] Since victims often seek help from Christian clergy or other pastoral caregivers, theological responses play a role in how victims understand their situations and whether they find safety from their abusers.

In many cases, pastors and pastoral counselors raise the issue of forgiveness with victims of domestic violence. Often victims, having noted the Gospel emphasis on forgiveness, struggle with whether and how to forgive their abusers. While certainly not all pastoral professionals advise women to remain in abusive marriages, many advocate forgiveness, either toward reconciling the marriage relationship or for the individual health of the victim. In this fourth chapter, I examine how women are sometimes encouraged to follow the example of Christ on the cross ("Father, forgive them"; Luke 23:34a) and to forgive without condition. I argue that this verse in fact reflects a *refusal* to forgive in such a circumstance, and thus it provides a positive model for victims of domestic violence to withhold forgiveness from unrepentant and potentially dangerous abusers. Considering that many women forgive and return to abusive partners only to be abused again, victims may be served by a reading of this text that encourages an intermediary step, such as prayer that makes way for careful discernment as called for in John 20:23 before forgiving.

I review the history of interpretation of Jesus's cry from the cross in order to show how the verse has been used in both ancient and contemporary contexts to promote unconditional forgiveness in the midst of suffering, as well as after the fact. In light of Jesus's other teachings on forgiveness in the Gospel of Luke (e.g., 17:3–4),

83. P. Tjaden and N. Thoennes, *Extent, Nature, and Consequences of Intimate Partner Violence: Findings from the National Violence against Women Survey*, Publication No. NCJ 181867 (Washington, DC: Department of Justice, 2000), iii, https://www.ncjrs.gov/pdffiles1/nij/181867.pdf.

some scholars assert that he withholds forgiveness in the absence of repentance.[84] His prayer for forgiveness is entirely consistent with his earlier call for enemy love (Luke 6:27–28), but it is not a direct act of forgiveness. In Luke, Jesus teaches a forgiveness that is conditioned on repentance, and his prayer on the cross illustrates this.

Next, I show how pastoral caregivers often apply explicit or tacit pressure on victims to forgive their abusers in ways that are similar to techniques used by forgiveness advocates in the other two case studies. Many pastors and counselors embrace the psychological model or unilateral and unconditional forgiveness and present this to victims as a biblical imperative. This forgiveness is given as the duty of the victim, as well as the only way to heal from abuse. I demonstrate how some pastoral caregivers downplay the role of repentance and conflate biblical and psychological understandings.

When Jesus prays from the cross, he turns the matter of forgiveness over to God. As he suffers violence and death, he demonstrates to victims that forgiveness in the midst of violence is not an obligation. This prayer in place of forgiveness gives victims who are concerned with following the biblical text another way to respond in the midst or aftermath of abuse. With this interpretation, victims maintain their moral agency and may faithfully imitate Christ without forgiving their abusers.

Reimagining forgiveness

In each of these three cases, well-meaning theologians, clergy, and counselors transform the biblical call for forgiveness as a bilateral process that has practical outcomes (restored relationships, reconciliation, community cohesion) into a pop-psychological notion that requires only emotional work on the part of the victim

---

84. See, for example, S. John Roth, "Jesus the Pray-er," *Currents in Theology and Mission* 33, no. 6 (2006): 497.

and little participation from the offender or the affected community. As such, the entire burden of repair rests on the victim. This book presents new interpretations of biblical texts toward reimagining forgiveness as bilateral and contingent.

Preserving the bilateral nature of forgiveness in accordance with the Scriptures offers victims a biblically based alternative to forgiving offenders. This allows victims to protect themselves in the wake of violence by refusing to forgive and reconcile with their abusers while remaining faithful to their religious convictions. The seventy-times-seven instructions, the Lord's Prayer, and Jesus's cry from the cross all contain a prescription for repentance as a necessary part of forgiveness.

It is not the purpose of this project to debunk or devalue forgiveness. On the contrary, I recognize that a process of repentance and forgiveness may be a powerful part of conflict transformation or relationship repair. Indeed, such repair is what is called for in the Gospel texts. However, I suggest that not every act of forgiveness is morally valuable or even appropriate. Following Margaret Urban Walker, I argue that the value of forgiveness is governed by its intentions and outcomes. She writes:

> An account of forgiveness needs to capture that part of forgiving that looks ahead hopefully to an uncertain future and not only to the part that looks to settle something in the past. There are conditions [i.e., whether the offender repents, whether that repentance is sincere, and whether that relationship is genuinely safe for the victim going forward] that make that hopefulness more or less risky, and understanding forgiveness as something of moral value involves understanding what conditions those are.[85]

---

85. Margaret Urban Walker, *Moral Repair: Reconstructing Moral Relations after Wrongdoing* (New York: Cambridge University Press, 2006), 151–52.

Thus forgiveness must not be idealized; every act of forgiveness is only as good as what it accomplishes. For example, if forgiving an unrepentant abuser opens the door for further abuse, such forgiveness is not morally good. Such a discerning account holds forgiveness accountable to the biblical view and provides a safeguard for acts of forgiveness that put the victim or others in danger by becoming again vulnerable, either physically or emotionally, to the offender.

Walker also argues that there are circumstances in which relationship repair may not be possible. She writes, "Where the reparative role of forgiveness is blocked or impossible due to some changeable feature of the situation, it may be true that to forgive under those conditions [lack of repentance, amends, or acknowledgment of harm] would be wrong."[86] For Walker, there are no negative moral implications for the victim who is unable or unwilling to forgive. She continues, "Holding wrongs 'unforgivable' is a way to mark the enormity of injury and the malignancy of wrongdoing as exceeding anything that could be made to fit back into a reliable framework of moral relations."[87] Walker focuses on the *end result* of forgiveness as well as the *act* of forgiveness before naming it as a virtue. According to Walker, forgiveness may not be possible. According to the biblical instructions, forgiveness may not be possible. But that failure does not indicate a moral failure on the part of the individual victim. This book is predicated on this careful and conditional understanding of the possibilities and limits of forgiveness.

86. Ibid., 178.
87. Ibid., 190.

2

———

Repentance and Repair, or "Ethical Bungee Jumping"? Forgiveness in the "Seventy-Times-Seven" Instructions and Victim-Offender Mediation

When Clair and Anna May Weaver were brutally murdered by their fourteen-year-old son Keith in 1991, the response from Landisville Mennonite Church was immediate. In addition to caring for surviving family members, Pastor Sam Thomas created support groups for the community and began providing legal and social assistance for Keith. In the early days after the murders, Thomas encouraged the congregation to "understand what it means to forgive," and to "think about their intent to forgive."[1]

---

1. Andrea Schrock Wenger, "How Does a Congregation Deal with a Triple Murder?," *Gospel Herald*, February 9, 1993, 6. The now-defunct *Gospel Herald* was a news organ of the Mennonite Church from 1908 to 1998. I received a scanned copy of this article courtesy of Colleen MacFarland of the Mennonite Church USA Archives on April 17, 2012.

A few months later, church members had established the "70×7 Fund" to help with the legal, therapeutic, educational, and personal needs of Keith Weaver. Through the fund, the congregation acknowledged their "biblical responsibility to have compassion for both victims and offenders and their desire to forgive and continue forgiving, even 'seventy times seven,' as Jesus called his disciples to do in Matthew 18."[2]

In reporting on these events, Andrea Schrock Wenger calls the fund a "modern response to an ancient command."[3] She presents the story of the church's actions as an example of restorative justice in action. Indeed, Howard Zehr, widely regarded as the founder of the restorative justice movement, cites the community's response as a shining example of right response to crime. He writes, "[The] only justice [is one] that treats each actor as a full participant . . . that encourages communication and empathy, that addresses the needs of victims as well as offenders."[4] Zehr cites the "70×7 fund" as a model of restorative justice practice. Its name, he observes, recognizes that "forgiveness [is] a decision that would need to be made over and over, 'seventy times seven.'"[5]

The church's response to the murder in their midst—as well as Zehr's analysis—goes to the heart of the restorative justice movement in which advocates offer an alternative to the so-called "retributive" criminal justice system and criticize its emphasis on punishment. Privileging such values as forgiveness and reconciliation, they emphasize the humanity and agency of the victim, the offender, and the community. In their view, the essence of crime is a broken

2. Ibid., 7.
3. Ibid.
4. Zehr, "Restoring Justice," in *God and the Victim: Theological Reflections on Evil, Victimization, Justice, and Forgiveness*, ed. Lisa Barnes Lampman and Michelle D. Shattuck (Grand Rapids, MI: Eerdmans, 1999), 159.
5. Ibid., 154.

relationship and the goal of restorative justice is to repair that breach.[6] Even when there was no relationship prior to the offense, many restorative justice advocates contend that the crime creates a relationship, and that relationship is worth restoring.[7] As Mark Umbreit observes, "Restoration of the emotional and material losses resulting from crime is far more important than imposing ever-increasing levels of costly punishment on the offender."[8]

In this chapter, I examine the intersection of Scripture and law in the restorative justice movement and specifically in the practice of victim-offender mediation (VOM). Since many restorative justice advocates cite biblical foundations for their work,[9] I address how they interpret the community instructions about forgiveness in Matt. 18:21–22 and Luke 17:3–4 and apply them in this context. Advocates often use these texts to promote unlimited and unconditional forgiveness. However, a closer look at the biblical texts demonstrates definite boundaries within the forgiveness instructions, boundaries that are often transgressed in VOM practices.

First, I review the history of interpretation of the so-called "seventy-times-seven" instructions on forgiveness. I show how these

6. On crime as broken relationship in restorative justice, see Howard Zehr, *Changing Lenses: A New Focus for Crime and Justice*, Christian Peace Shelf (Scottsdale, PA: Herald Press, 1990), 184; Daniel W. Van Ness, *Crime and Its Victims* (Downers Grove, IL: InterVarsity Press, 1986), 137; Elizabeth M. Bounds, "For Prisoners and Our Communities," in *To Do Justice: A Guide for Progressive Christians*, ed. Rebecca Todd Peters and Elizabeth Hinson-Hasty (Louisville, KY: Westminster John Knox Press, 1989), 37; Christopher D. Marshall, *Beyond Retribution: A New Testament Vision for Justice, Crime, and Punishment*, Studies in Peace and Scripture (Grand Rapids, MI: Eerdmans, 2001), 73; Stuart Wilson, "The Myth of Restorative Justice: Truth, Reconciliation and the Ethics of Amnesty," *South African Journal of Human Rights* 17 (2001): 553; Keith Allen Regehr, "Judgment and Forgiveness: Restorative Justice Practice and the Recovery of Theological Memory" (PhD diss., University of Waterloo, 2007), 37; Conrad G. Brunk, "Restorative Justice and the Philosophical Theories of Criminal Justice," in *The Spiritual Roots of Restorative Justice*, ed. Michael L. Hadley (Albany, NY: SUNY Press, 2001), 48.

7. Zehr, *Changing Lenses*, 51.

8. Mark S. Umbreit and Jean Greenwood, *Guidelines for Victim-Sensitive Victim-Offender Mediation: Restorative Justice through Dialogue*, U.S. Dept. of Justice, Office for Victims of Crime, NCJ 176346 (St. Paul, MN: Center for Restorative Justice and Peacemaking, 2000), 1.

9. See chapter 1, n. 78.

verses teach a forgiveness that is boundless but conditional, and I situate them in their context of a set of instructions intended to strengthen the nascent Christian community. In examining the process of forgiveness described in Matthew and Luke, I find that the call for repentance given explicitly in Luke 17:4 and implied in Matthew's discourse on community discipline (18:15–20) is highly valued among early church fathers and Reformers, but is often lost in the celebration of "radical forgiveness"[10] that is the hallmark of restorative justice and mediation practices. I also show how current interpretations enlarge the definition of forgiveness, downplay the role of repentance, and conflate the biblical instructions with contemporary psychological notions of forgiveness.

Next, I show how VOM practices are both consistent with and also antithetical to the biblical forgiveness instructions. Jesus's instructions—especially in Matthew—serve as directions for resolving conflicts within the community, a process that ideally ends in forgiveness. VOM follows this course to a point, especially by carefully delineating requirements for both victim and offender. However, by identifying a "forgiving" victim in conversation with a "repentant" offender as the basic structure, the very process contains pressure on each participant to behave in a particular way or risk termination of the mediation session.[11] Further, advocates tend to

10. See Brian Zahnd, *Unconditional? The Call of Jesus to Radical Forgiveness* (Lake Mary, FL: Charisma House, 2010), 82: "Restorative justice is . . . the kind of justice Jesus wants to bring to a broken world. This is the kind of justice that can happen when we choose to end the cycle of revenge. This is the kind of justice that can happen when we are more interested in restoration than retaliation." Restorative justice expectations for offenders span a spectrum from eliminating prisons to encouraging mediation as a complement to the criminal process. For an extended discussion of the variety of meanings of "justice" in restorative justice circles, see Zehr, *Changing Lenses*, 61–157. On justice as defined anew in each restorative justice context, see Jennifer Llewellyn, "Restorative Justice and Truth Commissions," in *Handbook of Restorative Justice*, ed. Gerry Johnstone and Daniel W. Van Ness (Portland, OR: Willan Publishing, 2007), 360.
11. Some VOM mediators discourage expressions of anger during mediation, and many cases are rejected for VOM if the victim is judged to be "too angry." As a result, victims must sublimate

draw the basis of their advocacy of forgiveness from contemporary visions of unlimited and unconditional forgiveness, both religious and psychological. While VOM mediators take care never to pressure victims to forgive, I show that implicit pressure and a preference for forgiveness exist.

In the murder case described above, the pastor warns, "It is not helpful at all to push forgiveness or to give pat answers."[12] But as the congregation acted out a specifically "restorative" vision of community justice, one of the first tasks of the ministry team was to help parishioners and the victim's family "understand what it means to forgive, and to . . . think about their intent to forgive."[13] At no point in this extended article about the murders and their aftermath does the author recount the words or behavior of the offender after his arrest. The article does not report whether he was apologetic or remorseful. For this community, supporting or forgiving Keith Weaver does not depend on his response.

Jesus's forgiveness instructions in Matthew and Luke

Two similar sets of teachings about forgiveness appear in Matthew and Luke:

Matt. 18.21–22	Luke 17.3–4
Then Peter came and said to him, "Lord, if my brother sins against me, how often should I forgive? As many as seven times?" Jesus said to him, "Not seven times, but, I tell you, seventy-seven times."	Be on your guard! If your brother sins, you must rebuke the offender, and if there is repentance, you must forgive. And if the same person sins against you seven times a day, and turns back to you seven times and says, "I repent," you must forgive.

negative emotions in order to fit within the VOM picture of what successful mediation looks like. See Jennifer Gerarda Brown, "The Use of Mediation to Resolve Criminal Cases: A Procedural Critique," *Emory Law Journal* 43 (1994): 1276.

12. Wenger, "How Does a Congregation Deal with a Triple Murder?," 8.

13. Ibid., 6.

In both passages, the verb ἀφίημι ("forgive") echoes the Lord's Prayer as well as the pronouncements of forgiveness in the healing of the paralyzed man (Matt. 9:2–8; Mark 2:2–12; Luke 5:17–26) and the sinful woman (Luke 7:36–50). In Matthew's version, Jesus gives a simple instruction: if a member of the church sins against you, then you must forgive seventy-seven times, that is, without limit. The Lukan formula is more complex. Instead of presenting forgiveness as an automatic response to wrongdoing, Jesus describes a bilateral process in which the offender must first show repentance before the victim is required to forgive.

Unlimited forgiveness

Scholars most commonly interpret Matthew's use of "seventy-seven" to mean that forgiveness should be boundless.[14] The number may also be an allusion to Gen. 4:24, where Lamech boasts that he will avenge himself seventy-sevenfold. Jesus's audience would have noticed this parallel and so regarded the instruction concerning unlimited forgiveness as the correction of Lamech's unrestricted revenge.[15] Understood as such, forgiveness serves to quiet, or offset, the desire for revenge. However, unlimited forgiveness may be as problematic as unlimited revenge in that it may excuse even ongoing offenses; a more effective antidote to unlimited revenge could be more careful consideration and moderation of both the forgiving and angry responses.

Others interpret the number seventy-seven as representing not the quantity but rather the ongoing character of forgiveness. Christoph

---

14. In Matthew, the command is to forgive seventy-seven times (ἑβδομηκοντάκις ἑπτά, which is often mistranslated as "seventy times seven times"). In Luke's version (17:3–4), the command is to forgive "seven times" (ἑπτάκις) if preceded by seven expressions of "I repent" (μετανοήσῃ). For the sake of expediency, I refer to these texts as the "seventy-times-seven" instructions or teachings.

15. Douglas R. A. Hare, *Matthew*, Interpretation (Louisville, KY: John Knox Press, 1993), 216.

Klein sees the command as less about quantity and more a way of life, "an understanding of reconciliation as a process, that needs to be repeatedly [and] constantly maintained, regularly nurtured and brought about, therefore pointing to the demand for a 'culture of reconciliation.'"[16] In this configuration, forgiveness as a way of life may not include a forgiving response to every instance of wrongdoing but rather a general disposition toward forgiving where possible.

In both Matthew and Luke, Peter questions whether one should forgive "seven times," which would have been a very large or even infinite number. This makes Jesus' multiplication of seven in his responses seem even more excessive.[17] Matthew's instruction for boundless forgiveness appears near the end of Jesus's discourse on community rule. In the preceding verses, Jesus advises his followers to rebuke other church members when they commit sins and to cast those who are not receptive to this rebuke out of the community (18:15–17). He tells Peter that he is obligated to forgive his "brother" (18:21) seventy-seven times. Similarly, in Luke Jesus instructs forgiveness of "your brother" (17:3) seven times a day as long as that disciple repents.[18] The familial language indicates that these instructions were intended to promote reconciliation within a specific community. Luke's addition of "a day" (τῆς ἡμέρας) to the instruction emphasizes the everyday character of this process.

16. Christoph Klein, *Wenn Rache der Vergebung weicht: Theologische Grundlagen einer Kultur der Versöhnung*, Forschungen zur systematischen und ökumenische Theologie 93 (Göttingen: Vandenhoeck & Ruprecht, 1999), 19 (translation mine). Original text: "Eines Verständnisses von der Versöhnung also Prozess, der immer wieder, ständig, regelmässig gepflegt und bewirkt, werden muss; sie ist somit Hinweis auf die Forderung einer 'Kultur der Versöhnung.'"
17. R. T. France, *The Gospel of Matthew*, NICNT (Grand Rapids, MI: Eerdmans, 2007), 700, 704–5; on seven as an infinite number, see my "Seventy Times Seven," in *The Dictionary of the Bible and Western Culture: A Handbook for Students*, ed. Michael Gilmour and Mary Ann Beavis (Sheffield, UK: Sheffield Phoenix Press, 2012), 482–83.
18. The NRSV renders ὁ ἀδελφός as "another member of the church" (Matt. 18:21) and "another disciple" (Luke 17:3).

Forgiveness and reconciliation are closely linked in these passages. Matthew and Luke both devote substantial effort to dealing with conflict and reconciliation within the community. Relationships in the church are worth restoring.[19] The exhortations in Matthew and Luke are limited to how church members should behave toward one another. The community cannot survive without an active effort to maintain and nourish relationships.[20] Forgiveness in these contexts is synonymous with reconciliation; in Jesus's teachings, forgiveness always involves the restoration of right relationship and reintegration into the community, whether that is a human community or the eschatological community of the saved. The current notion that forgiveness can begin and end with the individual victim, or achieve an emotional or psychological change, does not appear in Jesus's teachings.[21]

Reproving and repentance

While the teaching of unlimited forgiveness in Matthew seems antithetical to the immediately preceding instructions on strict discipline for unrepentant sinners (those not receptive to reproof should "be to you as a Gentile and a tax collector" 18:17), in fact they are complementary. Forgiveness should be unlimited, but not unconditional. Leviticus instructs, "You shall not hate in your heart anyone of your kin; *you shall reprove your neighbor*, or you will incur

---

19. Thomas G. Long, *Matthew*, Westminster Bible Companion (Louisville, KY: Westminster John Knox Press, 1997), 210. On forgiveness as a tool for community maintenance, see also Gordon M. Zerbe, *Non-Retaliation in Early Jewish and New Testament Texts: Ethical Themes in Social Contexts* (Sheffield, UK: Sheffield Academic Press, 1993), 204; and W. G. Thompson, *Matthew's Advice to a Divided Community* (Rome: Biblical Institute Press, 1970).

20. Dale C. Allison, "Matthew," in *The Oxford Bible Commentary*, ed. John Barton and John Muddiman (New York: Oxford University Press, 2001), 867; see also W. D. Davies and D. C. Allison, *Matthew 1–7*, ICC (London: T&T Clark International, 1988), 308.

21. David Konstan, *Before Forgiveness: The Origins of a Moral Idea* (New York: Cambridge University Press, 2010), 165–66.

guilt yourself" (19:17; emphasis mine). Correcting one's neighbor is, according to the Bible, not only a kind response; it is also an obligation. Further, as Davies and Allison observe, "The [early Christian] community would cease to be if it did not insist on [right behavior]. Thus the spirit of forgiveness cannot mean blindness and indifference to sin within the church."[22]

Matthew supplies only a general instruction on forgiveness, but Luke offers details on the mechanics of the process. Luke gives a pair of parallel examples: "If your brother sins, you must rebuke the offender, and if there is repentance, you must forgive. And if the same person sins against you seven times a day, and turns back to you seven times and says, 'I repent,' you must forgive" (17:3–4). Luke thereby presents a progression: *sin → rebuke → repent → forgive*. The second example is more specific: *sin seven times a day → turn back seven times a day → say, "I repent" → forgive*. In Luke's description, the process of forgiveness is an exchange between victim and offender with requirements on both sides. It follows that if any of the steps fails, the entire process fails. Luke makes clear that repentance is necessary for forgiveness.

In both the Gospels of Luke and Matthew, forgiveness material appears within a collection of community instructions. Where Matthew separates the process of reproof (18:15) from the command to forgive (18:22), Luke joins the two to demonstrate that forgiveness must be preceded by repentance (17:3–4). Repeated sins must be accompanied by repeated expressions of repentance before there can be repeated forgiveness (signified by the number seven).

The early church followed Luke's insistence on repentance. Concerning Matthew's verse about the one who is unwilling to be reproved being "as a Gentile and a tax collector" (18:17), John

---

22. Davies and Allison, *Matthew*, 308.

Chrysostom sees Matthew as imposing a limit on the command for forgiveness.[23] He rephrases Peter's question by adding a phrase: "How often then ought I to bear with him, *being told his faults, and repenting? Is it enough for seven times?*"[24] The addition of "being told his faults" and "repenting" to Matthew's text indicates the importance of both behaviors in the granting of forgiveness. For Chrysostom, repentance is such an integral part of the forgiveness instruction that he alters Peter's question in order to include the repentance behavior described in Luke.

Martin Luther makes a similar move. He writes, "As oft as thy brother asks forgiveness, thou shalt forgive him."[25] Again, repentance demonstrated by "asking forgiveness" is included in the formula. Luther considers the Matthean and Lukan versions of these texts to be interchangeable; his comment on Luke 17:1–4 cross-references Matthew 18.[26] Even in the midst of a sermon on Christ's voluminous grace and forgiveness, Luther incorporates a call to repentance: "Because Christ . . . set up and erected such a kingdom, as wherein is only grace, which must at no times cease, so that *if thou repent* all things will be wholly forgiven thee."[27]

Luther invokes Luke 24:47 ("Repentance and forgiveness of sins is to be proclaimed in his name to all nations") to demonstrate further the inexorable relationship between repentance and faith, which together open the way to forgiveness. According to Luther, repentance and faith cannot be understood separately. "These two

---

23. St. John Chrysostom, Homily 61 on Matthew, http://www.newadvent.org/fathers/200161.htm.
24. Ibid.
25. Martin Luther, in E. Mueller, ed., *Luther's Explanatory Notes on the Gospels*, trans. P. Anstadt (York, PA: P. Anstadt & Sons, 1899), 107; this is from Luther's commentary on Matt. 18:18–22. Here the translator renders Luther's text in language similar to the King James Version of the Bible.
26. Mueller, *Luther's Explanatory Notes*, 241.
27. Martin Luther, *Sermons on the Most Interesting Doctrines of the Gospel*, trans. J. Thornton (London: Paternoster-Row, 1830), 370 (emphasis mine).

are the first elements of Christian life," he writes. "Repentance or contrition and grief, and faith through which we receive the forgiveness of sins and are righteous before God. Both should grow and increase in us."[28] Even as the reformer sought to correct what he saw as the Catholic emphasis on human works as necessary for salvation, he held onto the call for repentance as a requirement for forgiveness.

John Calvin also focuses on the importance of repentance. He writes, "As repentance is a wonderful work of the Spirit, and is the creation of the new man, if we despise it, we offer an insult to God himself."[29] He considers the Matthean and Lukan instructions together: Matt. 18:21–35 (the seventy-times-seven instruction and the parable of the unforgiving servant) and Luke 17:4 (the seventy-times-seven instruction with the inclusion of repentance). His arrangement of the Gospel instructions presents a text that moves from the last line of the parable—"So likewise shall my heavenly Father do to you if you forgive not every one his brother from your hearts their offenses"—straight to Luke's instruction—"If the same person sins against you seven times a day, and turns back to you seven times and says, 'I repent,' you must forgive."[30] By joining the two scriptures in this way, he emphasizes the role of repentance in forgiveness. Thus for the Reformers repentance is an essential part of the process of forgiveness.

28. Martin Luther, "Instructions for the Visitors of Parish Pastors," in *Luther's Works: Church and Ministry II*, Luther's Works 40, trans. and ed. Conrad Bergendoff (Philadelphia: Muhlenberg Press, 1958), 277.
29. John Calvin, *Calvin's Bible Commentaries: Matthew, Mark and Luke, Part II*, trans. John King (Charleston, SC: Forgotten Books, 2007), 328.
30. Ibid., 325.

Unconditional forgiveness

Matthew and Luke present forgiveness instructions that demand concrete expressions (in Matthew, receptiveness to rebuke; for Luke, repentance), and early interpreters emphasize the bilateral process of repentance and forgiveness. However, contemporary voices from biblical studies, pastoral care, and psychology embrace a vision of forgiveness that has neither limit nor condition. Such forgiveness is then contained entirely in the emotional state of the victim, while the offender remains unrepentant or even unknown. In these scenarios, forgiveness is separated from reconciliation; it becomes a change of mind and heart, one that a victim is often pressured to perform. Underlying this idea are Jesus's instructions for unlimited forgiveness, which are understood as unconditional.[31]

Theologian and psychologist Lewis B. Smedes writes, "Forgiving is a gift, not a duty. It is meant to heal, not obligate. So the only good answer to Peter's question is: Use the gift as often as it takes to set you free from a miserable past you cannot shake."[32] David W. Augsburger cites both the Matthean and Lukan passages in his work on pastoral care, but like Smedes, he says nothing about repentance. "Jesus sets no limits, draws no line in the sand, defines no point when forgiving love can capitulate to evil and offer reactive violence. It is in this refusal of limits, this boundless and stubborn refusal to draw lines to define the intolerable, that we reflect the fullness of God's love."[33]

---

31. David Konstan offers an account of this shift in *Before Forgiveness,* 122–23. For examples of "seventy times seven" interpreted as a call for unconditional forgiveness, see Johann Christoph Arnold, *Seventy Times Seven: The Power of Forgiveness* (Farmington, PA: Plough Publishing House, 1997); Doris Donnelly, *Seventy Times Seven: Forgiveness and Peacemaking* (Erie, PA: Pax Christi USA, 1993); David Augsburger, *Seventy Times Seven: The Freedom of Forgiveness* (Chicago, IL: Moody Press, 1970); Thomas W. Buckley, *Seventy Times Seven: Sin, Judgment, and Forgiveness in Matthew* (Collegeville, MN: Liturgical Press, 1991); among many other textbooks, memoirs, and novels bearing this title and celebrating "the power of forgiveness."

32. Lewis B. Smedes, *The Art of Forgiving: When You Need to Forgive and Don't Know How* (New York: Random House, 1996), 161.

Both authors praise the unconditional and unlimited character of Jesus's teachings, but neither retains the original verse's emphasis on offender repentance.

Today, the phrase "seventy times seven" has become Christian shorthand for unconditional and unlimited forgiveness, especially forgiveness in situations of betrayal or violence. In *Seventy Times Seven: The Power of Forgiveness*, Johann Christoph Arnold relates a series of stories in which "real people" demonstrate forgiveness in difficult circumstances: a woman forgives her husband for molesting their daughter; a woman forgives and advocates for the man who kidnapped and murdered her daughter; parents forgive the drunk driver who killed their son.[34] These, Arnold writes, are "people who have the right to tell you that forgiveness is the only way to find healing."[35] He does not, however, question whether there are people who have the right to say that forgiveness is *not* the only way to heal. In his view, only forgiving victims may make such moral pronouncements. Arnold attests to the healing power of both forgiveness and repentance, but at no point does he posit the latter as a condition of the former.[36] In his view, human forgiveness is a reflection of Jesus's forgiveness, which knows no bounds.[37] Repentance can open the door to forgiveness, but forgiveness can and should take hold even in its absence. A church community's goal, he argues, "should never be punishment, but restoration."[38] However, avoiding punishment need not negate the role of repentance, whether in a church community or criminal process. Withholding forgiveness in the absence of repentance is not necessarily

33. David W. Augsburger, *Helping People Forgive* (Louisville, KY: Westminster John Knox Press, 1996), 143.
34. Arnold, *Seventy Times Seven*.
35. Ibid., back cover.
36. Ibid., 150.
37. Ibid., 157.
38. Ibid., 150.

synonymous with "punishment," and according to the instructions in Matthew and Luke, it is exactly what is called for.

Restorative justice and the forgiveness imperative

Forgiveness seventy-times-seven times is attractive as a community ethic in its simplicity and clarity. Teodor Costin notes the potential for such forgiveness to manifest in everyday life. He writes that the forgiveness teachings in Matthew, "which are powerfully radical and at the same time stand a realistic chance of being implemented, are rooted in a deep experience of an impartial God."[39] However, the biblical text does not portray God as "impartial." In Matthew especially, God is portrayed as a harsh judge prone to violent reactions, as seen in the parable of the unforgiving servant when the servant is "handed . . . over to be tortured" (18:34). Neither the Matthean nor the Lukan instructions on boundless forgiveness recommend impartiality; on the contrary, they provide guidelines for reproof and repentance, along with forgiveness that depends on both. The idea that these forgiveness instructions might reach into contemporary contexts with a "realistic chance" of being implemented is the kernel of the restorative justice movement. Drawing on a biblical vision of restoration of right relationship through repentance, forgiveness, and mutual respect, advocates propose alternatives to criminal justice that include restitution along with mediation (and ideally, reconciliation) between victim and offender.

Restorative justice advocates identify the movement against traditional criminal justice, or what they term a "retributive" system.[40]

---

39. Teodor Costin, *Il Perdono di dio nel Vangelo di Matteo: Uno studio esegetico-teologico*, Tesi Gregoriana Serie Teologia 133 (Roma: Editrice Pontificia Università Gregoriana, 2006), 223 (translation mine). Original text: "Tali affermazioni etiche di Matteo, con il loro forte radicalismo e, nello stesso tempo, con la loro reale possibilità di essere messe in pratica, sono radicate nella propria profonda esperienza di un Dio imparziale."

Claiming a biblical foundation, restorative justice shifts the focus away from the state and abstract legal concepts such as crime as a violation against the state[41] to focus on the effects of crime on relationships and the community. The restorative vision names three primary stakeholders: the victim, the offender, and the community in which the crime occurred[42] and insists that all three have an active role in seeking justice in the aftermath of crime. Justice is defined in terms of restoration of right relationship among individuals and communities rather than punishment of an offender. The victim takes the central role in this process, and the offender is encouraged to provide restitution to both the victim and the affected community, such as repayment of a loss or repair of damaged property. The personal needs of the victim and the offender rather than the state are at the forefront, and every attempt is made to resolve the conflict without adjudication or incarceration.[43]

Central to this vision of justice is a process called victim-offender mediation (VOM), in which the victim and the perpetrator sit together with a trained mediator in order to resolve questions and engage in dialogue about the offense and its effects. VOM reflects restorative justice's desire to incorporate civil dispute resolution techniques such as mediation and restitution into the process of addressing criminal wrongs.[44]

40. While restorative justice advocates position themselves against the "retributive" American criminal justice system, this is in fact a misnomer. Retribution (or deserved punishment) is only one justification for punishment in a system that also aims for deterrence, incapacitation, or rehabilitation. See Matthew Lippman, *Contemporary Criminal Law: Concepts, Cases, and Controversies*, 2nd ed. (Thousand Oaks, CA: SAGE Publications, 2010), 54–57.

41. Umbreit and Greenwood, *Guidelines*, 1; Zehr, *Changing Lenses*, 152.

42. Umbreit and Greenwood, *Guidelines*, 1.

43. For a narrative description of restorative justice principles—especially forgiveness—employed in the context of a murder trial, see Paul Tullis, "Can Forgiveness Play a Role in Criminal Justice?," *New York Times Magazine*, January 4, 2013, 28–38.

44. John Braithwaite, *Restorative Justice & Responsive Regulation* (Oxford: Oxford University Press, 2002), 239. See also Albert Fiadjoe, *Alternative Dispute Resolution: A Developing World Perspective* (New York: RoutledgeCavendish, 2004), 109–30.

More than one thousand VOM programs, both private and state funded, currently operate in North America and Europe.[45] Advocates cite high rates of emotional satisfaction for both victims and offenders.[46] Currently VOM is used primarily in juvenile cases, for first-time offenses, and for low-level property crimes, but advocates are pressing for its employment in cases of assault, rape, and even homicide (with surviving family members).[47] VOM provides a controlled setting in which victims can question offenders and offenders may explain or apologize for their actions. In some cases, offenders are offered reduced sentences in exchange for participating in mediation;[48] in others, VOM stands in for the criminal justice process altogether, which means no conviction and no state-imposed sentence when the mediation yields positive results and both parties are satisfied with the outcome.

45. Mark S. Umbreit and Jean Greenwood, *National Survey of Victim-Offender Mediation Programs in the United States*, Office for Victims of Crime, NCJ 176350 (St. Paul, MN: Center for Restorative Justice & Peacemaking, 2000), 3. In 2000, there were 315 programs in the United States and Canada, and 707 programs in Europe.

46. For surveys and figures, see Mark S. Umbreit, *Victim Meets Offender: The Impact of Restorative Justice and Mediation*, Criminal Justice Press (Monsey, NY: Willow Tree Press, 1994); Heather Strang, *Repair or Revenge? Victims and Restorative Justice* (Oxford: Clarendon Press, 2002); Umbreit and Greenwood, *National Survey*; among others.

47. See, for example, Sarah Eschholz et al., "Offenders' Family Members' Responses to Capital Crimes: The Need for Restorative Justice Initiatives," in *Current Perspectives in Forensic Psychology and Criminal Behavior*, ed. Curt R. Bartol and Anne M. Bartol, 3rd ed. (Los Angeles, CA: Sage Publications, 2012), 224; Mark S. Umbreit, William Bradshaw, and Robert B. Coates, "Victims of Severe Violence in Dialogue with the Offender: Key Principles, Practices, Outcomes and Implications," in *Restorative Justice in Context: International Practice and Directions*, ed. Elmar G. M. Weitekamp and Hans-Jürgen Kerner (Portland, OR: Willan Publishing, 2003), 123–44; Mark S. Umbreit, Betty Vos, Robert B. Coates, and Kathy Brown, "Victim-Offender Dialogue in Violent Cases: A Multi-Site Study in the United States," in *Restorative Justice: Politics, Policies and Prospects*, ed. E. van der Spuy, S. Parmentier, and A. Dissel(Cape Town: Juta, 2008), 22–39; and Mark S. Umbreit, *The Handbook of Victim-Offender Mediation* (San Francisco: Jossey-Bass, 2001), chapter 13: "Advanced Mediation and Dialogue in Crimes of Severe Violence" (255–90).

48. Martin Wright, "Victim-Offender Mediation as a Step towards a Restorative System of Justice," in *Restorative Justice on Trial: Pitfalls and Potentials of Victim-Offender Mediation—International Research Perspectives*, ed. Heinz Messmer and Hans-Uwe Otto (Dordrecht, The Netherlands: Kluwer Academic Publishers, 1992), 534.

Biblical foundations of restorative justice

Most early victim-offender mediation[49] programs were community-based nonprofit organizations, and many were located in and funded by religious groups, often Mennonite churches. The Mennonite Central Committee Office on Crime and Justice continues to provide training, resources, and funding support to VOM programs worldwide.[50] In a 2000 national survey, Mark S. Umbreit and Jean Greenwood identify the characteristics of VOM programs in the United States:[51] 22 percent surveyed were based in churches, and 39 percent of mediations took place in Christian or Jewish places of worship: churches, synagogues, or temples.[52]

Howard Zehr incorporates biblical material into his writings and sees the church as essential to the movement. "[VOM] desperately needs the church if it is to survive in a form that matters," he writes. "Motivated by a biblical vision of justice as restoration . . . the church can provide the kind of independent value base and independent institutional base which is necessary to carry the vision."[53] Zehr's "biblical vision of justice" is predicated on a broad definition of *shalom* that incorporates equal distribution of resources, peaceful social relationships, and a condition of honesty or "moral integrity."[54] All of this is "how God intends things to be."[55] Zehr interprets forgiveness as the highest goal for the social aspect of *shalom* as restoration of

---

49. The first organized victim-offender mediation programs (first called victim-offender reconciliation programs, or VORP) took place in the 1970s in Elkhart, Indiana and Kitchener, Ontario (http://www.vorp.org/history.shtml).

50. Marty D. Price, "Victim-Offender Mediation: The State of the Art," *VOMA Quarterly* 7, no. 3 (1996): 1.

51. Umbreit and Greenwood, *National Survey.*

52. Umbreit and Greenwood, *National Survey,* 5, 10. For VOM in church basements and classrooms, see also Robert B. Coates, "Mediation Observations: Case Examples and Analysis," in Umbreit, *Victim Meets Offender,* 119, 129.

53. Zehr, *Changing Lenses,* 174.

54. Ibid., 126–57.

55. Zehr, *Changing Lenses,* p. 132.

right relationship. Zehr cites multiple Old Testament texts as both positive and negative examples of *shalom*-as-justice (Lev. 24:19–20, "an eye for an eye"; 19:18, "do not seek revenge" but "love your neighbor"; 24:16, "anyone who blasphemes must be put to death"), but primarily he offers general statements not supported by biblical citations. Zehr cites only one New Testament text in support of his vision of biblical justice: "Therefore, since we are justified by faith, we have peace with God" (Rom. 5:1).

Zehr draws heavily on his Mennonite tradition by appealing to biblical principles that emphasize reconciliation and repair as primary goals.[56] As a result of crime, he writes, "[v]ictims and the community have been harmed and are in need of restoration."[57] Victims should be at the center of the justice-making process and offenders should "make things right."[58] The community should be the site of this justice process, and the goal is an idealized image of repaired relationships and wounds addressed by dialogue and restitution rather than trial and incarceration.

In some ways, restorative justice—and especially VOM—appear to bring the principles of the seventy-times-seven instructions into contemporary contexts in a productive way. The vision of conflict resolution presented by Jesus involves a dialogue that includes both forgiveness and repentance. The offender is held accountable by the community (in Matthew) or the victim (in Luke), and repentance opens the door for forgiveness, which is here synonymous with

---

56. On nonviolence in the Mennonite tradition, see Sally Engle Merry, "Mennonite Peacebuilding and Conflict Transformation," in *From the Ground Up: Mennonite Contributions to International Peacebuilding*, ed. Cynthia Sampson and John Paul Lederach (Oxford and New York: Oxford University Press, 2000), 203–17. The other texts in this volume are also instructive on nonviolence in the history of the Mennonite tradition.

57. Howard Zehr, *The Little Book of Restorative Justice*, The Little Books of Justice and Peacemaking (Intercourse, PA: Good Books, 2002), 64.

58. Ibid., 65.

restored relationship. For restorative justice advocates, that restored relation is the essence of justice.[59]

Howard Zehr cites the New Testament as a starting point. "We are called to forgive our enemies, those who harm us, because God has forgiven us," he writes. "We cannot be free as long as we are dominated by enmity."[60] Zehr cites Matt. 18:21–22 as a reversal of the "law of Lamech": "It is no accident, perhaps, that [Jesus] extends [this reversal] to seventy times seven, a number almost beyond imagination. From unlimited retaliation to unlimited love—we have come full circle."[61] He does not mention the Lukan version with its requirement for offender repentance.

The lack of emphasis on repentance in restorative justice literature is especially curious considering the prominence of repentance in the teachings of Jesus.[62] In Luke, Jesus states, "There will be more joy in heaven over one sinner who repents than over ninety-nine righteous persons who need no repentance" (Luke 15:7). Repentance is sometimes celebrated in restorative justice, but repentance has nothing to match the cachet of victim forgiveness. When advocates quote Scripture, they are most likely to cite the seventy-times-seven teachings, Jesus's cry from the cross, or the Lord's Prayer—all of which are easily extrapolated to support the kind of emotional and unilateral forgiveness that restorative justice advocates praise. Jesus's teachings about repentance carry as much weight in the Gospels as those on forgiveness.[63]

---

59. Marshall, *Beyond Retribution*, 35–96, esp. 92; Annalise E. Acorn, *Compulsory Compassion: A Critique of Restorative Justice*, Law and Society Series (Vancouver: UBC Press, 2004), 11.

60. Zehr, *Changing Lenses*, 45. Here, Zehr misquotes the biblical text; while Jesus does instruct his followers to "love your enemies" (Luke 6:27), nowhere does Jesus suggest that they should forgive their enemies.

61. Ibid., 150.

62. Jesus talks passionately about repentance multiple times in the Gospel literature: Matt. 4:17; 11:20–21; 21:32; Luke 5:31–32; 13:3–5; 15:7, 10; 17:3–4; 24:47.

63. While Jesus emphasizes the importance of repentance, he devotes more overall time to discussing forgiveness: Matt. 6:12, 14–15; 9:2–8; 12:31–32; 18:21–22, 23–35; 26:28; Mark

When an offender agrees to a mediation session, this hints at repentance, but it may or may not be articulated during the mediation session. And since offenders often have incentives to participate in mediation (such as reduced or dropped charges, reduced sentences, or increased privileges), victims may not simply assume that a cooperative offender is a repentant one.[64]

The writings of Christopher D. Marshall present another distorted view of biblical teachings in a presentation of biblically grounded restorative justice. He notes that the Lukan version of the seventy-times-seven command calls for repentance, but even so, he still manages a vision of unconditional forgiveness. "For a broken relationship to be restored, forgiveness by the victim alone is not enough; there must also be repentance by the offender," he writes. "But even if repentance is not forthcoming, even if the relationship cannot be restored, the disciple is still obligated to nurture forgiveness."[65] As if on cue, Marshall then cites Jesus's cry from the cross as a prooftext.

As restorative justice advocates map the biblical call for forgiveness onto their theories of how criminal justice should work, three themes emerge. First, biblical forgiveness is equated with unilateral, unconditional forgiveness. Second, the requirement for repentance is lost. And third, forgiveness gets defined as a psychological and emotional feat accomplished by the victim, regardless of whether the offender is present or shows remorse. In the ideal paradigm, a

2:2–12; 3:28–29; 4:10–12; 11:25; Luke 5:17–26; 6:37–38; 7:36–50; 11:3; 12:10; 17:1–4; 23:34; 24:46–47; John 20:22–23.

64. This is true especially in juvenile cases, when participation in mediation can mean dropped charges (or felony charges reduced to misdemeanors) and avoiding a criminal record. See Marian Liebmann, *Restorative Justice: How It Works* (London: Jessica Kingsley Publishers, 2007), 325; Wright, "Victim-Offender Mediation as a Step," 534; Declan Roche, *Accountability in Restorative Justice*, Clarendon Studies in Criminology (Oxford: Oxford University Press, 2003), 86.

65. Marshall, *Beyond Retribution*, 73.

remorseful offender sits across the table from a receptive victim and the mediation culminates in a catharsis of apology and forgiveness. But even absent this, an endlessly and unconditionally forgiving victim still suits the restorative purpose.

However, the conviction that a victim will be "healed" (or, made to feel better physically or emotionally) by forgiving and restoring a relationship with her attacker represents a major flaw in restorative justice thinking. As they conjure ideals of successful, forgiving VOM encounters, restorative justice advocates paint their bright picture against the dark backdrop of retributivism (a theory of justice that advocates the punishment of criminals). A false dichotomy emerges as restorative justice defines itself over and against so-called retributive justice. In the process, victims are limited to two options: they engage in VOM and follow its rules of engagement, or they reject the restorative path in favor of retribution. The idealized "forgiving victim" takes on a pernicious other, the ultimate VOM undesirable: the "angry victim."

Defining forgiveness

For restorative justice advocates, the primary point of departure from the biblical teachings is the definition of forgiveness. Where the seventy-times-seven instructions offer roles for both victim and offender toward forgiveness-as-reconciliation, restorative justice advocates isolate forgiveness as the most important and potentially most thrilling aspect of restoring right relation. In these pages I do not mean to suggest that restorative justice advocates should map their understandings of forgiveness exactly from the biblical text. Rather, I argue that a second look at the seventy-times-seven instructions could help to temper VOM's intense focus on the victim's response and prompt equal concern for the responses of both victim and offender. The bilateral vision of forgiveness presented in both Matthew and Luke stands to lighten the burden on the victim to forgive and stands to open new possibilities of restored relationship in which accountability and restitution play a larger role.

A salient problem in restorative justice literature is the conflation of biblical forgiveness with contemporary psychological definitions of the term. Howard Zehr starts out with the Bible but arrives at an unconditional forgiveness that the victim is obligated to undertake for her own good. "Forgiveness is letting go of the power the offense and the offender have over a person," he explains. "Without this experience of forgiveness, without this closure, the wound festers, the violation takes over our consciousness, our lives."[66]

Following Zehr, Marshall writes, "Forgiveness is a process whereby those who have been wounded let go of the power of the offense and the offender over them, and move toward freedom and wholeness."[67] Such understandings of forgiveness dismiss the role of repentance and emphasize the psychological task of the victim. "The offense" takes on a life of its own as an unfriendly ghost that torments the victim, and forgiveness is the only way she will overcome its power.

Restorative justice is better served by preserving the bilateral character of forgiveness presented in the biblical text that sees forgiveness and reconciliation as separately defined but closely linked. In her work on VOM,[68] Stephanie van de Loo highlights the difference between forgiveness (*Vergebung*) and reconciliation (*Versöhnung*). "Forgiveness means a change of attitude on the side of the hurt person regardless of the dispositions or behavior of the person who caused the hurt, such as insight, remorse, or repentance,"

---

66. Zehr, *Changing Lenses*, 47.
67. Marshall, *Beyond Retribution*, 73.
68. In Germany this practice is known as *Täter-Opfer-Ausgleich*, which translates to "offender-victim compensation."

she writes. "Reconciliation is a reciprocal process that requires both the injured person and the offender to assume responsibility for [dealing with the past] and also requires both to have the desire to improve relations going forward."[69] Van de Loo focuses on the "work of reconciliation" (*Versöhnungsarbeit*), a process that may include forgiveness and repentance but is not synonymous with these. For her, VOM at its best will be a reflection of God's reconciliation, or restored relationship, with humankind through Jesus.[70]

For the purposes of this chapter, I follow van de Loo in distinguishing between forgiveness and reconciliation. While these two ideas overlap nearly completely in the biblical text—that is, forgiveness does not exist apart from its tangible effect on the restoration of right relation—today they represent two very different ideas. In popular usage today, forgiveness is defined as giving up resentment, anger, or negative actions against the offender and *may* include—but not always (or necessarily)—the offender's expressions of remorse or repentance. Reconciliation refers to the restoration of right relationship between victim and offender. As van de Loo discusses it, reconciliation may include forgiveness, but it does not have to. For example, coworkers or family members may "agree to disagree," thus restoring relationships but not necessarily forgiving past behavior.[71]

69. Stephanie van de Loo, *Versöhnungsarbeit: Kriterien—theologischer Rahmen—Praxisperspektiven*, Theologie und Frieden (Stuttgart: W. Kolhammer, 2009), 16 (my translation). Original text: "Vergebung meint eine Einstellungveränderung auf der Seite der—im wörtlichen oder metaphorischen Sinn—verletzten, vergebenden Person die unabhängig geschieht von Dispositionen oder Verhaltensweisen der verletzt habenden Person wie beispielsweise Einsicht, Reue oder Umkehr; Versöhnung als wechselseitiger Prozess setzt hingegen bei verletzter und verletzt habender Person gleichermassen Verantwortungsübernahme für das Gewesene und den Willen zur Beziehungsverbesserung voraus."

70. Ibid., 136 and passim. On the atonement of Christ as reconciliation with humanity, see Rom. 5:10; 2 Cor. 5:18; Eph. 2:16; Col. 1:20.

71. On reconciliation without forgiveness, see Everett L. Worthington, "The Pyramid Model of Forgiveness: Some Interdisciplinary Speculations about Unforgiveness and the Promotion of Forgiveness," in *Dimensions of Forgiveness: A Research Approach* (Radnor, PA: Temple

Veneration of forgiveness

In restorative justice circles, forgiveness has become an idol. James Ptacek observes this veneration of forgiveness and its role in countering victims' anger. "In Restorative Justice training conferences and events that I have attended in the United States, there have been tables filled with books about forgiveness on display. … Forgiveness, then, seems to be a powerful emotional process that Restorative Justice harnesses."[72] Ptacek notes that restorative justice advocates claim an objective stance toward forgiveness even as they celebrate books and films on the topic. While restorative justice advocates generally agree that victims should never be pressured to forgive, they remain enamored with forgiveness at the level of mediator training. Often mediators are instructed to follow scripts that are "carefully designed to ensure that a process of emotional transformation [leading in the direction of forgiveness] takes place in a conference."[73] In such cases, while the participants are encouraged to "express disapproval about an offender's actions," this is matched by an emphasis on "the offender's intrinsic worth as an individual, 'separating the deed from the doer.'"[74]

Foundation Press, 1998), 129–30; Jeffrie G. Murphy, *Punishment and the Moral Emotions: Essays in Law, Morality, and Religion* (Oxford: Oxford University Press, 2012), 8–9, 56–57; Juergen Manemann, "Anthropological Remarks on Reconciliation after Auschwitz (Response)," in *After-words: Post-Holocaust Struggles with Forgiveness, Reconciliation, Justice*, ed. David Patterson and John K. Roth, The Pastora Goldner Series in Post-Holocaust Studies (Seattle: University of Washington Press, 2004), 131; Adam Morton, "What Is Forgiveness?," in *Ancient Forgiveness: Classical, Judaic, and Christian*, ed. Charles L. Griswold and David Konstan (Cambridge, UK: Cambridge University Press, 2011), 9; Brien Hallet, "To Forgive and Forget?," in *Fear of Persecution: Global Human Rights, International Law, and Human Well-Being*, ed. James D. White and Anthony J. Marsella (Lanham, MD: Lexington Books, 2007), 280.

72. James Ptacek, "Resisting Co-optation: Three Feminist Challenges to Antiviolence Work, in *Restorative Justice and Violence against Women*, ed. James Ptacek, Interpersonal Violence (Oxford: Oxford University Press, 2010), 22.

73. Roche, *Accountability*, 120; "Restorative Justice in Canada: What Victims Should Know" (prepared by the Canadian Resource Centre for Victims of Crime, 2011), 3; Zehr, *Changing Lenses*, 46; Umbreit, *Handbook*, 286–87.

74. Roche, *Accountability*, 120.

Declan Roche observes a tendency of restorative justice authors to elevate forgiveness to a supernatural level.[75] Other scholars revere the "magical"[76] or "miraculous"[77] powers of apology and forgiveness; and Conrad G. Brunk writes, "Offenders, victims, families, mediators, judges, and lawyers who participate all speak of the 'magic,' or 'deeply spiritual' aspects of the events that take place when offenders show repentance and victims are able to forgive."[78] These scholars name repentance as a part of the process, but their primary focus is on forgiveness.

Some argue that forgiveness is not only a moral obligation of the victim, but also necessary for restoring the offender as a productive member of society. Margaret Holmgren writes, "If the offender is forgiven by his victim, he may feel as if he has a new lease on life, or a second chance to be a decent, contributive member of society."[79] This carries resonances of the Christian notion that forgiveness may precede repentance so as to inspire it.[80] In Holmgren's lengthy treatise on the virtues of unconditional forgiveness, though, she offers scant anecdotal or statistical evidence of such positive outcomes. Indeed, many victims may not appreciate being loaded with the burden of restoring a violent offender to a positive place in the community.

The offender has no prescribed role in this process of unconditional forgiveness. Instead, Holmgren writes, "I argue that an attitude of unconditional genuine forgiveness is always appropriate and desirable from a moral point of view, regardless of whether the offender

---

75. Ibid., 9–10.
76. Heather Strang, "Justice for Victims of Young Offenders: The Centrality of Emotional Harm and Restoration," in *Restorative Justice for Juveniles: Conferencing, Mediation and Circles*, ed. A. Morris and G. Maxwell (Oxford: Hart Publishing, 2001), 186.
77. Marshall, *Beyond Retribution*, 284.
78. Brunk, "Restorative Justice and the Philosophical Theories," 51.
79. Margaret R. Holmgren, *Forgiveness and Retribution: Responding to Wrongdoing* (New York: Cambridge University Press, 2012), 269.
80. See the discussion of repentance inspired by forgiveness and "prevenient grace" in the introduction.

repents and regardless of what he has done or suffered."[81] A bilateral process of forgiveness may occur, she writes, but it will be sparked by this initial cultivation of "unconditional genuine forgiveness," which is the moral obligation of the victim.[82] Thus the fate of both victim and offender lies in the hands of the victim and depends on the victim's willingness to meet the offender face to face, listen to him, and bestow the powerful gift of forgiveness so that he may rejoin the community. According to Holmgren, the offender's only responsibility is to attempt to make restitution for the crime, and to behave better in the future.[83] These are major responsibilities, but they are not given as preconditions for victim forgiveness. Rather, Holmgren expects the victim to take a leap of faith and extend "unconditional genuine forgiveness" to any offender regardless of how he or she behaves. As with van de Loo above, such a view posits that victims must not only deal with their own injuries, but also help reform the offender.

Holmgren dismisses any value of resentment in favor of this unconditional forgiveness. Like other advocates of unilateral or unconditional forgiveness discussed here, she thus condemns victims for what may well be a reasonable response to being violated and at best a measure of self-respect.[84] In Aristotelian ethics, the absence of anger, and a willingness to forgive too easily, are signs of "small-souledness" or obsequiousness.[85] Nietzsche follows this line of thinking when he argues that forgiveness is a sign of weakness,

---

81. Holmgren, *Forgiveness and Retribution*, 10.
82. Ibid., 65.
83. Ibid., 269–71.
84. Thomas Brudholm, *Resentment's Virtue: Jean Améry and the Refusal to Forgive* (Philadelphia: Temple University Press, 2008), 4 and passim; Jeffrie G. Murphy, "Forgiveness and Resentment," in Jeffrie G. Murphy and Jean Hampton, *Forgiveness and Mercy*, Cambridge Studies in Philosophy and Law (Cambridge, UK: Cambridge University Press, 1998), 14–34, esp. 16–18.
85. Gregory Sadler, "Forgiveness, Anger, and Virtue in an Aristotelian Perspective," *Proceedings of the American Catholic Philosophical Association* 82 (2008): 235.

while revenge is a sign of self-respect: "Everybody will revenge [sic] himself unless he is without honor or full of contempt or full of love for the person who has harmed and insulted him."[86] Such revenge is a matter of "self-preservation" and "self-defense."[87] Gregory Sadler observes, "Not only are such non-forgiving responses merited [in Aristotelian thought], as well as protective of self and others in the community, they may even serve purposes of moral education both for the offender and for others."[88] Aristotle contemplates something that contemporary VOM advocates can't imagine—that there might be reform *without* forgiveness. It is nonforgiveness rather than forgiveness that stands to reform the offender, much in the same way that some theologians imagine that forgiveness may prompt repentance.

Another way restorative justice advocates revere forgiveness is by naming it as a gift—sometimes ineffable and always invaluable—that the victim might offer the offender. Stephanie van de Loo describes forgiveness as a "free gift" from the victim that is not synonymous with but may contribute to reconciliation. "Forgiveness as an interior process can only be a free gift from the victim," she writes. "In its interpersonal effects, forgiveness comes close to the concept of reconciliation."[89] Forgiveness here is figured as an internal, emotional process that may have a visible, outward effect in a reconciled relationship between the victim and the offender. This "free gift," even in the absence of repentance, may heal the breach on its own.

86. Friedrich Nietzsche, *On the Genealogy of Morals and Ecce Homo*, ed. and trans. Walter Kaufmann (New York: Vintage, 1989), 182.
87. Ibid., 180, 183.
88. Sadler, "Forgiveness, Anger, and Virtue," 235.
89. Van de Loo, *Versöhnungsarbeit*, 17 (translation mine). Original text: "Auch eine Bitte um Vergebung von Seiten der verletzt handenden Person ist als Beginn eines interpersonalen Prozesses denkbar, wobei die eigentliche Vergebung als innerer Prozess nur als freies Geschenk von der verletzten Person gewährt werden kann. Vergebung nähert sich so in ihrem interpersonalen Vollzug dem Versöhnungsbegriff an."

Christopher D. Marshall, however, describes a gift that is transactional and requires "moral effort" on both sides to be accomplished. He writes, "Forgiveness, by definition, is a gift freely given to the guilty party, otherwise it is not forgiveness. But it is not given cheaply, for it occurs in the moral space created by remorse, repentance, confession, and accountability, and demands moral effort on the part of both giver and receiver. But when it occurs, it lifts the shame of offending (and, indeed, the shame of victimhood) from the heads of those affected."[90] The gift of forgiveness, then, stands to release both victim and offender from being, well, *victim* and *offender*. It is a task that can only be accomplished by the victim, with some "moral effort" on the part of the offender as well. And even though forgiveness requires effort from both sides, it is still seen as a gift from the victim to the offender. This is not to say that all victims are opposed to such "gifts"; indeed, in many cases victims find listening to and forgiving offenders to be a rewarding and valuable part of recovering from the criminal offense. My point is that victims ought not be presented with forgiveness as the *only* way forward, and certainly not in the absence of offender participation.

The gift of forgiveness might also communicate renewed trust between victim and offender. Lode Walgrave writes, "Forgiving is a gift . . . because it conveys to [the offender] the victim's trust that he will refrain from causing further harm and opens hope for constructive relations in the future."[91] However, Walgrave does not discuss what the victim might base this trust on. Simply showing up for a mediation session does not, as noted above, signal offender repentance. The "hope for constructive relations in the future" is yet

---

90. Christopher D. Marshall, *Compassionate Justice: An Interdisciplinary Dialogue with Two Gospel Parables on Law, Crime, and Restorative Justice*, Theopolitical Visions 15 (Eugene, OR: Cascade Books, 2012), 243.
91. Lode Walgrave, *Restorative Justice, Self-Interest, and Responsible Citizenship* (Cullompton, UK: Willan Publishing, 2008), 117–18.

another burden for victims who wish no further contact with the offender. Such visions of the transformative power of forgiveness do not speak to the realities of reconstructing moral relations in the aftermath of crime. Forgiveness is not a magic wand that erases the threat of further victimization by a "forgiven" offender.

Marshall sees a gift-giving dynamic at play in the parable of the prodigal son (Luke 15:11–32). He observes, "As the [story] indicates, it is the positive bestowal of honor on the shamed party, not the reinforcement or clarification of their shame, that makes the critical difference. And the person best equipped to confer such honor on the wrongdoer is the victim of their offense."[92] Again, the onus is on the victim (here, the father) to dole out the gifts of honor and community wellness. Whether the wasteful son has any gifts to offer toward the restoration of honor and right relationship remains unknown. However, it is not clear that the parable offers the model that Marshall and others would like it to play in their discussion. At no point does the parable indicate that the father felt wronged by the prodigal son or in any way violated. Indeed, the father facilitated the initial dishonor by acceding to the younger son's request for his share of the inheritance. The father's response stands in contrast to the older brother, who fumes as the prodigal is welcomed home (15:28–30). And the father is not exactly a "victim"; indeed, he has power and resources to provide a welcome banquet without any apparent stress, nor does the parable describe any distress on his part. Thus the idea that this is a parable about forgiveness is in question. The father is "filled with compassion" (15:20, ἐδπλαλχνίδθη), but there is no reason to assume that he forgives his son for anything. In Luke, ἐδπλαλχνίδθη ("to be filled with compassion, pity, or sympathy"[93]) is also Jesus's response to the widow of Nain before he raises her only

---

92. Marshall, *Compassionate Justice*, 231.
93. BAGD, 770 (δπλαλχνίζομαι).

son from the dead (7:13). While this action could be considered a gift, there is nothing in this instance that suggests that ἐσπλαλχνίσθη has anything to do with forgiveness.

The gift status of forgiveness can be threatened if there is pressure to forgive, so restorative justice advocates direct mediators to avoid mentioning forgiveness at all costs, especially in the context of VOM. Thus most advocacy of forgiveness is implied or suggested rather than explicitly delivered. Howard Zehr writes, "Those who cannot find it in themselves to forgive [should not] be encouraged to feel an extra burden of guilt. Real forgiveness cannot simply be willed or forced, but must come in its own time, with God's help. *Forgiveness is a gift.* It should not be made into a burden."[94] Given Zehr's exaltation of the mystery and beauty of forgiveness, however, forgiveness appears to be a foregone conclusion even for those who resist at first.

Forgiveness and the VOM process

The preference for forgiveness is clear in restorative justice literature—along with warnings not to pressure victims—but the message is often mixed. John Braithwaite includes forgiveness on a "priority list of values" for victim-offender mediation even as he writes, "We actively seek to persuade participants that they ought to listen respectfully, but we do not urge them to forgive. It is cruel and wrong to expect a victim of crime to forgive."[95] However, Braithwaite goes on to declare the power of forgiveness and advocate its celebration in restorative justice circles. "This is not to say that we should not write beautiful books like [Desmond] Tutu's on the grace that can be found through forgiveness," he writes. "Nor does it

---

94. Zehr, *Changing Lenses*, 46 (emphasis mine).
95. John Braithwaite, "Principles of Restorative Justice," in *Restorative Justice and Criminal Justice: Competing or Reconcilable Paradigms?*, ed. Andrew von Hirsch, Julian V. Roberts, and Anthony Bottoms (Oxford: Hart Publishing, 2003), 12.

preclude us evaluating restorative justice processes according to how much remorse, apology, forgiveness and mercy they elicit."[96] Thus forgiveness emerges as a definite goal of restorative justice.

VOM proponents take special care not to pressure victims to forgive offenders. In fact, the first mediation programs were called "victim-offender reconciliation programs" (VORP), but advocates realized that "reconciliation" might sound too much like pressure to forgive and adjusted the title accordingly.[97] "The shift in terminology from VORP to VOM signaled a shift in focus, based on experience, from reconciliation to mediation as a defining characteristic of victim offender engagement."[98] I find this change to be a beneficial one. Victims of crime may be hesitant to engage in any process that envisions "reconciliation," or a restored relationship, as its desired outcome. Shifting the focus to the process (mediation) rather than a desired goal (reconciliation) leaves the possibilities open.

Forgiveness is the most mentioned unmentionable concept in all of restorative justice literature, especially when it comes to VOM. Writing with Marilyn Peterson Armour, Umbreit even refers to it as "the 'f' word" in the context of mediation.[99] However, in the same work Umbreit and Armour espouse its spiritual healing effects. They write, "Forgiveness, in the sense of letting go of anger and control over the outcome, also allows the victim to be whole again. This exercise of forgiveness relieves victims of the responsibility for their own anger, the crime, and the offender and replaces it with the

---

96. Braithwaite, "Principles of Restorative Justice," 13. Here he refers to Desmond Tutu, *No Future without Forgiveness* (New York: Doubleday, 1999).

97. Lorraine Stutzman Amstutz and Howard Zehr, *Victim Offender Conferencing in Pennsylvania's Juvenile Justice System* (1998), 6. http://www.emu.edu/cjp/publications/faculty-staff/rjmanual.pdf.

98. Howard J. Vogel, "The Restorative Justice Wager: The Promise and Hope of a Value-Based, Dialogue-Driven Approach to Conflict Resolution for Social Healing," *Cardozo Journal of Conflict Resolution* 8 (2007), 568.

99. Mark Umbreit and Marilyn Peterson Armour, *Restorative Justice Dialogue: An Essential Guide for Research and Practice* (New York: Springer Publishing Company, 2011), 230.

trust that *something else will prevent further crimes* toward themselves and others."[100] Umbreit and Armour do not define forgiveness any further than as a release of anger; they primarily discuss how amazing forgiveness is, and how important it is not to suggest it to victims.

Heather Strang, whose work focuses on victim emotions and careful attention to the needs of victims in restorative justice theory, also espouses forgiveness as the goal of the restorative justice encounter. For example, she concludes her article "Is Restorative Justice Imposing Its Agenda on Victims?" by pronouncing: "It is the work of a restorative justice encounter to engender emotions of remorse and forgiveness to the benefit of all participants. When that is achieved, then the restorative justice agenda has been fulfilled."[101]

Legal theorist Stephen P. Garvey considers the criminal justice process from the point of view of the offender and envisions punishment as a way to achieve restoration of relationships. For this punishment-as-restoration model to work, the victims must do their part. He writes, "*It reflects a moral failure* . . . for victims to withhold forgiveness unreasonably from offenders who have done all they can do to expiate their guilt. Forgiveness may not be obligatory, but neither is it always supererogatory. Forgiveness is something victims ought to give, even if they are not obligated to give it."[102] In this sense, victims are subjected to moral "Good Samaritan" laws; they are obligated to help out offenders by forgiving them. Not forgiving becomes an act of hostile neglect, just as forgiveness is seen above as a gift you are obligated to give.

---

100. Umbreit and Armour, *Restorative Justice Dialogue*, 75 (emphasis mine).
101. Heather Strang, "Is Restorative Justice Imposing Its Agenda on Victims?," in *Critical Issues in Restorative Justice*, ed. Howard Zehr and Barb Toew (Monsey, NY: Criminal Justice Press, 2004), 106.
102. Stephen P. Garvey, "Punishment as Atonement," *UCLA Law Review* 46 (1999): 1828 (emphasis added).

Here I engage the biblical text to counter Garvey's argument. It is only in cases where the offender's repentance is sincere (and this is a matter of the victim's judgment) that the question of "obligation" arises in the biblical instructions. According to the forgiveness instructions in Luke, forgiveness is required "if there is repentance . . . [and if the offender] says, 'I repent'" (17:3–4). In the context of mediation, such repentance takes the form of a speech act, as in the latter part of Luke's instruction. Gauging the sincerity of the offender's apology falls to the victim, just as in John 20:23 when Jesus authorizes the disciples to forgive and retain sins as they see fit.[103] If the victim judges the offender's repentance to be insincere or lacking, she may refuse to forgive. The "gift" of forgiveness has little meaning when it is offered based on false pretenses.

While I would argue that victims may not be obligated to forgive when certain conditions are not met, the question remains: Must the victim forgive when the offender *has* satisfied every requirement? For example, if the offender apologizes and the victim judges the apology to be sincere, and if the offender has made restitution to the victim and the community, is forgiveness absolutely required? Regarding the biblical instructions, it appears that forgiveness in such circumstances is compulsory. And in situations where the offender has met every demand of the victim and the justice system, I would not argue against forgiveness as a moral obligation. If the offender is sincere, if he is no longer a threat to the victim, and if restitution has been made, it may indeed be wrong to withhold forgiveness. And even if we were to take the biblical commands as absolute, as many Christians do, we should still consider what exactly that obligation would mean.

---

103. On victim forgiveness (and the tendency to forgive too easily), see Erin O'Hara and Maria Mayo Robbins, "Using Criminal Punishment to Serve Both Victim and Social Needs," *Law and Contemporary Problems* 72, no. 2 (Fall 2009): 207.

Whether restorative justice advocates discuss or stay quiet about forgiveness, the emphasis (and sometimes the measure of mediation success) is on the victim's ability—and often the victim's *obligation*—to accomplish it. Writing specifically about the offender's experience of VOM in a manual for mediators, Janet P. Schmidt suggests that mediators should push offenders toward repentance, which is the final step before they are able to ask for forgiveness.[104] However, later in the same manual, the authors also suggest building in "delays" in the mediations (such as delaying entering a room or waiting for papers to be signed) in order to make space for "spontaneous acts of contrition and forgiveness."[105] John Braithwaite presents a similar strategy. He offers forgiveness as the "prime example" of the values restorative justice practices should be designed to realize. "Many of us believe that if we can *create spaces* that give victims an opportunity to discover how they might bring themselves to forgive, this is the most important thing we can do," he writes.[106] Here again, forgiveness is an explicit agenda, and while Braithwaite knows better than to mention it in the mediation encounter, he advocates "creating spaces" where forgiveness might emerge. While some authors do mention repentance and contrition, these are optional and often get overshadowed in the emphasis on forgiveness.

To gain a local perspective on forgiveness and victim-offender mediation practices, in the spring of 2012 I contacted the Nashville Conflict Resolution Center. According to its website, the center mediates cases involving misdemeanor crimes in order to "[help] disputing parties communicate their needs and interests, express grievances and develop mutually acceptable solutions."[107] Forgiveness

104. Janet P. Schmidt, "The Offender's Journey," in Amstutz and Zehr, *Victim Offender Conferencing*, 18. http://www.emu.edu/cjp/publications/faculty-staff/rjmanual.pdf.
105. Amstutz and Zehr, *Victim Offender Conferencing*, 32.
106. Braithwaite, *Responsive Regulation*, 15 (emphasis mine).

is not a stated goal of this process, but it is a theme that undergirds the center's literature and workspace.

In the main room of the center, copies of Mark Umbreit's *Handbook for Victim-Offender Mediation* (with its hopeful words about forgiveness) line the bookshelves. Executive director Tamara Losel screened the "awe-inspiring" film "The Power of Forgiveness" as part of a "movie night" at the center in 2009, and she offers a review on the center's website. She writes, "As a mediator, I believe that our primary task is to bring more peace to this world. Virtues like love, compassion, forgiveness and mercy—key ingredients in the recipe for peace—must be studied and put into practice in our own lives."[108] Losel also acknowledges that she uses this film—which features Robert Enright, Everett Worthington, Fred Luskin, and other prominent figures in the "forgiveness movement" speaking enthusiastically about forgiveness—as part of all mediator-training courses at the center.[109]

Forgiveness and the rhetoric of VOM

VOM literature is replete with instructions on how *not* to mention forgiveness in the mediation context. Umbreit recommends mediators "listen for the issue of forgiveness either as an expectation of the offender or perhaps as a fear from the victim"[110] so they might step out of the way of it. He writes, "If forgiveness is to occur, it must be genuine and not contrived or done because someone thought the mediator expected it."[111] The bottom line for Umbreit is that it is not

---

107. Nashville Conflict Resolution Center website, http://www.nashvilleconflict.org/, accessed May 12, 2012.
108. Nashville Conflict Resolution Center, http://www.nashvilleconflict.org/conflict_resolution_education_programs/film_night, accessed May 12, 2012.
109. Tamara Losel, director, Nashville Conflict Resolution Center, personal e-mail communication, May 14, 2012.
110. Mark S. Umbreit, *The Handbook of Victim-Offender Mediation* (San Francisco: Jossey-Bass, 2001), 287.

a good idea to pressure victims into forgiving, primarily because this might prevent "genuine" forgiveness from taking hold.

In the *Handbook of Victim-Offender Mediation*, Umbreit issues a strong warning to mediators. He advises, "It is also important that mediators avoid the use of words such as *forgiveness* or *reconciliation*. Such words pressure and prescribe behavior for victims . . . Forgiveness may be expressed during the mediation session, but if the mediator so much as uses the word *forgiveness*, it may be destructive to the victim."[112] In spite of this instruction, Umbreit goes on to discuss forgiveness throughout the book in continuing to warn against its mention while simultaneously celebrating its amazing healing powers.[113] Victims are more likely to forgive, he argues, if the mediator doesn't mention forgiveness at all.[114] Thus the hush around forgiveness becomes a form of gentle coaxing.

Umbreit even devotes an entire subsection to the topic of forgiveness in a chapter on mediation possibilities in cases of severe violence. He writes, "Although forgiveness may be an outcome of the dialogue for some, it is not the goal of the program. Even if it is a goal of participants, there are limits as to how far such dialogues can move victim and offender . . . To forgive the [offender] for what he or she has done requires an almost superhuman effort."[115] Forgiveness cannot be a goal, then, because it takes *superhuman* emotional skills. This kind of language suggests that victims who are unwilling to forgive are unable to summon such a "superhuman effort."

The idealization of forgiveness in this context is especially problematic. Annalise Acorn notes the emotional allure of forgiveness in restorative justice processes, especially forgiveness in the wake of

111. Ibid., 287.
112. Ibid., 25.
113. Ibid., xxxii, 25, 63–64, 269–70, 272, 280, 281, 286, 287, 292.
114. Ibid., 25.
115. Ibid., 286.

an especially violent or heinous crime. "It appeals as an exhilarating form of ethical bungee jumping," she writes. "Forgiveness of the unthinkably egregious has more drama and is worth the effort because, if successful, it clearly counts as seriously impressive ethical and existential muscle-flexing."[116] As restorative encounters capitalize on catharsis, forgiveness offers a grand payoff.

In *Facing Violence: The Path of Restorative Justice and Mediation,* Umbreit and colleagues evaluate VOM programs in Texas and Ohio and show their preference for forgiveness in the criteria they use. They evaluate "the philosophical principles that shaped the program, the selection and training of volunteers, the preparation, meeting, and follow-up phases of the work, supervision and accountability, waiting list issues, *forgiveness*, and self care."[117] Forgiveness becomes just one more logistical issue on the list along with case selection and waiting list maintenance. That the presence of forgiveness is simply assumed at such a basic level demonstrates its ubiquity in VOM structures.

Keith Allen Regehr argues that the "hidden presence" of forgiveness in restorative justice dialogues should be more explicit.[118] "If Restorative Justice is to fully live up to its potential as a new way of doing justice, this presence [i.e., forgiveness] needs to become public and become a more explicit part of Restorative Justice practice," he writes.[119] However, later in the same text Regehr employs a familiar subversive strategy. He writes, "Despite its essential role in Restorative Justice, care must be taken not to impose a requirement of forgiveness on victims. Too strong a focus on the possibilities

---

116. Acorn, *Compulsory Compassion,* 10.
117. Umbreit, Vos, Coates, and Brown, *Facing Violence,* 70 (emphasis mine).
118. Regehr, "Judgment and Forgiveness," 39.
119. Ibid. Regehr locates this "biblical underpinning" in the general Hebrew terms, צדק (righteousness) and שׁולם (peace), expanding these to include forgiveness, justice, and well-being (41). He closely follows Zehr's discussion of "biblical justice" in *Changing Lenses* (151–52 and 184–85), which is also founded on general terms instead of specific scriptures.

for reconciliation and forgiveness can drive victims away from a willingness to be involved."[120] For Regehr, forgiveness is and ought to be the primary goal of restorative justice practices, but mediators must behave as though it is not in order to ensure its possibility.

Restorative justice advocates claim that forgiveness is not an explicit goal while simultaneously describing the healing effects "*if* it happens."[121] In practice, acknowledging the possible beneficial effects of forgiveness in the context of VOM is not necessarily a negative aspect of the process. The problem lies in the double-talk. Facilitators are careful not to mention forgiveness in the mediation encounter, but elsewhere advocates are writing about it, hoping for it, and carefully documenting and celebrating every time mediations result in forgiving responses.[122] VOM advocates are not unaware of the tendency toward double-talk. Mark S. Umbreit and Marilyn Peterson Armour acknowledge this "paradox of forgiveness" in an article by that title. "The more one talks about [forgiveness]," they argue, "the more likely [it] will be heard as behavioral prescriptions, and the less likely victims will participate and have the opportunity to experience elements of forgiveness and reconciliation."[123]

The forgiveness hush is directed at coaxing victim responses, but there is no equivalent surge of books and articles about how best to tiptoe around issues of repentance or remorse (because it would follow that advocates would need to avoid prescribing responses for offenders as well as victims). Since the forgiveness burden is on the victim, there is not as much urgency about how to approach

120. Regehr, "Judgment and Forgiveness," 109–10.
121. Umbreit, *Victim Meets Offender*, 157; Braithwaite, "Principles of Restorative Justice," 12–13; Holmgren, *Forgiveness and Retribution*, 99; Walgrave, *Restorative Justice, Self-Interest*, 18.
122. Umbreit and Armour, *Restorative Justice Dialogue*, 231; Umbreit and Greenwood, *National Survey*; Susan Jennifer Szmania, "Beginning Difficult Conversations: An Analysis of Opening Statements in Victim Offender Mediation/Dialogue" (PhD diss., University of Texas at Austin, 2004), 114–15; Strang, *Repair or Revenge?*, 110–11.
123. Armour and Umbreit, "Paradox of Forgiveness," 493.

offenders. The willingness to engage in mediation is often an indicator of remorse, and since the encounter is a conversation, a spoken apology is often forthcoming. Another reason the literature devotes less attention to speaking with offenders is that they may already be incarcerated and, as a result, face-to-face preparation with a mediator prior to the encounter may be limited.[124]

Analyzing VOM rules and expectations

Another way pressure on victims to forgive offenders is manifested in VOM comes with the mandatory preparation and extensive rules for mediation encounters. VOM requires particular behaviors for both victim and offender. Victims who are angry, vengeful, and potentially disrespectful are excluded from participation. Likewise, apathetic and nonremorseful offenders are also excluded. By removing undesirable emotions and behaviors from the mediation, the stage is set for victim forgiveness and offender remorse. In some cases, these boundaries might be helpful, but in others they serve to stifle victim expressions of anger and hurt much in the same way VOM activists claim that the criminal justice system stifles emotional responses from both victims and offenders.[125] I argue that such negative emotions, especially on the part of the victim, have every place in the context of VOM.

Mark S. Umbreit suggests "Guidelines for Victim-Sensitive Mediation and Dialogue with Offenders."[126] He starts by affirming the victim's choice of a time and place for the mediation session as well as the option to bring one or two support persons. Under

124. Note the outlines for victim and offender premediation preparation given in the Victim-Offender Mediation Association's "Recommended Ethical Guidelines"; the program for victim preparation is nearly twice as long as the offender's and includes much greater discussion of feelings (http://www.voma.org/docs/ethics.pdf).
125. Marty Price, "Personalizing Crime: Mediation Produces Restorative Justice for Victims and Offenders," *Dispute Resolution Magazine*, Fall 2001, http://www.vorp.com/articles/justice.html.
126. Umbreit, *Handbook*, 19–34.

the heading "Careful Screening of Cases," he writes, "It is important in the mediation process that offenders take responsibility for their participation in the crime and proceed willingly to mediation."[127] From the outset, then, VOM is only open to offenders who acknowledge guilt and approach the process with contrition. The "Careful, Extensive Preparation of the Offender" emphasizes that offenders must delve into their feelings about the crime(s) and their own experience as victims in order to foster empathy for the victim.[128] Likewise, "Careful, Extensive Preparation of the Victim" includes helping victims with "preliminary brainstorming about the ways their losses and needs might be addressed."[129]

VOM demands certain "ground rules," primarily "allowing each person to speak without interruption and speaking and listening respectfully."[130] Arguing and emotional outbursts risk termination of the mediation session. Offenders must admit guilt, and victims must listen without interruption to their explanations and/or apologies. The complex superstructure of rules surrounding the process runs counter to one of the most common restorative justice complaints about the traditional system, namely that its procedures take precedence over personal and emotional outcomes for the stakeholders.[131]

These ground rules draw boundaries around what it means to be a victim in the context of restorative justice. George Pavlich identifies two characteristics of victimhood that seem to be nonnegotiable. First, he identifies a "contingent ontology"; that is, being a victim is transient, and restorative justice processes imagine "moving beyond" the victim identity.[132] The goal is the "non-victim sense of self," and

127. Ibid., 26.
128. Ibid., 28.
129. Ibid., 31.
130. Ibid., 41.
131. Zehr, *Changing Lenses*, 211.

restorative justice practices like VOM are designed to assist with this forward motion into a nonvictim future.[133] Restorative justice defines itself as empowering and serving the needs of victims, but at the same time it seeks to shed that label.[134] I contend that the label of victim need not indicate weakness or inferiority, only one's status of having been subjected to a crime. VOM advocates who focus on discarding the victim identity assign a negative value to the label by suggesting that it should be discarded. For most victims, however, simply abandoning a label does nothing to change the fact that they have been victimized.

Further, Pavlich points to the structure of the pre-mediation process as containing a bias toward this type of victim identity (a victim who wants to escape the victim label) as well as a preference for a forgiving victim. He notes Heather Strang's emphasis on victim preparation: "*Insufficient preparation of victims* (and of offenders) regarding their role in the conferences, their expectations about the outcome, and their rights in terms of requesting reparation can have serious negative consequences for victims."[135] Pavlich questions the need to "prepare" a victim to enter an encounter where she will play the role of victim. He wonders whether victimization alone shouldn't be enough to qualify a victim for the role. Rather, what is happening is that mediators and other restorative justice advocates are interested in preparing a particular *kind* of victim. "'Preparing' is thus an important point at which subjects are socialized into the

---

132. George Pavlich, *Governing Paradoxes of Restorative Justice* (London: GlassHouse Press, 2005), 52–53.

133. Ibid., 52. For a perspective on restorative justice as helping victims move beyond "wallowing in victimhood," see David Smock, "The Process of Forgiveness," in *No Enemy to Conquer: Forgiveness in an Unforgiving World*, ed. Michael Henderson (Waco, TX: Baylor University Press, 2009), 28.

134. Pavlich, *Governing Paradoxes*, 60: "There is therefore a tragic incongruity involved in promoting a justice that empowers victims *as* victims, and which depends essentially on the continued presence of victims."

135. Strang, *Repair or Revenge?*, 150 (emphasis in original).

basic tenets of restorative justice's victim identity," Pavlich writes. This includes "encouraging them to adopt an identity that focuses on losses (material, emotional and relational), needs and resolutions to these."[136]

Using Umbreit's guidelines, Pavlich identifies the "restorative victim" as one who keeps her emotions under control, never becomes "abusive or revengeful," is reasonable about restitution, and is forgiving whenever possible.[137] "As such," he writes, "we have at least a sense of the 'ideal type' of victim identity that restorative justice processes are designed to restore and reconcile with a broader community."[138] Victim-offender mediation programs should include all manner of victims: angry and outraged in addition to conciliatory and forgiving. Instead, the current agenda for VOM is to help victims release or overcome anger rather than express it at length in a mediation session. Indeed, mediation sessions risk being terminated if a victim becomes too angry.[139]

Once angry and disruptive victims are screened out, forgiveness is much more likely. Pavlich concludes that while VOM programs vary in their tone and design, "[a]ll embrace equivalents of a secular confessional in which the victim is required—as a condition of participating in the process—to adopt a delimited identity designed to help bring about restoration [in the form of forgiveness or even a restored relationship]."[140] Forgiveness—or the hope for forgiveness—is central to this identity, with some form of it nearly a requirement for sitting on the opposite side of this "secular confessional." In this metaphor, the victim sits in the place of the priest, and she is fully expected to fill her role by forgiving the

136. Pavlich, *Governing Paradoxes*, 54–55.
137. Ibid., 57.
138. Ibid.
139. Umbreit, *Handbook*, 61.
140. Pavlich, *Governing Paradoxes*, 56.

offender. Except here, the victim's role exceeds that of a priest. A priest in the confessional must simply absolve—or communicate God's forgiveness to—the penitent. In the VOM encounter, the victim not only communicates the absolution, but does the forgiving as well. Furthermore, she is restricted from assigning some form of penance as a priest might do (e.g., six Hail Marys, a dozen Our Fathers), lest her unconditional forgiveness begin to look like a conditional exchange.

Declan Roche observes the power of language in the VOM process. "Participants in restorative meetings are still expected to master a language—not the formal, dispassionate language of the courtroom—but the nuanced and complex language of the emotions," he writes. "Some will be highly proficient at expressing their feelings, able to communicate convincingly remorse and sorrow, forgiveness and empathy. Some [offenders] will master it so well they can abuse it—using rhetoric to deceive, manipulate, and flatter."[141] Not every VOM participant will be able to master this "nuanced and complex" emotional language in ways that are beneficial. Some victims may use it as a weapon against the offender or vice versa.

On this point, Annalise Acorn warns, "Apology and forgiveness, the primary method of restorative repair, can often be anything but healing. They can be essential weapons for placing an offender in a position to inflict new wounds and reopen old ones."[142] Either victim or offender may use the mediation encounter as an opportunity to unleash harsh words against the other. However, the VOM guidelines, which attempt to regulate the encounter so that it does not deteriorate into a shouting match, often overcorrect and reach for an opposite extreme in which anger and resentment have almost

141. Roche, *Accountability*, 113–14.
142. Acorn, *Compulsory Compassion*, 74.

no place in the process. Insofar as anger is permitted, it is only in service to the restorative ideals of forgiveness and reconciliation. Acorn writes, "Restorative justice hopes that, by making appropriate space for the controlled expression of mean-spirited desires, we can transform them into healthy desires for right-relation."[143] There is no reason to believe that every victim approaches a VOM encounter with hopes for forgiveness and renewed relationship. Some may simply want answers about why they were targeted, or even an apology. The offender has something the victim wants—usually, this is information—and VOM gives the victim a way to get it. Righteous indignation and anger about lost property or physical injury are not unreasonable emotions. Requiring a victim to "respect" the offender precludes the expression of such emotions. While VOM sessions should not be occasions for verbal or physical assaults, lifting the prohibition on anger could result in more victim participation in and satisfaction with the process.

Victim intentions and VOM outcomes

The staunchest champions of restorative justice promote mediation and reconciliation in cases of violent crimes by strangers.[144] Here, the ideal of right relation prevails regardless of whether a relationship preexisted between the victim and the offender. The crime has created a relationship, and that relationship is worth restoring.

In restorative justice, healing is a primary goal, and that includes healing of both parties after stranger crimes, including "opportunities for forgiveness, confession, repentance, and reconciliation."[145] Howard Zehr writes, "Some of this must take place between

143. Ibid., 52.
144. Umbreit, *Handbook*, 255–90: chapter 13, "Advanced Mediation and Dialogue in Crimes of Severe Violence."
145. Zehr, *Changing Lenses*, 51.

individuals and their God, their church, and their community. But involved also is the relationship between victim and offender, a relationship which if it did not exist before the offense, does now."[146] However, restoring relationships after stranger crimes may be a moral impossibility. Margaret Urban Walker writes, "When a crime victim has been unjustly harmed by a stranger, the offense creates a relationship where there was none before. Forgiveness cannot aim at the restoration of relationship here, unless this means restoring the fact that *no* relationship exists, just as no relationship existed before the crime."[147] Here, the value of forgiveness might trump the impossibility of restoring right relationship in the aftermath of a crime by a stranger. By focusing so closely on forgiveness as the ideal outcome, advocates may unwittingly press victims to reengage with their attackers in service to this ideal.

However, victims may reject VOM and restorative principles for a number of reasons that have nothing to do with retribution. Not all victims are angry. Not all are choosing between fantasies of forgiveness and fantasies of revenge. As Susan Jacoby observes, "Boundless vindictive rage is not the only alternative to unmerited forgiveness."[148] Judith Lewis Herman demonstrates in her study of responses to crime that many victims actually seek a third option: incapacitation.[149] They want neither to embrace nor to punish the offender; they just want the offender to stay away from them. Victims who hold this simple hope of safety may not be interested in restorative practices, but this does not mean that they are seething with revenge and should be viewed negatively. Some victims just

---

146. Ibid.
147. Margaret Urban Walker, *Moral Repair: Reconstructing Moral Relations after Wrongdoing* (New York: Cambridge University Press, 2006), 159.
148. Susan Jacoby, *Wild Justice: The Evolution of Revenge* (New York: Harper and Row, 1988), 362.
149. Judith Lewis Herman, "Justice from the Victim's Perspective," *Violence against Women* 11 (2005): 578.

want to be left alone. Since the majority of VOM cases are referred by the district attorney's office, victims may experience pressure as those in authority suggest they participate. They may reject the suggestion for a variety of reasons, including concern for emotional or physical safety, but they should not be characterized as angry or vengeful just for passing on that opportunity. Annalise Acorn argues that the goals of restorative justice reach beyond what victims and communities (and even offenders) might expect in the aftermath of crime. She writes, "[Restorative justice] requires that we build better, more respectful, more mutual relationships than those that existed prior to the wrong. It reaches toward an idealized state of right-relationship as its model of the just."[150]

According to Herman's study of victim responses to crime, some victims wanted or valued apologies; others recognized the potential for further abuse or manipulation if they open themselves to such communication.[151] Some victims are more than happy to let the state step in as the arbiter of justice. Restorative justice is built on the assumption that mediations are in the best interest of victims, offenders, and the community, with forgiveness gleaming as the ideal outcome. But for many victims the refusal to forgive an unrepentant attacker becomes a measure of self-protection and self-respect.[152] Often, suggesting that a victim engage in a dialogue with the offender serves as another victimization in itself. Martha Minow observes, "To expect survivors to forgive is to heap yet another burden on them."[153]

---

150. Acorn, *Compulsory Compassion*, 22.
151. Herman, "Justice from the Victim's Perspective," 597.
152. On this point, see Murphy, "Forgiveness and Resentment," 16; Brudholm, *Resentment's Virtue*, 4.
153. Minow, *Between Vengeance and Forgiveness: Facing History after Genocide and Mass Violence* (Boston, MA: Beacon Press, 1998), 17.

Polarizing only two options—retribution or forgiveness—leaves out the meaningfulness of safety that is their goal. Margaret Holmgren, for example, does not address the issue of the victim's safety in her discussion of the "paradigm of forgiveness." She theorizes forgiveness as a moral ideal with retribution as its evil opposite: "Retributive reactive attitudes are rejected ... it is ultimately appropriate and desirable from a moral point of view for [crime victims] to adopt an attitude of unconditional genuine forgiveness toward the offender."[154] She does not acknowledge that victims may withhold forgiveness (or refuse to engage in mediation) for reasons other than retributive goals.

Instead, as Herman demonstrates, victims may hold the very reasonable fear of being reoffended. Holmgren demands a level of trust that a victim may not be able to or want to manufacture in order to bestow this gift on the offender. She discounts the possibility of more complex victim responses in the title of her book: *Forgiveness and Retribution*, which are, as she describes with her subtitle, the primary *Responses to Wrongdoing*.[155] Suggesting that victims are morally obligated to forgive and portraying nonforgiving victims as vengeful and hate-filled serves only to amplify the offense they already suffer.

Conclusion

With its promises of healing and moral accomplishment, a particular ideal of forgiveness has become the shining star of restorative justice theory and practice. The structure and rules of VOM, along with the undercurrent of forgiveness rhetoric, create an environment in which susceptible victims are led, implicitly but palpably, toward

154. Holmgren, *Forgiveness and Retribution*, 261.
155. Holmgren, *Forgiveness and Retribution*.

accepting an obligation to forgive their offenders, while angry and more emotionally complicated victims are screened out of the process. In describing the mediation encounter, advocates proclaim the importance of not mentioning forgiveness or pressuring victims to forgive; but forgiveness remains the goal of the mediation process—sometimes explicitly stated—and thus remains the agenda hidden in plain sight. To the degree victims are aware of the expectation that they forgive—for example, as they might be simply from reading literature promoting the mediation process—they may experience that expectation as an obligation, even as a burden. That burden may well be corrosive to the sense of self-respect that has already been damaged by the offense, especially in heinous cases. And that burden is not balanced by an equal emphasis on the expectation that the offender will express and demonstrate repentance as a condition of receiving forgiveness. This is seen in books and articles celebrating the miraculous healing effects of forgiveness, in subtle questions posed by mediators, and in the biblical principles that undergird the origins and processes of restorative justice.

In the case of the triple murder in the Mennonite congregation, "developing the intent to forgive" was an immediate concern. Congregants and family members called on the biblical instruction of forgiveness "seventy times seven" as they worked to support the young man who murdered his family. And yet, they embraced only the forgiveness command, thus disregarding the complexity of the teaching that also called for reproof (Matthew) and repentance (Luke) in order for forgiveness to take hold. While early interpreters of the seventy-times-seven instructions emphasize the role of repentance in this bilateral process of forgiveness, contemporary readers of the Bible—and especially advocates of practices like VOM who profess to put these Bible passages into concrete action—tend to adopt a unilateral vision that incorporates modern psychological definitions of forgiveness as an emotional task that concerns primarily the victim.

In their focus on community repair, VOM practices are faithful to the New Testament vision. Both the seventy-times-seven instruction and VOM value community cohesion and harmony. The dialogic structure of VOM opens the way for a repentance-forgiveness exchange, but advocates who dream of unilateral, unconditional forgiveness downplay this bilateral opportunity. Instead, they laud forgiveness as *the* way to restore the relationship and provide beneficial emotional effects for both victim and offender. The assumption is always that the relationship should be restored, or at least attempts should be made toward that goal. However, many victims may enter into mediation with little interest in restoring a relationship, especially in the case of stranger crimes. Other goals might include having questions about the crime answered and gaining a sense of future security.[156] For VOM advocates who claim a biblical warrant, a closer focus on victim-offender dialogue and forgiveness-repentance exchange could stand to lighten the pressure on the victim, hold the offender responsible, and produce a more desirable outcome for the victim, the offender, and the affected community.

Acorn underscores the heady idealism and grandiose fantasies of forgiveness and right relation inherent in restorative justice literature. "The seductive vision of restorative justice seems, therefore, to lie in a skillful deployment—through theory and story—of cheerful fantasies of happy endings in the victim-offender relation, emotional healing, closure, right-relation, and respectful community," she writes. "Yet, as with all seductions, the fantasies that lure us in tend to be very different from the realities that unfold. And the grandness of the

---

156. Acorn, *Compulsory Compassion*, 86.

idealism in these restorative fantasies, in and of itself, ought to give us pause."[157]

Forgiveness may well be restorative and admirable, but it should be judged by its effects, not simply by its expression.[158] The victim alone cannot repair the broken relationship; rather, such a process must be nurtured by the offender in the form of repentance, apology, reparation, or remorse. This is what is described in the seventy-times-seven instructions, and this is a more constructive vision of how VOM encounters might look. Configuring forgiveness as a unilateral, unconditional initiative, to be achieved emotionally by the victim as a moral obligation (as many of the above authors do) renders the offender's contribution desirable, but optional. VOM advocates do not dismiss the role of offender repentance and apology, but at the end of the day what they celebrate most is victim forgiveness. When forgiveness is unilateral and unconditional, the only necessary work is the victim's.

Any account of forgiveness must not only seek to settle something in the past, but also look toward what future landscape that forgiveness creates.[159] Repair of a torn fabric is valuable only in its strength to withstand or prevent future tears. Such a process must involve effort on the part of both victim and offender. Forgiveness may not always succeed. This is true in the biblical seventy-times-seven instructions, and it is true in VOM practices that maintain a reciprocal understanding of reconciliation. Without question, though, the past and the hoped-for future, along with the victim-offender dialogue, determine the possibility and value of forgiveness.

---

157. Ibid., 16.
158. Walker, *Moral Repair*, 169.
159. Ibid., 151–52.

3

———

Community Cohesion, or a Hegemony of Harmony? Forgiveness in the Lord's Prayer and in Post-apartheid South Africa

On April 16, 1997, in the small coal-mining and cattle-farming town of Vryheid in KwaZulu Natal, Bettina Mdlalose took her seat before the Human Rights Violations Committee (HRVC) of the South African Truth and Reconciliation Commission (TRC). She was there to testify about the night of April 19, 1990, when her son was killed.[1]

1. What follows is taken from the testimony of Bettina Mdlalose and Thandi Mdlalose, Human Rights Violations Committee Proceedings held at Vryheid (Durban), April 16, 1997; full transcript available at the Official Truth and Reconciliation Commission Website: http://www.justice.gov.za/trc/hrvtrans/vryheid/vryheid1.htm (my redaction). Mrs. Mdlalose's testimony is also discussed by the following authors: Claire Moon, *Narrating Political Reconciliation: South Africa's Truth and Reconciliation Commission* (Lanham, MD: Lexington Books, 2008), 112; Daniel Philpott, *Just and Unjust Peace: An Ethic of Political Reconciliation* (Oxford: Oxford University Press, 2012), 278; Thomas Brudholm, *Resentment's Virtue: Jean Améry and the Refusal to Forgive* (Philadelphia: Temple University Press, 2008), 31; Annelies Verdoolaege, "The Human Rights Violations Hearings of the South African TRC: A Bridge between Individual Narratives of Suffering and a Contextualizing Master-Story of

"The police arrived at night at about twelve midnight," she began. "They knocked at the door and I asked, 'Who are you?' They said they were police. I opened the door. . . . Now they started looking, searching for [my son]. . . . They went outside to get one white police, and they were almost breaking the door open, and they shot instantly right in the bedroom."

She continued, "They left and I went in the room, found out that they had already shot him. I tried to see if there were any signs of vitality and to no avail. They came back again and said, 'This one is dead, and leave him just like that.'"

She went on to describe how the police removed her son's body, her struggle to reclaim it, and how the police disrupted the funeral with tear gas. When she finished, she acknowledged that the perpetrators had not come forward and had not applied for amnesty. Even so, the commissioner asked her, "If they come to you and ask for forgiveness would you be prepared to sit down with them, shake hands with them, and reconcile with them? Would you be prepared to talk to them?"

Mrs. Mdlalose replied, "I don't think I will allow such an opportunity."

Apartheid (literally, "apart-ness") was a system of legislated racial segregation and white political domination in South Africa from 1948 to 1993.[2] Under apartheid, everything from park benches and bathrooms to land, education, and political status was racially determined. Black Africans—who made up 80 percent of the

Reconciliation" (Ghent University, Belgium, 2002), paper online at the TRC Research Website: http://cas1.elis.ugent.be/avrug/trc/02_08.htm.

2. Roger B. Beck, *The History of South Africa*, The Greenwood Histories of the Modern Nations (Westport, CT: Greenwood Press, 2000), 125–54; Robert Ross, *A Concise History of South Africa*, 2nd ed., Cambridge Concise Histories (Cambridge, UK: Cambridge University Press, 2008), 122–173; Patty Waldmeir, *Anatomy of a Miracle: The End of Apartheid and the Birth of the New South Africa* (New York: W. W. Norton & Co., 1997), xiii–xiv.

population—along with "coloured" (Asian or mixed-race people) were forced to live separately from whites and afforded limited freedom of movement; some were banished to quasi-autonomous "homelands" or *bantustans*. While racial segregation began in colonial times under Dutch and British rule, apartheid as an official policy was introduced when the National Party took power in 1948.

The hearings of South Africa's Truth and Reconciliation Commission began in 1995 to address human rights violations and other wrongdoings committed during the apartheid regime in which black and "coloured" (Asian or mixed-race) South Africans were forced to live separately from whites and with significantly fewer rights, a system that was often enforced by violent means. The commission was divided into three parts: the Human Rights Violations Committee, which heard testimony of victims; the Reparation and Rehabilitation Committee, which assisted victims in recovery and awarded monetary reparations (mostly symbolic); and the Amnesty Committee, which reviewed applications for amnesty from those who committed crimes under apartheid. The TRC was meant to supplant a criminal process by giving victims a forum in which to be heard and perpetrators the opportunity to make full confessions in exchange for amnesty. All of this was carried out in service to South Africa's transition to democratic rule.

The 1995 Promotion of National Unity and Reconciliation Act[3] established the TRC to deal formally with crimes committed under apartheid by both the government and the anti-apartheid combatants. Led by Desmond Tutu, a high-profile anti-apartheid activist and retired Anglican archbishop, the act presents the mandate of the TRC:

---

3. The full text of the Promotion of National Unity and Reconciliation Act, No. 34 is available here: http://www.justice.gov.za/legislation/acts/1995-034.pdf.

To provide for the investigation and the establishment of as complete a picture as possible of the nature, causes and extent of gross violations of human rights . . . emanating from the conflicts of the past, and the fate or whereabouts of the victims of such violations; the granting of amnesty to persons who make full disclosure of all the relevant facts relating to acts associated with a political objective committed in the course of the conflicts of the past during the said period; affording victims an opportunity to relate the violations they suffered; the taking of measures aimed at the granting of reparation to, and the rehabilitation and the restoration of the human and civil dignity of, victims of violations of human rights; reporting to the Nation about such violations and victims; the making of recommendations aimed at the prevention of the commission of gross violations of human rights.[4]

It was the great hope of the TRC that a thorough airing of the truth would be "a means to reconcile a fractured nation and heal the wounds of its troubled soul."[5]

With regard to reconciliation, Mark R. Amstutz joins a number of people who judge the TRC to be a success: "[It] represents the most successful governmental initiative to promote peace and harmony through the discovery and acknowledgment of truth."[6] However, others criticize the TRC for its overemphasis on forgiveness in the service of reconciliation and its questionable rhetorical tactics used to urge victims in that direction.[7] This chapter makes its contribution to

4. Promotion of National Unity and Reconciliation Act.
5. Priscilla B. Hayner, *Unspeakable Truths: Transitional Justice and the Challenge of Truth Commissions*, 2nd ed. (New York: Routledge, 2011), 183.
6. Mark R. Amstutz, *The Healing of Nations: The Promise and Limits of Political Forgiveness* (Lanham, MD: Rowman and Littlefield Publishers, 2005), 209.
7. For considerations of problematic discussions of forgiveness in the TRC and post-apartheid South Africa, see Antjie Krog, *Country of My Skull: Guilt, Sorrow, and the Limits of Forgiveness in the New South Africa* (New York: Three Rivers Press, 1999), esp. 202; Verdoolaege, "Human Rights Violations Hearings"; Annelies Verdoolaege, "Reconciliation: The South African Truth and Reconciliation Commission; Deconstruction of a Multilayered Archive" (PhD diss., Universiteit Gent, 2005), esp. 48; Lyn S. Graybill, *Truth and Reconciliation in South Africa: Miracle or Model?* (Boulder, CO: Lunne Rienner Publishers, 2002), 32, 34, 43, 50; Graeme Simpson, "'Tell No Lies, Claim No Easy Victories': A Brief Evaluation of South Africa's Truth and Reconciliation Commission," in *Commissioning the Past: Understanding South Africa's Truth and Reconciliation Commission*, ed. Deborah Posel and Graeme Simpson (Johannesburg:

that discussion through an analysis of the language of forgiveness that permeated the TRC process.

While what follows is a critique of the forgiveness rhetoric of Desmond Tutu and the TRC, it should not be taken as a dismissal of the entire process. Let me be clear: The TRC was a remarkable experiment in alternative justice and moral repair. The victories of this process must not be overlooked: the cycles of racial violence fueled by apartheid have largely ended, democratic elections are standard, and black, white, and coloured people live in the same communities, study in the same schools, and enjoy the same freedoms. I might go so far as to join with others who call the TRC miraculous, both in its intention and its effect. That a truth commission could successfully supplant a criminal system and offer something like justice to victims, perpetrators, and the affected community is a beacon of hope.

Witwatersrand University Press, 2002), 239–40; Thomas Brudholm, "On the Advocacy of Forgiveness after Mass Atrocities," in *The Religious in Responses to Mass Atrocity: Interdisciplinary Perspectives*, ed. Thomas Brudholm and Thomas Cushman (New York: Cambridge University Press, 2009), 124–53; Audrey R. Chapman, "Perspectives on the Role of Forgiveness in the Human Rights Violations Hearings," in *Truth and Reconciliation in South Africa: Did the TRC Deliver?*, ed. Audrey R. Chapman and Hugo van der Merwe, Pennsylvania Studies in Human Rights (Philadelphia: University of Pennsylvania Press, 2008), 66–89; Martha Minow, *Between Vengeance and Forgiveness: Facing History after Genocide and Mass Violence* (Boston, MA: Beacon Press, 1998), 17–19 and passim; Richard A. Wilson, *The Politics of Truth and Reconciliation in South Africa: Legitimizing the Post-Apartheid State*, Cambridge Studies in Law and Society (Cambridge: Cambridge University Press, 2001), 174; Stuart Wilson, "The Myth of Restorative Justice: Truth, Reconciliation and the Ethics of Amnesty," *South African Journal of Human Rights* 17 (2001): 548; Annelies Verdoolaege, *Reconciliation Discourse: The Case of the Truth and Reconciliation Commission*, Discourse Approaches to Politics, Society and Culture (Amsterdam: John Benjamins Publishing Company, 2008); Annalise E. Acorn, *Compulsory Compassion: A Critique of Restorative Justice*, Law and Society Series (Vancouver: UBC Press, 2004), 72; Brudholm, *Resentment's Virtue*, esp. 21–62; Ari Kohen, "The Personal and the Political: Forgiveness and Reconciliation in Restorative Justice," in *Faculty Publications: Political Science*, Paper 34 (University of Nebraska-Lincoln, 2009), 416–17; Colleen Murphy, *A Moral Theory of Political Reconciliation* (Cambridge, UK: Cambridge University Press, 2010), 1–17; Jacques Derrida, *On Cosmopolitanism and Forgiveness*, trans. Mark Dooley and Michael Hughes (New York: Routledge, 2001), 41–42.

But like any institution, the TRC was flawed. Today, it leaves behind unprosecuted former combatants who refused to apply for amnesty, persistent and abject poverty among the formerly oppressed communities, and a "new civil religion" of racial reconciliation that is already under strain.[8] The systemic racism many had hoped the TRC would address is still a reality.[9] I am critical not of the political aspirations or the symbolic importance of the TRC; rather, I am troubled by the language used to pressure victims into forgiving perpetrators in service of the new South Africa.

Appeals for forgiveness in the name of national unity and reconciliation are not uncommon in the Human Rights Violations Committee (HRVC) transcripts, and often they come directly from the chairperson of the TRC, Archbishop Desmond Tutu. Many victims acquiesce to the calls for forgiveness, and they are lavishly praised. There are also, however, witnesses like Bettina Mdlalose. She refuses to forgive the men who shot her son; she will not even face them. With one sentence, Mdlalose rejects the TRC's overarching narrative of forgiveness as healing and national reconciliation.

This narrative is seen primarily in the writings of Desmond Tutu and crystallized in the title of his memoir of the TRC, *No Future without Forgiveness*. Here Tutu issues the most famous forgiveness imperative associated with the TRC: "Without forgiveness, there is no future."[10] He contends that victims must forgive in order to ensure

---

8. Waldmeir, *Anatomy of a Miracle*, 254.
9. Megan Shore, *Religion and Conflict Resolution: Christianity and South Africa's Truth and Reconciliation Commission* (Burlington, VT: Ashgate Publishing, 2009), 81; Heidi Grunebaum and Yazir Henri, "Where the Mountain Meets Its Shadow: A Conversation of Memory and Identity and Fragmented Belonging in Present-Day South Africa," in *Homelands: The Politics of Space and the Poetics of Power*, ed. Bo Strath and Ron Robins (Brussels: Peter Lang, 2003), 267–83.
10. Tutu, *No Future without Forgiveness* (New York: Doubleday, 1999), 165, 260, 273, 279, 282; see also Tutu, "Without Forgiveness There Is No Future," in *Exploring Forgiveness*, ed. Robert D. Enright and Joanna North (Madison: University of Wisconsin Press, 1998), xiii–xiv; Desmond Tutu, Symposium contribution in Simon Wiesenthal, *The Sunflower: On the Possibilities and*

the reconciliation of South Africa because such magnanimity among victims is the only way to quell resentment and end violence.

However, applicants for amnesty are not required to apologize or show remorse, and Tutu has not yet produced a corresponding volume called *No Future without Repentance*. The forgiveness ideal presented to victims in South Africa is both unconditional and a national imperative. If there is no future without forgiveness, then the entire burden of the future is on the victims.

In addition, Tutu's account generally rejects the potential value of negative emotions such as resentment, outrage, and anger. He denounces those emotions in his post-TRC work (he notes the "corrosive" effects of anger on the common good, for example),[11] and yet his own anti-apartheid speeches, sermons, and writings demonstrate how the negative emotions can fuel social action. Resentment, outrage, anger, and even the refusal to forgive can demonstrate self-respect and a commitment to justice—namely, holding offenders accountable for their actions. The fall of the apartheid government and the institution of the TRC could not have come about without the decades of righteous indignation that fueled the anti-apartheid movement.

Reflecting on the end of the apartheid era in South Africa, Tutu posits that forgiveness is essential not only for transforming conflict, but for all human relations from the creation of Adam and Eve to the present.[12] "Forgiveness is an absolute necessity for continued human existence," he writes.[13] However, forgiveness is reactive and relies on the presence of wrongdoing, as well as a community that

Limits of Forgiveness, rev. and exp. ed. (New York: Schocken Books, 1998), 268; Meinrad Scherer-Emunds, "No Forgiveness, No Future: An Interview with Archbishop Desmond Tutu," *U.S. Catholic* 65, no. 8 (2000): 24–28; Tutu, *God Is Not a Christian: And Other Provocations* (New York: HarperOne, 2011), 25–36.

11. Tutu, *No Future*, 31.
12. Tutu, "Without Forgiveness," xiii.
13. Ibid.

is constantly being defined by that wrongdoing and forgiveness as a mode of repair. To be sure, certain instances of forgiveness may form constructive and even admirable ways to rebuild a community in the aftermath of systemic violence such as apartheid, but forgiveness is not the only way forward; it is conditional (depending on perpetrator repentance) and contextual (defined or limited by circumstance and setting), and it is not always a morally appropriate response. I argue that, because forgiveness is always contextual, it does not always provide a fitting foundation for a national ethic.

In this chapter I use the Lord's Prayer as a lens to think about how forgiveness might be understood in the context of conflict transformation (the process by which societies in conflict, such as South Africa under apartheid, transform that conflict into peaceful outcomes), particularly the TRC and South Africa's transition to democratic rule. First, I consider how the Lord's Prayer operates as a tool for social cohesion in the Gospels of Matthew and Luke. I show that the prayer—which is first of all a *community* prayer—depicts a vision of forgiveness that equally values asking for forgiveness from God and forgiving others. In both Gospels, but especially Matthew, the prayer demonstrates the importance of community harmony for being in right relationship with God. Next, I examine debt language in the prayer ("forgive us our debts" in Matt. 6:12; "we forgive everyone indebted to us" in Luke 11:4) and evaluate its usefulness and limits in contemporary interpretations. The prayer contains a repentant plea for forgiveness ("forgive us") as well as a commitment to forgiving others ("as we forgive"), thus demonstrating the bilateral character of forgiveness.

In the years leading up to the TRC, Tutu acknowledged the interdependence of repentance and forgiveness in the Lord's Prayer. In 1990, when the Dutch Reformed Church confessed and apologized for providing theological support for the apartheid government, Tutu responded with an appeal to the reciprocal forgiveness presented in the Lord's Prayer. He explains, "I cannot, when someone says, 'Forgive me,' say, 'I do not.' For then I cannot pray the prayer that we prayed, 'Forgive us, as we forgive.'"[14] While Tutu often touts unconditional, unilateral forgiveness of victims, here he emphasizes the importance of an exchange of repentance and forgiveness. He says, "When that confession of wrongdoing is made, those of us who have been wronged must say, 'We forgive you.'"[15]

Not all amnesty applicants viewed their testimony as confessions or expressions of repentance in this sense, and applicants were not required to apologize or otherwise express remorse for their crimes. Since amnesty was not awarded by the TRC as a gift but rather in exchange for information in the form of truthful testimony, testimony before the Amnesty Committee did not constitute the kind of confession of sin depicted in the Lord's Prayer. As a result, Tutu's charge for victims to respond to "that confession of wrongdoing" with forgiveness rings hollow since testimony before the Amnesty Committee was not seen as a "confession of wrongdoing" in the sense Tutu implies.

In the Gospels, both Matthew and Luke provide conditions for interpersonal forgiveness, as seen in the previous chapter. There is no instruction relating to unconditional forgiveness. The Lord's Prayer prescribes community solidarity by way of a bilateral understanding of forgiveness in which believers must ask for forgiveness as often as they dispense it. In this case, forgiveness is not just an emotion or speech act that makes everything right. Rather, forgiveness here is an element of reconciliation that requires work from all sides in order to establish right relationship in community and with God.

---

14. Tutu, *God Is Not a Christian*, 31, citing Tutu's words with the South African Council of Churches in Mogopa in 1983.
15. Ibid., 29.

In the context of the TRC, forgiveness was necessary for reconciliation. However, the term "reconciliation" was highly contested, with some arguing that it demanded "contrition, confession, forgiveness and restitution,"[16] and others calling simply for "peaceful coexistence."[17] The TRC defined "reconciliation" as "both a goal and a process" for both individuals and communities.[18]

For the purposes of this chapter, I define reconciliation as the repair or restoration of a broken relationship, both between human beings and communities at large. In the case of South Africa, reconciliation means the restoration of peaceful community relations in the wake of apartheid. The reconciliation at stake in the TRC is between black and coloured South Africans who were oppressed by the white apartheid government, as well as between perpetrators of apartheid or anti-apartheid violence (of all races) and their victims.

Building on the analysis of reciprocal forgiveness in the Lord's Prayer, the second part of this chapter focuses on the rhetoric of forgiveness of the TRC and particularly its chairperson. Tutu draws heavily on the African concept of *ubuntu*, which he calls "the African *Weltanschauung*."[19] The essence of *ubuntu*, he explains, is the recognition that all human beings are interconnected, and therefore the suffering of any affects the health of the whole.[20] This notion of inherent interdependence undergirds the TRC and the drive toward reconciliation. Tutu enlarges the concept to introduce Christian language of forgiveness to the TRC proceedings, and a future based on reconciliation becomes a future based on forgiveness. As a result, victims were sometimes implicitly pressured by commissioners to

16. Chapter 5, "Concepts and Principles," in *Truth and Reconciliation Commission of South Africa Report*, 5 vols. (Cape Town: Juta, 1998), 1:108.
17. Ibid., 108.
18. Ibid., 106.
19. Tutu, *No Future*, 31.
20. Ibid.

forgive. The presence of clerical garments, prayer, and candles contributed to the general religious character of the hearings, which supplied implicit moral pressure to forgive. Throughout the proceedings, Tutu and other commissioners abundantly praised testifiers who agreed to forgive, both in and out of the hearing rooms.

In addition, Tutu promotes a biblical imperative to forgive (based primarily on the Lord's Prayer [see above], the seventy-times-seven instructions, and Jesus's cry from the cross, "Father, forgive them") that is based on decidedly *non*biblical understandings of forgiveness. He defines forgiveness using therapeutic terms such as "healing" and "catharsis," urges victims to forgive without apology or even the presence of the perpetrators, and repeatedly states in his writings, "To forgive is not just to be altruistic. It is the best form of self-interest."[21] As a result, the project of reconciliation depends wholly on emotional feats of forgiveness accomplished by the victims. I contend that reconciliation based on one-sided forgiveness stands to be shakier than its bilateral counterpart. In addition, such constant pressure to forgive and celebration of forgiveness marginalize victims who are unable or unwilling to forgive those who tortured them, terrorized them, and murdered their loved ones.[22]

---

21. Tutu, *No Future*, 31, 35; Desmond Tutu, interview by Marina Cantacuzino for The Forgiveness Project, London, UK, June 1, 2003, http://theforgivenessproject.com/stories/desmond-tutu-south-africa/; Scherer-Edmunds, "No Forgiveness, No Future," 26.
22. No provisions were made for psychological follow-up with victims who testified before the HRVC or whose perpetrators applied for amnesty, so I cannot speak to the experience of victims whose anger and outrage might have changed in the years since the close of the TRC. On this topic, see Timothy Sizwe Phatathi and Hugo van der Merwe, "The Impact of the TRC's Amnesty Process on Survivors of Human Rights Violations," in Chapman and van der Merwe, *Did the TRC Deliver?*, 137. On the lack of follow-up with victims, see also Graybill, *Miracle or Model?*, 84; Brandon Hamber, *Transforming Societies after Political Violence: Truth, Reconciliation, and Mental Health*, Peace Psychology Book Series (London: Springer Science Business Media, 2009), 58.

Forgiveness in the Lord's Prayer

Perhaps the most familiar canonical instruction on forgiveness comes in the Lord's Prayer in Matthew and Luke:

Matt. 6:9–13	Luke 11:2–4
Pray then in this way: Our Father in heaven,	When you pray, say:Father, hallowed be your name.
hallowed be your name.	Your kingdom come.
Your kingdom come.	Give us each day our daily bread.
Your will be done,	And forgive us our sins,
on earth as it is in heaven.	for we ourselves forgive everyone
Give us this day our daily bread.	indebted to us.
And forgive us our debts,	And do not bring us to the time of trial.
as we also have forgiven our debtors.	
And do not bring us to the time of trial,	
but rescue us from the evil one.	

Here I demonstrate that this prayer contains not only an imperative for human beings to forgive, but also an expression of repentance. While the words of confession ("Forgive us our debts"; Matt. 6:12//"Forgive us our sins"; Luke 11:4) are directed at God, they constitute a general disposition of repentance for past transgressions.

The extended prayer in Matthew begins with *"Our* Father" and implies a community of believers praying together.[23] In both Matthew and Luke, Jesus teaches his followers to pray in the first-person plural.[24] Darrell Bock writes, "As disciples come before the Father, they are to affirm their unity and share a sense of family."[25] The prayer contains hoped-for ideals for the new community:

---

23. Nicholas Ayo, *The Lord's Prayer: A Survey Theological and Literary* (Lanham, MD: Rowman & Littlefield, 1992), 21.
24. Where Matthew has "Our Father" (πάτερ ἡμῶν), Luke's prayer is addressed simply to "Father" (πάτερ). Following this, both prayers are given in the first-person plural.
25. Darrell L. Bock, *Luke*, IVP New Testament Commentary Series (Downers Grove, IL: InterVarsity Press, 1994), 203.

enough food, forgiveness within the group, and protection from temptation and hardship. The communal groundwork of the Lord's Prayer establishes a framework for the health and strength of the community.

The prayer as preserving community order

The use of the first-person plural in both versions of the Lord's Prayer emphasizes the importance of preserving community unity. In Matthew, the instruction is to pray to "*Our* Father," not "*My* Father." In both Matthew and Luke, the petitions follow: "Give *us*" our daily bread, "forgive *us*" our debts or sins, and "do not bring *us*" to the time of trial. The Lord's Prayer is a corporate prayer. The command to forgive ensures that interpersonal conflicts will not threaten the health of the group. In addition, the prayer serves as a foundational story for the community; when the members pray together, they proclaim who they are in relation to God and each other.[26] According to the Didache, the community was to pray these words together three times a day; the promises and pleas of this prayer were deeply ingrained in the character of the community.[27]

Cyprian, third-century bishop of Carthage, also emphasizes the corporate character of the Lord's Prayer. He writes, "Our prayer is public and common. When we pray, we pray not for one, but for the whole people, because we the whole people are one ... one should thus pray for all, even as He Himself bore us all in one."[28] In the thirteenth century, St. Thomas Aquinas also underscores the prayer's

---

26. James D. G. Dunn, "The Tradition," in *The Historical Jesus in Recent Research*, ed. James D. G. Dunn and Scot McKnight, Sources for Biblical and Theological Study 10 (Winona Lake, IN: Eisenbrauns, 2005), 168.

27. "Pray this three times each day" (Didache 8:3); see also Aaron Milavec, *The Didache: Text, Translation, Analysis, and Commentary* (Collegeville, MN: The Liturgical Press, 2003).

28. Cyprian, "On the Lord's Prayer." Quoted in John Alfred Faulkner, *Cyprian the Churchman* (Cincinnati, OH: Jennings and Graham, 1906), 142.

importance for the community by insisting that the corporate power of the prayer transcends individual wrongs, for the voice of the prayer is the voice of the church as a whole. He writes, "The Lord's Prayer is pronounced in the common person of the whole Church, and so if anyone say the Lord's Prayer while unwilling to forgive his neighbor's trespasses, he lies not."[29] Even one who is not forgiving may say this prayer as a part of the common voice. Aquinas focuses on the all-forgiving nature of God (who abides by the instruction to forgive boundlessly [Matt. 18:22]) rather than on the possibility that unforgiving Christians may be excluded from the new covenant.

The two parts of the forgiveness prayer represent the roles in such a forgiveness dialogue that may lead toward reconciliation: one asks for forgiveness, while the other extends forgiveness. Both actions are necessary for a reconciled community. Warren Carter writes, "The request for forgiveness recognizes that the one praying has violated human dignity and not met divine and human demands. It requests God's faithful and inclusive love to set aside the debts and renew relationships and community. . . . Asking God for such mercy means releasing others from their failed obligations also."[30] I do not mean to suggest that sins against God and sins against other human beings are interchangeable, or that asking God's forgiveness stands in for asking forgiveness of others. Rather, the idea is simply that human repentance (expressed to God) and human forgiveness are dependent on each other.

Petitioning God to set aside one's debts and promising to express a simultaneous generosity demonstrate a desire to reconcile relationships marred by sin, on the part of both the penitent and other members of the community. This turning toward a changed

---

29. Thomas Aquinas, *Summa Theologica*, second part of the second part, question 83, http://www.ccel.org/ccel/aquinas/summa.SS_Q83_A16.html. Here he indicates that even the unforgiving member may speak forgiveness as a part of the body of the church.

30. Carter, *Matthew and the Margins*, 167–68.

relationship is exactly what is suggested by μετάνοια, the Greek word most often translated as "repentance" in the New Testament. Annemarie S. Kidder also notes the complementary elements in the Lord's Prayer:[31] it is a prayer of repentance ("forgive us") as much as forgiveness ("we forgive"). Every member of the community—sinner or sinned against, debtor or lender—makes a contribution to unity.

While the repentance portion of the prayer is not necessarily directed at a specific victim to address a specific crime, it does contain an apology as an expression of remorse. "Forgive me" (along with "I'm sorry" or "I repent," as seen in Luke 17:4) is a common phrase in the language of religious confession as well as spoken apology.[32] Indeed, "Forgive me, Father, for I have sinned," is the opening of the traditional formula for Roman Catholic confession (an occasion for repentance),[33] and in the Anglican tradition penitents pray, "Have mercy on us and forgive us."[34] Both petitions are rooted in the Lord's Prayer and taken as elements of penitential confessions. Edward Hanna observes, "Without sincere sorrow and purpose of amendment, confession avails nothing, the pronouncement of absolution is of no effect, and the guilt of the sinner is greater than before."[35] The person praying makes a general expression of repentance for past wrongs and pledges to forgive others in return.

Matthew's two-verse addendum to the Lord's Prayer underscores the connection between right relation in the community and divine

---

31. Annemarie S. Kidder, *Making Confession, Hearing Confession: A History of the Cure of Souls* (Collegeville, MN: The Liturgical Press, 2010), 203.

32. Linda Radzik, *Making Amends: Atonement in Morality, Law, and Politics* (Oxford: Oxford University Press, 2009), 56; Nick Smith, *I Was Wrong: The Meanings of Apologies* (New York: Cambridge University Press, 2008), vi, 263n17.

33. "In confession we have the opportunity to repent and recover the grace of friendship with God" (United States Conference of Catholic Bishops [USCCB], "The Sacrament of Penance," http://www.usccb.org/prayer-and-worship/sacraments/penance/).

34. *Book of Common Prayer* (New York: Seabury Press, 1979), 360.

35. Edward Hanna, "The Sacrament of Penance," *The Catholic Encyclopedia*, 15 vols. (New York: Robert Appleton Company, 1911), vol. 11, http://www.newadvent.org/cathen/11618c.htm.

forgiveness: "For if you forgive others their trespasses, your heavenly Father will also forgive you; but if you do not forgive others, neither will your Father forgive your trespasses" (6:14–15). It is impossible for God to be in relationship with a community that does not get along internally. That Matthew reiterates the prayer's forgiveness instruction testifies to its importance.

Sin as debt

Where Matthew has, "And forgive us our debts [ὀφειλήματα], as we also have forgiven our debtors [ὀφειλέταις]" (6:12), Luke instructs, "And forgive us our sins [ἁμαρτίας], for we ourselves forgive everyone indebted to us [ὀφείλοντι]" (11:4). Luke indicates that God may forgive the sins of human beings but then grounds the possibilities of human forgiveness in the metaphor of "debts" (or, "those indebted to us"). Matthew offers an exact parallel between divine and human forgiveness (both forgive "debts").[36]

Luke differentiates the human ability to forgive debts from God's capacity to forgive sins, but Matthew assigns to both the power to forgive "trespasses" (παράπτωμα) in the two-verse addendum. John Nolland observes, "The switch from 'debts' to 'transgressions' [or trespasses], which Matthew uses only in vv. 14–15, confirms that [Matthew] intended 'debts' in v. 12 to be an image for wrongdoings."[37] Thus in both Matthew and Luke the human willingness to forgive debts both literal and figurative is a

---

36. The verb translated as "forgive" (ἄφες [ἀφίημι]) is the same in both prayers and is used throughout the New Testament to indicate forgiveness of financial debt as well as wrongdoing (Matt. 6:9–13, 14–15; 9:2–8; 12:31–32; 18:21–22, 23–35; Mark 2:2–12; 3:28–29; 4:10–12; 11:25; Luke 5:17–26; 7:36–50; 11:2–4; 12:10; 17:1–4; 23:34; John 20:22–23; Acts 2:37–39; 8:22; Rom. 4:7; James 5:15; 1 John 1:9; 2:12). See Rudolf Bultmann, "ἀφίημι," in *Theological Dictionary of the New Testament*, ed. G. Kittel and G. Friedrich (Grand Rapids, MI: Eerdmans, 1964), 1:509; and Gary A. Anderson, *Sin: A History* (New Haven, CT: Yale University Press, 2009), esp. 27–39.

37. John S. Nolland, *The Gospel of Matthew: A Commentary on the Greek Text*, NIGCT (Grand Rapids, MI: Eerdmans, 2005), 293–94.

precondition for divine forgiveness. The prayer presumes that human beings have the ability to forgive both financial debts and personal trespasses.

The nature of forgiveness in the Lord's Prayer

In the history of interpretation of the Lord's Prayer there are numerous understandings of the forgiveness it describes. Parallels to the Matthean follow-up to the Lord's Prayer appear in both Mark and Luke. Mark, who does not include (or perhaps does not know) the Lord's Prayer, gives this admonition: "Whenever you stand praying, forgive, if you have anything against anyone; so that your Father in heaven may also forgive you your trespasses [παραπτώματα]" (11:25).[38] Mark's use of παράπτωμα for trespasses echoes Matthew's two-verse coda where the word is used twice. Παράπτωμα appears only once in Mark, suggesting a familiarity with or independent attestation of the parallel texts in Matthew and Luke.[39] Matthew's shift indicates that he means the language of debts to be related to these trespasses. As opposed to the more serious ἁμαρτίας (Luke 11:4), which signifies crimes against both other human beings and God, παραπτώματα are literally "false steps" or transgressions against others.[40] Matthew's follow-up is concerned with linking the resolutions of interpersonal disputes with God's own forgiveness of those transgressions.

Luke also offers an additional reciprocal formula, although it is detached from the prayer and uses different language. Luke writes, "Do not judge, and you will not be judged; do not condemn, and you will not be condemned. Forgive [ἀπολύετε], and you will be

---

38. The nrsv gives the following note: "Other ancient authorities add verse 26, 'But if you do not forgive, neither will your Father in heaven forgive your trespasses.'"

39. John R. Donahue and Daniel J. Harrington, *Mark*, SP (Collegeville, MN: The Liturgical Press, 2002), 330.

40. BAGD, 627 (παράπτωμα).

forgiven [ἀπολυθήσεσθε]; give, and it will be given to you" (6:37). This verse marks the only time in the Gospels in which the NRSV translates the verb ἀπολύω as "forgive." Elsewhere the NRSV renders this word as "send away," "depart," "divorce," or "release."[41] Every other discussion of interpersonal or divine forgiveness in the Gospels uses the verb ἀφίημι. Both verbs have the literal sense of "letting go"; both can indicate the forgiveness or release of a debt.[42] The semantic range of these terms indicates that forgiveness was understood in this context to have perceptible outcomes of release and liberation from the effects of wrongdoing as from debt.

In the parable of the unforgiving servant (Matt. 18:23–35), Jesus describes a servant whose enormous debt is forgiven by a king. When that servant then refuses to forgive the small debt of his fellow slave, the king throws him into prison to be tortured and reinstates his debt. Matthew uses ἀπολύω alongside ἀφίημι in this story to describe the king's response to the servant's pleas: "And out of pity for him, the lord of that slave released [ἀπέλυσεν] him and forgave [ἀφῆκεν] him the debt" (18:27). This proximity suggests that Jesus plays on the similarity of being released from slavery and having a debt released; the semantic ranges of both words are nearly identical. Here, debt forgiveness and release from captivity are related. The parable presents forgiveness as not reciprocal but as progressive: if one is forgiven a debt, one is obligated to forgive his or her debtors, just as the Lord's Prayer describes.

However, in the Pauline literature, God's forgiveness was understood to be grounded in the death and resurrection of Jesus.

41. Elsewhere in the New Testament, ἀπολύω is taken to mean "send away" (Matt. 14:15, 22, 23; 15:23, 32, 39; Mark 6:36, 45; 8:3, 9; Luke 8:38; 9:12; Acts 13:3; 15:30), "depart" (Luke 2:29; Acts 28:25), "divorce" (Matt. 1:19; 5:31, 32; 19:3, 7, 8, 9; Mark 10:2, 4, 11, 12; Luke 16:18), or "release" (Matt. 27:15, 17, 21, 26; Mark 15:6, 9, 11, 15; Luke 13:12; 14:4; 22:68; 23:16, 17, 18, 20, 22, 25; John 18:39; 19:10, 12; Acts 3:13; 4:21, 23; 5:40; 15:33; 16:35, 36; 17:9; 19:41; 23:22; 26:32; 28:18; Heb. 13:23).

42. BAGD, 95–96 (ἀπολύω), 125 (ἀφίημι).

Thus forgiveness was seen as a consequence of and response to God's forgiveness (as given in Eph. 4:32, "be kind to one another, tenderhearted, forgiving one another, as God in Christ has forgiven you," and Col. 3:13, "Bear with one another and, if anyone has a complaint against another, forgive each other; just as the Lord has forgiven you, so you also must forgive").[43] The idea that mutual forgiveness was a strict requirement for receiving God's forgiveness would have seemed to contradict early Christian writings that locate forgiveness not in the teachings of Jesus, but in the death and resurrection of Christ.

Early Christian interpreters of the Lord's Prayer emphasized the themes of divine reciprocity and right relationship to God. Tertullian (160–225) shifts the emphasis from forgiveness to repentance: "A petition for pardon is a full confession; because he who begs for pardon fully admits his guilt."[44] Cyril of Alexandria (376–444) and Gregory of Nyssa (335–95) both posit that human forgiveness provides a model for God's own behavior.[45] Cyril writes, "[Jesus] first commands them to ask forgiveness of the sins they commit and then to confess that they entirely forgive others. They ask God to imitate the patience that they practice."[46] Augustine (354–430) interprets the prayer both as a call for almsgiving ("so that God may give to you what you give to [the poor]")[47] and a remedy, or discipline of penance. The emphasis for these early interpreters is on the practical

43. Tobias Hägerland, *Jesus and the Forgiveness of Sins: An Aspect of His Prophetic Mission* (Cambridge, UK: Cambridge University Press, 2011), 63. In these verses, as in most New Testament discussions of forgiveness outside the Gospels, the word translated as "forgive" is χαρίζομαι.
44. Tertullian, Chapter VII, The Sixth Clause, from "On Prayer," http://st-takla.org/books/en/ecf/003/0030751.html.
45. Gregory of Nyssa, *Discourse Five, Forgive Us Our Debts as We Forgive Our Debtors. And Lead Us Not into Temptation, but Deliver Us from the Evil One*; Cyril of Alexandria, "On Prayer," in *Ancient Christian Commentary on Scripture: New Testament III: Luke*, ed. Arthur A. Just (Downers Grove, IL: InterVarsity Press, 2003), 188.
46. Cyril of Alexandria, "On Prayer," in Just, *Ancient Christian Commentary*, 188.

relationship between forgiving and being forgiven. They most often see the practice of forgiveness as a work that both responds to and secures God's forgiveness.

Martin Luther identifies a problem with the prayer's formula of reciprocal forgiveness. He writes, "It looks besides as if the forgiveness of sins was gained and merited by our forgiving. What would then become of our doctrine that forgiveness comes alone through Christ and is received by faith?"[48] The idea that salvation comes through the practice of human forgiveness assaults the very core of Luther's program of salvation by faith alone. Luther interprets the prayer as a call for peace and unity among the Christian community. Its utterance forms a strong bond and prevents factions and discord. Interpersonal forgiveness, according to Luther, is then not a requirement but rather evidence of divine forgiveness. He explains, "The external forgiveness which I practically show is a sure sign that I have the divine forgiveness of my sins."[49] In this view, forgiveness on earth is God's forgiveness made manifest; it binds the community together.

John Calvin reads the prayer with a similar emphasis on God's unlimited mercy. God's forgiveness is not conditional on mutual human forgiveness. The prayer for forgiveness, he writes, "the Lord intended, partly to comfort the weakness of our faith." Thus the prayer contains an assurance of forgiveness more than a command. Like Luther, Calvin regards human forgiveness as a sign of and not a condition for divine forgiveness. "For [the Lord] has added this as a sign, that we may be as certainly assured of remission of sins being

---

47. Augustine, Sermon on the Liturgical Seasons, 3.6 sermons 184-229Z, in *The Works of St. Augustine: A Translation for the Twenty-First Century*, trans. Edmund Hill (Hyde Park, NY: New City Press, 1995), 107.
48. Martin Luther, *Commentary on the Sermon on the Mount* (5:14–15), trans. Charles A. Hay (Philadelphia: Lutheran Publication Society, 1892).
49. Ibid.

granted us by him, as we are certain and conscious of our granting it to others."[50] In Calvin's view, forgiveness becomes less an imperative on Christians than an inevitable outcome of faith. Along with Luther, he plants the seed of unconditional, unilateral forgiveness developed later by Tutu.

Some contemporary scholars assert that the loving nature of God takes precedence over the threat of exclusion as a result of nonforgiveness. Like Luther, they suggest that making God's love dependent on forgiveness amounts to works righteousness and threatens the central Protestant doctrine of salvation by grace alone. Arthur W. Pink writes, "My capacity to forgive others seems inconsistent and incomplete at best. Will God's forgiveness be the same for me? The thought is horrifying!"[51] Questioning the idea that the forgiveness petition contains a precondition, he suggests that it is instead an example of Jesus's use of hyperbole to make his point. Pink writes, "It shocks us. How dare we beg for grace with no intention of extending that same grace to others?"[52] The outrageous idea that God's forgiveness might be conditional is meant to shock people into practicing forgiveness.

Nicholas Ayo reads the prayer's forgiveness petition as a description rather than condition. He writes, "'Forgive us as we forgive' need not imply human initiative with God's mercy. It may rather point to a parallel in the kind of forgiveness being asked. Forgive us *just as* or *even as* we forgive others."[53] Understood this way, the prayer offers an illustration, something more like Cyril of Alexandria's interpretation. The meaning is not, "Forgive us *because* we forgive," but "Forgive us *in the same way we do when* we forgive."

---

50. John Calvin, *Institutes of the Christian Religion*, vol. 2, Book III.

51. Arthur W. Pink, *The Beatitudes and the Lord's Prayer* (Grand Rapids, MI: Baker Books, 1979), 150.

52. Ibid., 151.

53. Ayo, *Lord's Prayer*, 80.

Ayo writes, "We learn of God's ways by analogy with the human ways we have known. It is hard to imagine how anyone could comprehend God's forgiveness if they had never been forgiven during their lifetime."[54] This interpretation transforms forgiveness from an imperative to an ideal or ambition. Forgiveness, when it happens, can be a powerful and loving gesture. We may hope that God will behave in this way toward us in light of our sins. These scholars remove the moral imperative, implied by the petition, that we must forgive, and thus the character of repentance is lost. Since God's forgiveness is a foregone conclusion, the petition is more a rote exercise than an earnest pleading.

Like the early church fathers, Desmond Tutu calls on the reciprocal formula in the Lord's Prayer to illustrate the necessity of human forgiveness in the service of God's collaborative kingdom. He writes, "Extraordinarily, God, the omnipotent One depends on us, puny, fragile, vulnerable as we may be, to accomplish God's purposes for good, for justice, for forgiveness and healing and wholeness."[55] He quotes Augustine on this interdependence: "God without us will not as we without God cannot."[56] However, John Dominic Crossan points out that this is "magnificently misquoted" by Tutu; the actual words of Augustine are, "God made you without you, but he doesn't justify you without you."[57]

In misquoting Augustine's maxim, Tutu makes God's action entirely dependent on human participation: "God without you will not." His misquotation loses the sense of omnipotence and autonomy Augustine ascribes to God: "God made you without you"; for

54. Ibid.
55. Tutu, *No Future*, 158.
56. Ibid.
57. John Dominic Crossan, *The Greatest Prayer: Rediscovering the Revolutionary Message of the Lord's Prayer* (New York: HarperCollins, 2010), 94; Augustine of Hippo, "Sermon 169," in Vol. 3, *The Works of St. Augustine*, 231.

Augustine, God waits for right human action to justify (or make right before God). Both sides of this sentence imply God's ultimate power. Tutu's version implies a mutual dependence that is absent in Augustine's original words. Tutu implies that God may refuse to forgive unless human beings forgive, but he also wants to say that human beings have a limited capacity to forgive without God. Human beings and God, then, are equal partners in forgiveness; each depends on the other to make it happen. The sense of human pleading with God for forgiveness, which I see as an act of repentance, gets lost in this teamwork formulation.

Forgiveness in post-apartheid South Africa

In 1985, a group of unnamed, black South African theologians came together to write the Kairos Document, a statement on the country's political crisis and practices of apartheid, and especially on the state and church theologies undergirding those practices. While Desmond Tutu did not sign the document, he is thought to be its architect and he publicly supported its ideas.[58] The document proposes a contextual theology, called "prophetic theology," that demands justice as a necessary condition for reconciliation. The Kairos theologians write,

> No reconciliation is possible in South Africa without justice. What this means in practice is that no reconciliation, no forgiveness and no negotiations are possible without repentance. The Biblical teaching on reconciliation and forgiveness makes it quite clear that nobody can be forgiven and reconciled with God unless he or she repents of their sins. Nor are we expected to forgive the unrepentant sinner. When he or she repents we must be willing to forgive seventy times seven times but before that, we are expected to preach repentance to those who sin against us or against anyone. Reconciliation, forgiveness and

---

58. John Allen, *Rabble-Rouser for Peace: The Authorized Biography of Desmond Tutu* (New York: Free Press, 2006), 288.

119

negotiations will become our Christian duty in South Africa only when the apartheid regime shows signs of genuine repentance.[59]

Like Bonhoeffer, the Kairos theologians will not stand for cheap grace. There can be no forgiveness without its outward manifestation of reconciliation (the restoration of right relationship), and no reconciliation without justice. For them, "true and lasting justice" involves a change in social structures that is accomplished by those who are oppressed (i.e., it comes from the bottom, not the top).[60] Forgiveness, they argue, is contextual. It becomes a "Christian duty" only when repentance and justice also reign. The body politic, like the body of Christ, must be nourished by both forgiveness *and* repentance.

This necessary relationship is manifested in the Lord's Prayer where the petition for forgiveness and the commitment to forgive are intertwined, although they form a triangular relationship rather than a reciprocal one: the general repentance is aimed at God, the promised forgiveness is extended to fellow human beings, and the hoped-for forgiveness flows from God. This does not preclude interpersonal repentance. Rather it implies that asking for forgiveness (from God or from one's neighbor) should be a regular discipline. However, the TRC abandons the Kairos emphasis on repentance in favor of a notion of forgiveness as unconditional and a source of individual healing.

The end of apartheid

In 1962, the United Nations established the UN Special Committee against Apartheid. By 1968, the UN was urging member countries to suspend all trade and cultural relations with South Africa.[61] As

59. Kairos Theologians, *The Kairos Document: Challenge to the Church; A Theological Comment on the Political Crisis in South Africa* (Johannesburg: Skotaville Publishers, 1986), 10.
60. Ibid., 12.

anti-apartheid resistance grew in South Africa, it was met with rising repression and violence from the apartheid government. In 1990, the president of South Africa, F. W. de Klerk, began negotiations with the African National Congress (ANC) to end apartheid. In 1994, Nelson Mandela—who had been jailed for twenty-seven years as a result of his opposition leadership—became South Africa's first democratically elected president.[62]

The religious character of the TRC

Within the hearing rooms and especially in public perception, forgiveness played a prominent role in the TRC. In its final report, the commission is transparent about the introduction of Christian language and imagery into the official process. Central to this boosting of forgiveness was Desmond Tutu. He promoted a vision of forgiveness that is unconditional and that he equated with being human, and he lavished enormous praise on victims who forgive their perpetrators.

At the time of the TRC, Desmond Tutu was serving as the first black Anglican archbishop of Cape Town. His presence in the hearings was visually striking. He dressed in full bishop's vestments: a long, purple cassock with a clerical collar and large crucifix. He opened sessions with prayer and lit candles on tables covered with white cloths.[63] As an active participant especially in the HRVC

61. United Nations General Assembly, "The Policies of Apartheid of the Government of South Africa," December 2, 1968, A/RES/2396, http://www.unhcr.org/refworld/docid/3b00f1d74.html.

62. Waldmeir, *Anatomy of a Miracle*, xiv; Beck, *History of South Africa*, xxv.

63. Piet Meiring, "The *Baruti* versus the Lawyers: The Role of Religion in the TRC Process," in *Looking Back Reaching Forward: Reflections on the Truth and Reconciliation Commission of South Africa*, ed. Charles Villa-Vicencio and Wilhelm Verwoerd (Cape Town: University of Cape Town Press, 2000), 123. On the "religious" character of the hearings, see also Verdoolaege, "Reconciliation," 49; Brudholm, "On the Advocacy of Forgiveness," 144; Acorn, *Compulsory Compassion*, 72; Derrida, *On Cosmopolitanism and Forgiveness*, 42; Brudholm, *Resentment's Virtue*, 53.

hearings, Tutu not only convened the proceedings but also questioned witnesses. Even after some commissioners voiced concerns that the hearings were "far too 'religious,'" Tutu persisted. As the story goes, he tried to open a session in Johannesburg without praying and found that he could not. "We cannot start without having prayed," he announced. "Close your eyes!"[64]

At the hearings, Tutu prayed not only to a "God of justice" but specifically "in the name of Jesus."[65] He told "the victims of apartheid crimes that we must forgive because God forgives us and because we ask God's forgiveness every day when we pray the Lord's Prayer." Allan Aubrey Boesak and Curtiss Paul DeYoung write, "By doing that, the TRC not only Christianized the process, it has set the standards for reconciliation for the victims of apartheid crimes, most of them black Christians who take their faith very seriously indeed."[66] Muslim victim Farid Esack reflects on the Christian character of the commission. "On the day of my testimony," he says, "I spoke critically to an all-Christian panel, headed by an archbishop sitting under a huge crucifix in a church hall."[67] The use of Christian imagery and language in the hearings created additional moral dilemmas for victims—such as difficulty with forgiveness and whether one is obligated to forgive unrepentant perpetrators—that went largely unaddressed throughout the hearings.[68]

Tutu also heavily promoted the idea of *ubuntu* alongside the Christian language of forgiveness. He writes, "*Ubuntu* . . . is to say,

64. Meiring, "*Baruti* versus the Lawyers," 124.
65. Allen Aubrey Boesak, "'Just Another Jew in the Ditch': Incarnated Reconciliation," in *Radical Reconciliation: Beyond Political Pietism and Christian Quietism*, ed. Allan Aubrey Boesak and Curtiss Paul DeYoung (Maryknoll, NY: Orbis Books, 2012), 63.
66. Ibid. On the imperative to forgive in the Lord's Prayer, see also Tutu, *The Rainbow People of God: The Making of a Peaceful Revolution*, ed. John Allen (New York: Doubleday, 1994), 224.
67. Quote in P. G. J. Meiring, "Truth and Reconciliation in South Africa: The Role of the Faith Communities," *Verbum et Ecclesia* 26, no. 1 (2005): 168. However, Esack is mistaken about the "all-Christian panel"; there was actually one Hindu member of the commission, Yasmin Sooka.
68. Shore, *Religion and Conflict Resolution,* 143.

'My humanity is caught up, is inextricably bound up, in yours.'[69] *Ubuntu* calls for justice that restores broken relationships rather than punishes or retaliates because relationships are primary. "Human community is vital for the individual's acquisition of personhood," writes Michael Battle in his explication of *ubuntu* in Tutu's theology.[70] Human beings are only persons insofar as they are social beings.

The language of *ubuntu* appears in the Promotion of National Unity and Reconciliation Act as a founding principle of the TRC: "There is a need for understanding but not for vengeance, a need for reparation but not for retaliation, a need for *ubuntu* but not for victimization."[71] There is a parallel relationship among *ubuntu*, understanding, and reparation. Tutu also equates *ubuntu* with forgiveness,[72] but the official language of the TRC does not; rather, the call for *ubuntu* is defined over and against "victimization," and thus implies that forgiveness and the common good must include an end to violence.[73] By merging forgiveness and *ubuntu*, Tutu invokes not only a Christian duty to forgive, but also an imperative that goes to the very heart of victims' African identity.

Tutu also calculates that *ubuntu* is equal to forgiveness, and thus to being human. He writes, "We say that a human being is a human being because he belongs to a community, and harmony is the essence of that community. So *ubuntu* actually demands that you forgive, because resentment and anger and desire for revenge undermine harmony. In our understanding, when someone doesn't

---

69. Tutu, *No Future*, 31.
70. Michael Battle, *Reconciliation: The Ubuntu Theology of Desmond Tutu* (Cleveland, OH: Pilgrim Press, 1997), 37. See also De Gruchy, *Reconciliation*, 91; and Tutu, *No Future*, 54.
71. Promotion of National Unity and Reconciliation Act.
72. Tutu, *No Future*, 31, 54.
73. Promotion of National Unity and Reconciliation Act.

forgive, we say that person does not have *ubuntu*. That is to say, he is not really human."[74]

Lyn Graybill is critical of such a vehement commitment to forgiveness in service of community harmony. She writes, "An inherent danger arises when a social order is enshrined around collective solidarity rather than civil liberties. Victims are expected to forgive and accept into the fold the perpetrator in the interests of traditional African values, and may feel guilty if they cannot."[75] Thus a victim who stands up for herself in anger or outrage excludes herself not only from the reconciled community but also from what makes her African and what makes her human.

Tutu's language of forgiveness was not always welcome to HRVC witnesses. One victim testifies, "The Government is telling us, saying that we must forgive the perpetrators. It is very difficult to forgive someone who was an enemy. . . . We cannot forgive them because they are still our enemy."[76] Tutu responds, exasperated: "After ten years we want to see results. We do not want to see that we have wasted our time. We also noted the requests you mentioned [that the perpetrators be brought forward and the police held accountable]. Some of them are very difficult, because we are trying to reconcile and to forgive each other in this country."[77] With these words, Tutu sets the entire project of national reconciliation and forgiveness against the earnest entreaties of this witness. Ostensibly, the work of the TRC will be wasted if this witness refuses to forgive and keeps requesting to see the perpetrators held accountable.

---

74. Desmond Tutu, quoted in Waldmeir, *Anatomy of a Miracle*, 254.
75. Graybill, *Miracle or Model?*, 34.
76. Testimony of Zimasile Joseph Bota, HRVC, Grahamstown, April 7, 1997, http://www.justice.gov.za/trc/hrvtrans/gtown/bota.htm.
77. Ibid.

In praise of forgiving victims

Far more common than confrontations with unforgiving witnesses in the TRC hearings are compliments to victims who extended forgiveness, even to unrepentant or unknown perpetrators. Beth Savage, for example, was severely wounded by a grenade attack during a wine-tasting party at her golf club in King William's Town in 1992. While Savage and all of the guests at the event were white, it is not clear whether the club registered any official support of apartheid policies. The guerilla wing of the Pan-African Congress (APLA, or Azanian People's Liberation Army) claimed responsibility, and the perpetrators received amnesty in 1998.[78] During her earlier HRVC testimony, Savage spoke charitably of her attacker. She testifies, "What I would really, really like [is] to meet that man that threw that grenade in a attitude of forgiveness and hope that he could forgive me too for whatever reason."[79] To this, Desmond Tutu responds:

> Thank you, I just want to say, we are, I think a fantastic country. We have some quite extraordinary people. . . . I think it just augers [sic] so wonderfully well for our country. We thank you for the spirit that you are showing and pray that those who hear you, who see you will say, "Hey, we do have an incredible country with quite extraordinary people of all races." And it is important for us to know that in the struggle, awful things happened on both sides, and that we in this Commission should seek to be revealing all the truth about our country.[80]

In his memoir, Tutu recounts this incident and offers further praise. He writes, "That ought to leave people quite speechless with the wonder of it all and make you want to be still in the presence of

---

78. Amnesty Hearing, April 6, 1998: http://www.justice.gov.za/trc/amntrans/el/eln4.htm.
79. Testimony of Beth Savage, HRVC, East London, April 17, 1996, http://www.justice.gov.za/trc/hrvtrans/hrvel1/savage.htm.
80. Ibid.

something so sublime, filled to overflowing with a sense of deep thankfulness that nearly all the victims, black and white, possessed this marvelous magnanimity."[81] Beth Savage, with her humility and expression of unconditional forgiveness, is the kind of victim the TRC prizes.

Johan Smit, a white man whose eight-year-old son was killed in a bomb blast near Durban in 1985, earns similar accolades after testifying that he could empathize with the perpetrators.[82] Tutu says, "The people of this country are incredible and the testimony that you have just given is something which people really admire. Our hats off to you and we would really like to express our appreciation and thanks to God that he created people like yourself, and that the reason why we still have this hope that reconciliation will triumph in the end is because there are people like yourself."[83] In his memoir, he cites Smit as another extraordinary example of South African forgiveness.[84]

Nor does Tutu limit his praise to South Africans. He also lauds the parents of slain Fulbright scholar Amy Beihl (they started a foundation for youth in the township where she was killed),[85] the widows of the Craddock Four (they want to forgive even though they don't know whom to forgive),[86] and in a puzzling non sequitur, he gives several pages to the forgiving mother of a kidnapped girl in Montana and an Irishman who forgave his daughter's killers.[87]

When Gregory Edmund Beck testified that Nelson Mandela inspired him to forgive the (unknown) men who shot and wounded him, Tutu congratulated him: "Ultimately if we are going to have

81. Tutu, *No Future*, 147.
82. Testimony of Johan Smit, HRVC, Johannesburg, April 29, 1996, http://www.justice.gov.za/trc/hrvtrans/methodis/smit.htm.
83. Ibid.
84. Tutu, *No Future*, 35–36, 152.
85. Ibid., 152–53.
86. Ibid., 147–49.
87. Ibid., 155–58.

the change then it is clear that forgiveness, reconciliation, are quite central to that process, and justice is an element of it as well. But forgiveness ultimately is to say you give people the chance to change. You open a door for someone to move from a dark past to a new and enlightened present and future."[88] Not only is forgiveness essential for national reconciliation, it is also the key to a productive future for the offender. Tutu continues, "All of us need to change, all of us are wounded people, all of us are traumatized people, all of us are people who need to forgive and who also need to be forgiven."[89] Here he equalizes all people: those who were victims of apartheid violence, and those who committed the violent crimes. All are equally "wounded"; all are equally "traumatized." Victims should forgive not because perpetrators repent or ask for forgiveness, but because *all* people need to be forgiven by God and each other.

There is very little room for responses other than forgiveness in the rhetoric of the TRC and the new South Africa. In some cases, commissioners appeared to restate witness remarks to conform to the underlying narrative of forgiveness. Audrey R. Chapman writes, "Whether intentionally or not, commissioners frequently seemed to misinterpret comments of deponents. Not infrequently a deponent told the commissioners that he would not forgive anyone, with the commissioner ignoring or misconstruing the statement in his summary remarks."[90] For example, Margaret Madlana—whose twelve-year-old son was murdered by police—testified, "I don't see the opportunity of me forgiving anyone" (here a note in the transcript indicates, "witness upset").[91] The commissioner responded,

---

88. Testimony of Gregory Edmund Beck, HRVC, Johannesburg, April 29, 1996, http://www.justice.gov.za/trc/hrvtrans/methodis/beck.htm.
89. Ibid.
90. Chapman, "Perspectives," 79.
91. Testimony of Margaret Madlana, HRVC, Alexandria, October 29, 1996, http://www.justice.gov.za/trc/hrvtrans/alex/madlana.htm.

"It doesn't have to be this human rights hearing, they can come to the amnesty so that they as perpetrators should come before the people and tell the truth so that people like you can be able to forgive and reconcile."[92] Rather than allowing her anger to stand, he reinstates forgiveness as the ultimate goal and defers it toward a future amnesty hearing.

In addition to being a prized goal of the TRC, forgiveness emerges in Tutu's writings as a fundamental part of being human. In one interview he waxes rhapsodic about the forgiving response of one of the TRC witnesses. He marvels, "How fantastic to see this young girl, still human despite all efforts to dehumanize her."[93] Accordingly, *not* to forgive is to be less than human. Even after being a victim of severe violence, she hangs onto her humanity; forgiveness is the clear sign of this.

Tutu's praise for forgiveness is expansive. After the gallery erupts in forgiving applause of the contrite perpetrators of the Bisho Massacre, when police killed twenty-eight black activists during a protest march in 1992, Tutu reflects, "It was as if someone had waved a special magic wand which transformed anger and tension into this display of communal forgiveness and acceptance of erstwhile perpetrators."[94] According to Tutu, even God is impressed with all this forgiveness. He writes, "God has looked and seen all these wonderful people who have shone in the dark night of evil and torture and abuses and suffering, shone as they have demonstrated their nobility of spirit, their magnanimity as they have been ready to forgive."[95]

Years after the close of the commission, Tutu describes its work as a veritable theophany. He says:

92. Ibid.
93. Tutu, interview by Cantacuzino; very similar language appears in Tutu, *No Future*, 31.
94. Tutu, *No Future*, 151.
95. Ibid., 158; see also Brudholm, "Advocacy of Forgiveness," 142–43.

The whole spirit of our process at the Truth and Reconciliation Commission was marked by an incredible generosity. When we had listened to the testimony of people who had suffered grievously and it all had worked itself out to the point where they were ready to forgive and embrace the perpetrators, I would frequently say, "I think we ought to keep quiet now. We are in the presence of something holy. We ought metaphorically to take off our shoes because we are standing on holy ground."[96]

Thomas Brudholm notes that this religious orientation offers little alternative for victims besides signing on to the religious-redemptive narrative. He writes, "I would suggest that this kind of religious praise and celebration of forgiveness offer an all too sanguine perspective. There is apparently no such thing as inappropriate forgiving and there is a fancy for the telling of uplifting stories and redemption."[97] On the "holy ground" of the TRC, which is also "breathtaking,"[98] "extraordinary,"[99] and under the sway of the "special magic wand,"[100] withholding forgiveness strikes a sour note indeed.

Tutu's immense praise of forgiving victims, coupled with the language of forgiveness for the sake of national unity and also for the sake of "healing," necessarily created a pressure among those waiting to testify.[101] The hearings were broadcast daily on television and radio with weekly recaps distilling the highlights.[102] One young victim remarked in a newspaper interview, "What really makes me angry

---

96. Desmond Tutu, quoted in Peter Sanford, "Out of Africa," *Catholic Herald*, January 30, 2004, http://archive.catholicherald.co.uk/article/30th-january-2004/7/ut-of-frica. For taking off one's shoes on the holy ground instantiated by the TRC's forgiving victims, see also Tutu, radio interview by Krista Tippett, *On Being*, American Public Media, April 29, 2010; Tutu, Symposium contribution in Wiesenthal, *Sunflower*, 267; Tutu, "Foreword" in *Forgiveness and Reconciliation: Religion, Public Policy, and Conflict Transformation*, ed. Raymond G. Helmick and Rodney L. Peterson (Philadelphia: Templeton Foundation, 2001), xii; among others.
97. Brudholm, "Advocacy of Forgiveness," 144.
98. Tutu, *No Future*, 147.
99. Ibid., 86, 118, 154.
100. Ibid., 151.
101. Amstutz, *Healing of Nations*, 202.
102. Minow, *Between Vengeance and Forgiveness*, 60, 72.

about the TRC and Tutu is that they are putting pressure on me to forgive. . . . The oppression was bad, but what is much worse, what makes me even angrier, is that they are trying to dictate my forgiveness."[103] Like Bettina Mdlalose in this chapter's opening story, other victims and survivors reject the idea of forgiveness on its face.

Tutu addresses the issue of withholding forgiveness only once in his memoir, and even then it becomes a catalyst for another panegyric on forgiving victims. He writes, "Of course there were those who said they would not forgive. That demonstrated for me an important point that forgiveness could not be taken for granted; it was neither cheap nor easy. As it happens, these were the exceptions. Far more frequently what we encountered was deeply moving and humbling."[104] Unforgiveness, then, only serves to highlight how challenging and remarkable an achievement forgiveness really is.

The specific forgiveness of the TRC

Perpetrators who appeared before the Amnesty Committee were offered amnesty in exchange for a full disclosure of events; they were not required to apologize or show remorse. There were more specific requirements for amnesty: the crime had to have been committed between March 1, 1960 and December 6, 1993, it had to have been politically motivated, and the act had to have been proportional to its motives. When amnesty was granted, it took immediate effect, and the applicant was exempt from criminal and civil liability.[105] The hearings of the Amnesty Committee and the Human Rights Violations Committee were held separately and victims had few opportunities to face their perpetrators. As a result, the forgiveness

103. "Kalu," quoted in Wilhelm Verwoerd, "Forgive the Torturer, Not the Torture," *Sunday Independent* (Cape Town), December 6, 1998.
104. Tutu, *No Future*, 271.
105. Verdoolaege, *Reconciliation Discourse*, 15.

promoted by the TRC was most often unilateral and unconditional. With offenders not required to apologize to victims or even face them to hear their testimony, forgiveness was solely the work of victims.

This separation of victims from offenders posed no problem for Tutu. In fact, throughout his writings during and after the TRC, he offers unconditional forgiveness the most praise. For example, the daughter of one of the Craddock Four, whose killers were not identified, famously affirmed, "We do want to forgive but we don't know whom to forgive."[106] Tutu highlights this incident in his memoir and even lifts this quotation into the title of the chapter celebrating examples of forgiveness.[107]

Tutu frequently presses victims to forgive without knowing who was responsible for the crimes against them, much less receiving words of repentance. He considers this kind of forgiveness to be "Christ-like." He writes, "Jesus did not wait until those who were nailing him to the cross had asked for forgiveness. He was ready, as they drove in the nails, to pray to his Father to forgive them."[108] He argues that victims must not wait for confession or repentance before they offer forgiveness. Consequently, forgiving an unknown and unrepentant perpetrator becomes the height of moral virtue, comparable to that of the crucified Christ. I return to Jesus's prayer on the cross (Luke 23:34) in the next chapter; here it is worth noting that Jesus does not appear in Luke to be particularly enthusiastic about forgiving his attackers, and there is no evidence that he was already considering this forgiveness as he was being fastened to the cross.

Such imitation sets an almost impossibly high and disproportionate standard for victims of systematic abuses who are asked to move

---

106. Tutu, *No Future*, 149.
107. Ibid., 121–60.
108. Ibid., 272. See also Desmond Tutu, *God Has a Dream: A Vision of Hope for Our Time* (New York: Doubleday, 2004), 56.

forward and live peacefully alongside those who had abused them. Thomas Brudholm and Arne Grøn write, "The question is whether victims of gross injustices should be held to the example of the crucified Christ. After all, there are a number of salient moral and ontological differences between the situation of Christ and that of the human survivor of genocidal violence."[109] Issuing a prayer of forgiveness at the moment of death does not have the same implications as forgiving one's rapist or torturer who may then go on to occupy the same neighborhood and enjoy the same freedoms as the victim.

Tutu also extols the therapeutic benefits of unconditional forgiveness. He writes, "Forgiving means abandoning your right to pay back the perpetrator in his own coin, but it is a loss that liberates the victim. In the commission we heard people speak of a sense of relief after forgiving."[110] This may be so, but it is a mistake to map a small selection of victim responses onto all victims of apartheid. Not all of them subscribed to Tutu's Christian version of forgiveness, were receptive to the TRC's rhetoric of forgiveness, or felt liberated upon "forgiving" unrepentant perpetrators. In fact, many victims of apartheid violence were Muslim, Jewish, Hindu, Baha'i, and Buddhist, to name a select few. These groups were marginalized by the apartheid regime based on religion and race, or religion-as-race.

Since perpetrators were required neither to apologize nor to show remorse, if the new South Africa's reconciliation was to be founded on forgiveness, it had to be unconditional. The fact that perpetrators were not compelled to demonstrate repentance was the primary reason the Roman Catholic Church in South Africa as well as many

---

109. Thomas Brudholm and Arne Grøn, "Picturing Forgiveness after Atrocity," *Studies in Christian Ethics* 24 (2011): 169.
110. Tutu, *No Future*, 272.

Protestant denominations found the TRC an unacceptable solution for conflict transformation.[111] For example, Alex Boraine—deputy chair of the TRC and an ordained Methodist minister—argues that forgiveness is only one ingredient in a larger process of reconciliation that must include "confession, repentance, restitution, and forgiveness."[112] Even Tutu, at the beginning of the TRC, had emphasized forgiveness, an emphasis that shifted during the course of the TRC's work as high-level architects of apartheid proved unwilling to present themselves before Tutu's moral tribunal.

Both Tutu and the TRC adopted wholesale a therapeutic, psychological understanding of forgiveness. Not only is forgiveness considered a political necessity for the future of South Africa, but it is also considered essential for recovery from trauma and mental health in general. In his appraisal of the TRC, Jeffrie Murphy observed, "arguments grounded in trendy notions of mental health where such gems of psychobabble as 'closure' and 'a time for healing' are the order of the day."[113] As such, forgiveness becomes its own mode of psychotherapy toward a kind of healing only it could accomplish. The idea of forgiveness, which in this case is conflated with national reconciliation and sound mental health, takes on a life of its own in the TRC and surrounding literature.

---

111. Stephen Cherry, "Forgiveness and Reconciliation in South Africa," in *Forgiveness in Context: Theology and Psychology in Creative Dialogue*, ed. Fraser Watts and Liz Gulliford (London: T&T Clark International, 2004), 166.

112. Alex Boraine, *A Country Unmasked: Inside South Africa's Truth and Reconciliation Commission* (Oxford: Oxford University Press, 2000), 360.

113. Murphy, *Punishment and the Moral Emotions: Essays in Law, Morality, and Religion* (Oxford: Oxford University Press, 2012), 147. See also Amstutz, *Healing of Nations*, 209; Pumla Gobodo-Madikizela, *A Human Being Died That Night: A South African Story of Forgiveness* (New York: Houghton Mifflin, 2003), 97; Acorn, *Compulsory Compassion*, 71. On forgiveness related to healing and closure, see Tutu, *No Future*, 179 and 270 (healing), and 143, 188, 212 (closure); Tutu, *God Has a Dream*, 53 ("the process of requesting and receiving forgiveness is healing and transformative for all involved").

The emotional, therapeutic character of the hearings is well known. Lyn Graybill remarks, "As long as there had been crying, commissioners said that healing had occurred."[114] Such valuing of emotion and catharsis led to some critics dubbing the TRC the "Kleenex commission."[115] Tutu's own metaphors reflect this emphasis on emotion. In explaining how South Africa's process of forgiveness and reconciliation should proceed, Tutu provides the analogy of a husband-and-wife quarrel.[116] "Tutu anticipates and desires an amazing euphoric catharsis," Annalise Acorn observes. "[He] speaks of the process of dealing with the atrocities of apartheid as akin to husband and wife making up after a fight. The route is apology and forgiveness. The destination is loving embrace."[117] In this vision, the future of South Africa is rendered as star-crossed lovers sprinting toward each other on a beach at sunset after a long estrangement, all injuries and harsh words forgotten regardless of who inflicted the wounds.[118]

A case study in negative emotions: Desmond Tutu prior to the TRC

Tutu finds that victims who do not forgive are "consumed by bitterness and hatred"[119] and "consumed by ... a lust for revenge."[120] He continues, "Not to forgive leads to bitterness and hatred, which, just like self-hatred and self-contempt, gnaw away at the vitals of one's being."[121] Such presentations leave victims no choice; either

---

114. Graybill, *Miracle or Model?*, 83; also noted in Wilson, *Politics of Truth and Reconciliation*, 120.

115. Verdoolaege, *Reconciliation Discourse*, 83; see also Tutu, *No Future*, 163.

116. Desmond Tutu, "Foreword by Chairperson," in *Truth and Reconciliation Commission of South Africa Report*, 5 vols (Cape Town: Juta, 1998), 1:18–19. The report was released on March 21, 2003, and is available in its entirety at the following address: http://www.justice.gov.za/trc/report/index.htm.

117. Acorn, *Compulsory Compassion*, 72, 115.

118. Tutu, "Foreword by Chairperson," 1:18.

119. Tutu, *No Future*, 120.

120. Tutu, "Foreword by Chairperson," 1:18.

121. Tutu, *God Has a Dream*, 54.

they forgive or they will find themselves gnawed at and consumed by these negative passions.

While Tutu devotes many pages to denouncing resentment, anger, and outrage, a close examination of his work leading up to the TRC demonstrates that such "negative" emotions were actually a driving force. The forceful rhetoric of forgiveness does not appear in Tutu's writings until the early 1990s, when the end of apartheid was imminent and the TRC under negotiation. A consideration of the totality of Tutu's work, especially his social justice work in the fight against apartheid, yields a case study in favor of negative emotions in the service of social change and self-respect, as well as against unconditional forgiveness as the path to harmony.

Tutu's corpus of writings, speeches, and sermons spans five decades. He is continuously engaged with the biblical text, but his exegesis shifts around the time of the institution of the TRC. Until that time, Tutu's theology centered on a God of justice and liberation. He cites the Exodus story as paradigmatic for black South Africans, and Jesus as a savior who is "setting God's children free."[122] He emphasizes God's preferential option for the oppressed and downtrodden when he writes, "God can't help it. He always takes sides. He is not a neutral God."[123] He argues that God is a liberator "who leads His people out of every kind of bondage, spiritual, political, social and economic, and nothing will thwart Him from achieving the goal of the liberation of all His people and the whole of His creation."[124] Tutu notes that the chief concern of God and Christ's work on earth is reconciliation, but he does not mention the role of human forgiveness in this divine project.[125]

122. Desmond Tutu, "The Role of the Church in South Africa (1981)," in *Hope and Suffering: Sermons and Speeches* (Grand Rapids, MI: Eerdmans, 1984), 82–83.
123. Desmond Tutu, "The Divine Intention (1982)," in *Hope and Suffering*, 177.
124. Ibid., 155–56.
125. Ibid., 166.

Nowhere in his earlier work does Tutu mention forgiveness as a mode of conflict transformation. The Jesus who instructs his followers to "be ready to [forgive] not just once, not just seven times, but seventy times seven, without limit"[126] is replaced by the prophet Jesus who preaches "release to the captives" (Luke 4:18–19). Tutu says, "Jesus seems to sum up His ministry with the words from Isaiah. We see that this liberation is meant to be total and comprehensive."[127] Tutu does not marshal the motif of the forgiving Jesus until the fall of apartheid when Jesus becomes a model for victim forgiveness.

Composed in 1985, the Kairos Document, to which Tutu was an unnamed contributor, also does not call for unconditional forgiveness. Instead, it promotes justice and reconciliation *with* *repentance*: "No reconciliation, no forgiveness and no negotiations are possible without repentance."[128] The tone of this document is indignant. Forgiveness is only mentioned in one paragraph, and there it is coupled with the charge for repentance. "As disciples of Jesus we should rather promote truth and justice and life at all costs, even at the cost of creating conflict, disunity and dissension along the way," the authors affirm. The Kairos Document calls for change, not forgiveness, and if the road to change includes "conflict, disunity, and dissension," so be it.

A few years after the publication of the Kairos Document, South Africa moved from apartheid to the transitional period of the TRC, and Tutu's role shifted from apartheid fighter to reconciliation leader. While this change in context calls for different tactics, his wholesale denunciation of anger and veneration of unconditional forgiveness disregard the constructive value of anger and overstate the political usefulness of forgiveness.

---

126. Tutu, *No Future*, 273.
127. Desmond Tutu, "The Story of Exodus 2 (1978)," in *Hope and Suffering*, 57.
128. Kairos Theologians, *Kairos Document*.

Anger and righteous indignation fueled the nonviolent protest movement against South Africa's apartheid government. Exemplifying this, Tutu's sermons and speeches during that time called for action, not forgiveness. While Tutu sometimes looks to a future when the perpetrators of apartheid might be forgiven (he writes, "The victims of injustice and oppression must be ever ready to forgive. That is a gospel imperative"),[129] the time for forgiveness has not yet arrived. In a taped message to the TransAfrica Forum in the U.S. in 1984, Tutu is exasperated. He says, "We have been deeply hurt. Blacks are really expendable in the view of the mighty U.S. … You can't really trust Whites. When it comes to the crunch . . . Whites will stick by their fellow whites."[130] But in the end, Tutu is not discouraged. He concludes, "Freedom is coming. We will be free whatever anybody does or does not do about it."[131] In a magazine article around the same time, he makes an ominous prediction. He writes, "I [said] last year that within five to ten years we will have a Black Prime Minister. Will this happen reasonably peacefully or after much violence or bloodshed? This is the context in which the PFP [the Progressive Federal Party, which advocated a federal system in place of apartheid] and White opponents of apartheid have to decide."[132]

Tutu was "vociferous" in his role as a leader in the United Democratic Front (UDF), a prominent anti-apartheid organization.[133] He led marches and protests, and he called for change. He says, "There is nothing the government can do to me that will stop me from what I believe is what God wants me to do.

129. Tutu, *God Is Not a Christian*, 28 (excerpt from a 1990 speech at a conference of South African churches).
130. Desmond Tutu, "Black South African Perspectives and the Reagan Administration," in *Hope and Suffering*, 116 (capitalization in original).
131. Ibid., 117.
132. Desmond Tutu, "The Role of White Opposition in South Africa," in *Hope and Suffering*, 124.
133. Graybill, *Miracle or Model?*, 31.

I cannot help it when I see injustice. I cannot keep quiet."[134] He did not stop. He raised his voice, he pointed his finger, and he shook his fist. He was very often and very publicly angry. And yet this anger did not corrode his sense of *summum bonum*; it fueled it. He embraced nonviolent struggle, but he also embraced *struggle*.[135]

When he was awarded the Nobel Prize for Peace in 1984, Desmond Tutu gave an impassioned speech about the conditions in South Africa under apartheid. He observes, "There has been little revulsion or outrage at this wanton destruction of human life in the West," and he questions why. Clearly *he* is revolted and outraged. He says, "Enough is enough. God created us for fellowship. . . . If we want peace, so we have been told, let us work for justice. Let us beat our swords into ploughshares."[136] Tutu does not mention forgiveness once in this speech.

Another instance of righteous anger occurred when United States President Ronald Reagan decided not to impose sanctions on South Africa in 1986. Tutu snapped, "Your president is the pits as far as blacks are concerned. I think the West, for my part, can go to hell."[137] There is no public indication that Tutu ever reversed himself and "forgave" the Reagan administration, although considering his speaking engagements and visiting professorships in the United

134. Tutu, "Divine Intention," 187.
135. Tutu's expressions of anger in the face of injustice did not end with apartheid. For example, in 2011 he publicly excoriated the ANC government for refusing an entry visa to the Dalai Lama. In 2012, he refused to share a stage with former British prime minister Tony Blair because of Blair's involvement in the war in Iraq. See David Smith, "Desmond Tutu Attacks South African Government over Dalai Lama Ban," *The Guardian*, October 4, 2011, http://www.guardian.co.uk/world/2011/oct/04/tutu-attacks-anc-dalai-lama-visa; and Oliver Wright, "Desmond Tutu Quits Summit with Tony Blair over Invasion of Iraq," *The Independent*, August 29, 2012, http://www.independent.co.uk/news/world/politics/desmond-tutu-quits-summit-with-tony-blair-over-invasion-of-iraq-8084805.html.
136. Desmond Tutu, "Nobel Lecture, December 11, 1984," in *Nobel Lectures, Peace 1981–1990*, ed. Tore Frängsmyr and Irwin Abrams (Singapore: World Scientific Publishing Co., Singapore, 1997), 120.
137. Desmond Tutu, quoted in the *Los Angeles Times*, June 22, 1986, http://articles.latimes.com/1986-07-22/news/mn-30949_1_south-africa.

States and Europe, we may assume that on some level he has reconciled with "the West."

On a visit to Yad Vashem in 1989, Tutu boldly proposed that Jews—not just Holocaust survivors, but all Jews, and especially Israelis—direct their forgiving energies toward Palestinians. He suggested that forgiveness could be a positive by-product of the extermination of European Jewry. After drawing a direct analogy between treatment of Palestinians in the occupied territories and South Africa under apartheid, he says, "Our Lord would say that in the end the positive thing that can come is the spirit of forgiving, not forgetting." He continues with a prayer that packs a passive-aggressive punch: "God, this happened to us. We pray for those who made it happen, help us to forgive them and help us so that we in our turn will not make others suffer."[138]

Later in a newspaper article on the topic, he suggested that Israelis were perpetrating another Holocaust on displaced Palestinians. He asks, "Have our Jewish sisters and brothers forgotten their humiliation? Have they forgotten the collective punishment, the home demolitions, in their own history so soon?"[139] Earlier he distorted the pay-it-forward model seen in the parable of the unforgiving servant (and to an extent, in the Lord's Prayer). In his questions, it is suffering—not forgiveness—that should prompt future benevolence. Holocaust survivor Ruth Kluger remarks on this idea that past suffering should warrant future goodwill with regard to the Palestinian conflict. She writes, "Auschwitz was no instructional institution. . . . You learned nothing there, and least of

138. Desmond Tutu, quoted in Allister Sparks and Mpho Tutu, *Tutu: Authorized* (New York: HarperOne, 2011), 239; see also Alan Cowell, "Tutu Urges Israelis to Pray for and Forgive Nazis," *New York Times*, December 28, 1989, http://www.nytimes.com/1989/12/27/world/tutu-urges-israelis-to-pray-for-and-forgive-nazis.html.
139. Desmond Tutu, "Apartheid in the Holy Land," *Guardian*, April 28, 2002, http://www.guardian.co.uk/world/2002/apr/29/comment.

all humanity and tolerance."[140] But Tutu reduced the Nazi horror to "humiliation," and doesn't recall that the Holocaust was much more than "collective punishment [and] home demolitions." In fact, the concentration camps, medical experiments, and forced labor were hardly "punishment," if punishment implies past wrongdoing. Tutu contends that the Holocaust should inspire reconciliation between Arabs and Israelis. He calls for "peace based on justice," which he defines as withdrawal from the occupied territories and the establishment of a Palestinian state, because this is "God's dream." He does not mention forgiveness in his prescription for a peaceful solution to the Israeli–Palestinian conflict. By writing under the title "Apartheid in the Holy Land," it is clear which side Desmond Tutu holds responsible. The answer here is not forgiveness.

The crusader Jesus of Tutu's earlier writings stands in stark contrast to the Jesus who appears in his work during and after the TRC. In a 1990 sermon, he writes, "If there is to be reconciliation, we who are the ambassadors of Christ, we to whom the gospel of reconciliation has been entrusted, surely we must be Christ's instruments of peace. We must ourselves be reconciled. The victims of injustice and oppression must be ever ready to forgive. That is a gospel imperative. [Wrongdoers must apologize,] and the wronged must forgive."[141] In this case, Tutu merges the prophetic Jesus with the forgiving one by preserving the call for repentance as a requirement for forgiveness. However, in this same text he also calls on the crucified Christ as a model for perfect love and unconditional forgiveness. He writes, "We expect Christians to be people filled with love. We expect Christians to be people who forgive as Jesus forgave even those who were nailing him to the Cross."[142]

---

140. Ruth Kluger, *Still Alive: A Holocaust Girlhood Remembered* (New York: The Feminist Press, 2001), 65.
141. Tutu, *Rainbow People of God*, 222.
142. Ibid., 131.

Desmond Tutu is passionate in his depiction of Jesus as the model of unconditional forgiveness. When asked if he thought Jesus would forgive the Nazis if Jesus were a Holocaust survivor, he invokes the prayer from the cross ("Father, forgive them") and ties it to the reciprocal forgiveness depicted in the Lord's Prayer. "From the paradigm that Jesus provided . . . it wasn't as if he was talking about something that *might* happen," he explains. "He was actually experiencing one of the most excruciating ways of being killed, and yet he had the capacity to live out a prayer that he taught Christians, that we can expect to be forgiven only insofar as we are ready to forgive."[143] Here Tutu connects the Lord's Prayer with the prayer from the cross but leaves out the seventy-times-seven instructions in Matthew and Luke, both of which call for repentance as a prerequisite for forgiveness.

In the mid-1990s, Tutu submitted an essay in response to Holocaust survivor Simon Wiesenthal's hypothetical query: Would you have forgiven the dying Nazi soldier who asked for my forgiveness? In his answer, Tutu invokes the amazing acts of forgiveness he encountered in the TRC. He writes, "There are others who say they are not ready to forgive, demonstrating that forgiveness is not facile or cheap. It is a costly business that makes those who are willing to forgive even more extraordinary."[144] However, he very carefully dodges the question and instead points to the awe-inspiring post-prison forgiveness offered by Nelson Mandela to his persecutors, along with Jesus's prayer from the cross (Luke 23:34a). He closes his essay on a familiar note that doesn't answer the question of whether he would forgive the soldier: "[Forgiveness] is practical politics. Without forgiveness there is no future."[145] Of course, post-

---

143. Tutu, *God Is Not a Christian*, 27.
144. Desmond Tutu, Symposium contribution in Wiesenthal, *Sunflower*, 267.
145. Ibid., 268.

apartheid South Africa and post-Holocaust Europe are entirely different landscapes. In South Africa, the TRC facilitated testimony from victims and offenders with strict amnesty requirements. While there was no official mechanism for victims to face their offenders, the TRC allowed victims to tell their stories and offenders to be held accountable. By the time Tutu wrote his reply, most victims and offenders of the Holocaust were dead.

In 1995, Tutu visited Rwanda with a church delegation a year after nearly one million people were killed in the genocide there. Speaking to a group of government officials and diplomats, he charges them with the task of justice as reconciliation. He says, "There can be no future without forgiveness. There will be no future unless there is peace. There can be no peace unless there is reconciliation. But there can be no reconciliation before there is forgiveness. And there can be no forgiveness unless people repent."[146] Just a year or two later, Tutu would be presiding over the TRC and urging victims to forgive unknown and unrepentant perpetrators. When his memoir appeared in 1999, his promotion of unconditional forgiveness had expanded even further. With no requirement for perpetrators to apologize or show remorse in the amnesty hearings, forgiveness most often begins and ends with the victims.

A case study in negative emotions: Desmond Tutu after the TRC

By the time *No Future without Forgiveness* is published in 1999, the image of a Jesus who forgives his murderers even as they are nailing him to the cross has become Tutu's central model for forgiveness. Tutu explains that Jesus forgave his executioners "and he even provided an excuse for what they were doing." He continues by clarifying the implications of this interpretation for victims and

146. Tutu, *God Is Not a Christian*, 35.

survivors at the TRC. "If the victim could forgive only when the culprit confessed," he reasons, "then the victim would be locked into the culprit's whim, locked into victimhood, whatever her own attitude or intention." [147] Thus, he links unconditional forgiveness both to being a good Christian and to being released from "victimhood." No longer is Jesus's primary role as a model for fighting injustice. Now the crucified Christ stands as a covictim and the epitome of the right response to suffering in his unconditional forgiveness.

In a 2000 interview with the BBC, Desmond Tutu remarks, "Resentment and anger are bad for your blood pressure and your digestion." Such comments about the deleterious effects of anger appear throughout his work. He writes, "Social harmony is for us the *summum bonum*—the greatest good. Anything that subverts, that undermines this sought-after good, is to be avoided like the plague. Anger, resentment, lust for revenge, even success through aggressive competitiveness, are corrosive of this good."[148] Anger interferes with forgiveness and *ubuntu*, he argues, and without *ubuntu*, one cannot be truly human.[149]

But Tutu's expressions of righteous indignation did not end with apartheid. When the Dalai Lama was denied an entry visa to South Africa to attend Tutu's eightieth birthday celebration in 2011, Tutu publicly exploded: "Our government is worse than the apartheid government because at least you would expect it with the apartheid government. Let the ANC know they have a large majority. Well, Mubarak had a large majority, Gaddafi had a large majority. I am warning you: watch out. Watch out!"[150] To this tirade, the official

147. Tutu, *No Future*, 272.
148. Tutu, *No Future*, 31.
149. Tutu, quoted in Waldmeir, *Anatomy of a Miracle*, 254.
150. Tutu, quoted in Smith, "Desmond Tutu Attacks South African Government."

ANC response included a request for Tutu to "calm down." He continued with a serious threat: "You, President Zuma and your government, do not represent me. I am warning you, as I warned the [pro-apartheid] nationalists, one day we will pray for the defeat of the ANC government."[151]

In August 2012, Tutu pulled out of a summit because of the presence of former British Prime Minister Tony Blair, whom Tutu charged with invading Iraq based on false intelligence about weapons of mass destruction. His office stated, "Morality and leadership are indivisible. In this context, it would be inappropriate for the Archbishop to share a platform with Mr. Blair."[152] It is clear that expressions of anger are essential elements of Tutu's sense of moral protest. In light of all his calls for forgiveness, however, it is surprising that he would be so public in his displays of this "corrosive" quality.

Tutu's condemnation of anger, resentment, outrage, and other negative emotions overlooks an important point. It is the expression of these emotions by protesters that got South Africa to the point where a TRC could become possible. In the immediate context of conflict transformation, forgiveness is perhaps a value worth promoting, along with repentance and reconciliation. However, acts of forgiveness did not fuel the apartheid resistance. Anger and outrage have their place, and Tutu's life is a clear example of this.

At one point, the post-TRC Tutu even explicitly endorsed the constructive value of anger. In a rare moment of openness to negative emotions, he said, "[These] are all part of being human. You should never hate yourself for hating others who do terrible things: the depth of your love is shown by the extent of your anger."[153] However, this was a rare moment indeed; Tutu's main line both during and after

151. Tutu, quoted in ibid.
152. Wright, "Desmond Tutu Quits Summit."
153. Tutu, interview by Cantacuzino.

the TRC as that anger is corrosive of social harmony, and those who do not forgive will be consumed by anger and resentment. He wrote, "In our African worldview, the greatest good is communal harmony. Anything that subverts or undermines this greatest good is ipso facto wrong, evil. Anger and a desire for revenge are subversive of this good thing."[154]

In the above examples, Desmond Tutu's anger and righteous indignation were most often directed *outside* the community to promoters of apartheid and countries that supported the apartheid state. Regarding relations *inside* the community—that is, those who would comprise the new South Africa—Tutu is vehement in his warnings about the "corrosive" effects of anger.[155] Such a distinction is visible in the seventy-times-seven instructions in Matthew and Luke. These texts frame the call for forgiveness with "brother" language: "If my brother (ἀδελφός) sins against me" (Matt. 18:21); "If your brother (ἀδελφός) sins" (Luke 17:3). This familial language indicates that the instructions apply to intracommunity conflict resolution. However, Tutu eschews anger and promotes forgiveness between both groups: the victims of apartheid and the perpetrators of those crimes. During and after the TRC, his language expands to cover all participants in the new South Africa: all victims should forgive so the new community may cohere and flourish. Anger—regardless of whom it is directed toward—is *verboten*. According to Tutu, sublimating anger is the answer for resolving conflict both inside and outside the various stakeholder communities in the TRC and the new South Africa.

---

154. Tutu, *God Is Not a Christian*, 24.
155. Tutu, *No Future*, 31, 35; Tutu, *God Has a Dream*, 54 (here corrosive anger is equated with nonforgiveness).

In praise of negative emotions

As demonstrated by Tutu's anger and outrage at the apartheid government, negative emotions—including resentment and the refusal to forgive—might actually serve a constructive purpose. Graeme Simpson writes, "The discourse of 'forgiveness' embroidered much of the Commission's work, [but] it is equally arguable that true reconciliation in South Africa will more likely be achieved by integrating the anger, sorrow, unresolved trauma and other complex feelings of victims, rather than by suppressing them."[156] Jeffrie G. Murphy similarly observes, "Just as indignation or guilt over the mistreatment of others stands as emotional testimony that we care about them and their rights, so does resentment stand as emotional testimony that we care about ourselves and our rights."[157] Thus resentment—sometimes manifested in a refusal to forgive—can be a signal of self-respect and self-worth.

This valuation of the negative emotions provides a counter to Tutu's forgiveness rhetoric. Thomas Brudholm writes, "Preservation of outrage or resentment and the refusal to forgive and reconcile can be the reflex expression of a moral protest and ambition that might be as permissible as the posture of forgiveness."[158] He also questions the TRC's commitment to restoring relationships and asks whether all relationships between victims and offenders were even *worth* restoring. He writes, "The person who does not forgive those who wronged his or her next of kin is not likely to shrivel in existential desolation. Not all relationships are worthy of restoration, and maintaining networks of humane relationship is hardly possible on the basis of an attitude that makes a hegemony of harmony."[159]

156. Simpson, "'Tell No Lies,'" 239–40.
157. Murphy, *Punishment*, 11.
158. Brudholm, *Resentment's Virtue*, 4.
159. Ibid., 48–49.

With regard to scriptural precedent for Tutu's condemnation of anger, there is no indication in the Gospels that anger, outrage, and indignation are destructive or inappropriate emotions. Jesus famously "cleanses" the temple by overturning tables and lambasting merchants and money changers (Mark 11:13–19; Matt. 21:12–17; Luke 19:45–48; John 2:13–22), and he also withers a fig tree (Mark 11:20–24; Matt. 21:18–22). He calls Pharisees "a brood of vipers" (Matt. 23:33) and rails at the scribes and Pharisees, "Woe to you, hypocrites!" (Matt. 23:13–15). Jesus "becomes angry" (ἀγανακτέω)[160] when the disciples try to keep the children from him and he rebukes them severely (Mark 10:13–15).

In these accounts and others, Jesus's anger is a response to injustice or infidelity. Even in the case of the fig tree, which symbolizes the destruction of Jerusalem, Jesus's anger is a motivating force for positive change. In addition to freely expressing his anger, Jesus never actively forgives another person for any wrongdoing against him personally.[161] He does not forgive the scribes and Pharisees for their hypocrisy, he does not forgive the merchants and money changers in the temple, and he does not forgive the disciples for their doubt (although he does reconcile with them). Jesus does not employ forgiveness as a mode of social change or conflict transformation. Further, in his anger Jesus is not "consumed by bitterness and hatred,"[162] as Tutu describes. Most often, his anger plays a constructive role.

After submitting the TRC's final report in 1998, Tutu notes Jesus's propensity for anger. "Our Lord was very forgiving," he says, "but he faced up to those he thought were self-righteous, who were behaving

---

160. BAGD, 4 (ἀγανακτέω).
161. Many interpret Jesus's prayer from the cross ("Father, forgive them"; Luke 23:34a) as an act of forgiveness. I hold that this is an example of praying for one's persecutors (Luke 6:28) and not a first-person act of forgiveness. See the following chapter for a full discussion of this verse.
162. Tutu, *No Future*, 120.

in a ghastly fashion, and called them a 'generation of vipers.'"[163] He continues, "Forgiveness doesn't mean turning yourself into a doormat for people to wipe their boots on. . . . There is necessarily a measure of confrontation. People sometimes think that you shouldn't be abrasive. But sometimes you have to be to make people acknowledge that they have done something wrong."[164] Here Tutu shifts the definition of forgiveness to include confrontation and reproof. And yet this is not the vision of forgiveness he advocates in his other writings and speeches in which anger and outrage are equated with nonforgiveness, which is non-*ubuntu* and therefore also inhuman.[165]

Forgiveness is an insufficient national ethic

Angry voices and continued protests ushered in a time when a truth commission working toward national reconciliation was possible in South Africa. Perhaps the transformation could not have occurred without the violent protests of anti-apartheid resistance.[166] In any case, it is clear that acts of forgiveness did not lead the way. Unconditional forgiveness of unknown perpetrators did not transform and overturn the apartheid government.

In the context of any oppressive regime, forgiveness does not necessarily work as a driving force for change, as Tutu's early writings show. Forgiveness in such contexts may even allow or embolden oppressors to continue their persecution. Instead, morally

---

163. Tutu, *God Is Not a Christian*, 38.
164. Ibid.
165. Tutu, *No Future*, 31.
166. For example, Nelson Mandela led the armed resistance of the ANC's military wing. "Violence would begin whether we initiated it or not," he said (quoted in Anthony Sampson, *Mandela: The Authorized Biography* [New York: Random House, 1999], 145). Other armed resistance groups took action against apartheid, such as the Pan-African Congress's armed wing, APLA (Azanian People's Liberation Army), which took aim at white civilians in the St. James Church massacre in Cape Town in 1993 as well as other attacks.

valuable responses may include negative emotions such as anger and indignation that call for justice and change.

Forgiveness as a sustaining political ethic misses the mark; there can be either constant harmony or constant forgiveness. There cannot be both. Forgiveness is reactive; it needs disruptions in the harmony to take hold. There is no forgiveness without victims, and there are no victims without wrongdoing. Further, it may not be a good idea to mix personal forgiveness with political aims. Rajeev Bhargava writes, "One cannot forgive for the future good of the society, if personal costs are excessive. The good of the community cannot provide reasons for unconditional forgiveness."[167] However, as seen in his responses to victim testimonies, Tutu presents victim forgiveness as essential for a reconciled South Africa.

Ernesto Verdeja argues against such harnessing of victims' emotional responses. He writes, "The state cannot, of course, decree forgiveness. But though forgiving should be a free and unencumbered act, its de facto institutionalization in some truth commissions (such as South Africa's) or in official apologies gives victims little free space for opposing it and demanding instead some sort of accountability."[168] Thus depicting reconciliation as dependent on victim forgiveness is coercive. Verdeja concludes, "Forgiveness may be morally praiseworthy, but it should not serve as the lodestar of reconciliation."[169]

A vision of the future that uses forgiveness as the basis for reconciliation and an end to all conflict can also preclude legitimate political debate by framing relations only in terms of good feelings

---

167. Rajeev Bhargava, "Restoring Decency to Barbaric Stories," in *Truth v. Justice: The Morality of Truth Commissions*, ed. Robert I. Rotberg and Dennis Thompson (Princeton, NJ: Princeton University Press, 2000), 62–63.
168. Ernesto Verdeja, *Unchopping a Tree: Reconciliation in the Aftermath of Political Violence* (Philadelphia, PA: Temple University Press, 2009), 16.
169. Ibid.

and harmony.[170] In such a utopia, negative emotions like resentment, anger, and outrage have no place. But defining relationships in terms of forgiving abuse creates a community of constant pardon. Such an emphasis on forgiveness then paves the way for miscreants who know that no matter what they do, the onus will be on the victims to forgive them.

Tutu's view of forgiveness has not changed since the close of the TRC. Indeed, most of his writings in the last fifteen years capitalize on this veneration of forgiveness, with several books repeating verbatim his effusive praise for unconditional forgiveness.[171] It is clear that he intends this message to be universal and timeless. Indeed, Tutu exhorts, "Forgiveness is practical politics," not only during but also after the close of the TRC and into the future of the relegitimized state.[172] As far as Tutu is concerned, this applies not only to South Africa, but to every human community.[173]

In her proposal for a moral theory of political reconciliation, Colleen Murphy considers whether the TRC should serve as a model for other transitional contexts. The TRC's emphasis on forgiveness-as-reconciliation is problematic for a number of reasons, especially the attempt to map the model of interpersonal forgiveness onto political contexts. "In transitional contexts, the conception of a prior,

---

170. Ibid., 17. Harmony is defined as peaceful relations characterized by forgiveness and reconciliation among former enemies and community members (3).

171. Pages of verbatim repeated text carry the theme of unconditional forgiveness across several decades of Tutu's writings: *The Rainbow People of God* (1994; the volume collects Tutu's letters and sermons 1974–94), *No Future without Forgiveness* (1999), "Without Forgiveness There Is No Future" (1998), *The Sunflower* symposium response (1998), *God Has a Dream* (2004), "Faith and the Problem of Evil and Suffering" (2010), *God Is Not a Christian* (2011).

172. The phrase "Forgiveness is practical politics" appears in the 1998 *TRC Report* (5:351), *The Sunflower* symposium response (268) in 1998, "Without Forgiveness There Is No Future" (xii) in 1998, and *God Has a Dream* (53) in 2004.

173. See Tutu, "Foreword by Chairperson," 22; *No Future*, 31, 35, 196. Tutu expands his philosophy to apply to all of humanity: "To work for reconciliation is to want to realize God's dream for humanity—when we will know that we are indeed members of one family, bound together in a delicate network of interdependence. . . . True forgiveness deals with the past, all of the past, to make the future possible" (*No Future*, 274).

normal, acceptable political relationship that has been ruptured by wrongdoing does not pertain," writes Murphy.[174] In personal relationships, the wrongdoing might be an aberration, but in political contexts it has been and might continue to be the rule. She continues, "Urging forgiveness and the overcoming of resentment in contexts where wrongdoing is systematic and ongoing seems at best naïve and at worst a form of complicity in the maintenance of oppression and injustice."[175] Thus in some cases forgiveness fuels the discontent rather than helps to resolve it. That is not to say that forgiveness is inappropriate for *any* political context, only that it risks suggesting a simple, emotional solution to complex, multilayered political problems.

The TRC's vision of forgiveness and reconciliation depends on an idealized vision of harmony with Edenic overtones. Tutu writes in his foreword to the *TRC Report*, "We are sisters and brothers in one family—God's family, the human family. Let us move into the glorious future of a new kind of society where people count, not because of biological irrelevancies or other extraneous attributes, but because they are persons of infinite worth created in the image of God."[176] This vision suggests a hope for the future as it recalls the past harmony of an original human family. Claire Moon writes, "Reconciliation is a story told in a single word. It tells a tale of prior harmony, a rupture (wrong perpetrated) and a subsequent reunion, predicated here on the confessional and forgiveness. Reconciliation relates these implied events in a causal and linear fashion—harmony, rupture, reunion—and prefigures narrative closure as reconciliation, the end point of the story."[177]

---

174. Murphy, *Moral Theory*, 10–11.
175. Ibid., 11.
176. Tutu, "Foreword by Chairperson," 22.
177. Moon, *Narrating Political Reconciliation*, 119.

This vision of reconciliation requires both victims and offenders to cast their testimonies in terms of hope for the future as a return to an Edenic ideal rather than moving forward and confronting the complicated present moment. Moon observes:

> [The TRC's] workings were most powerfully manifest through its retrospective structuration of the individual testimonies where victims were largely compelled to speak in terms of reconciliation rather than revenge and seek restorative justice which sought to endow them with a recognition of their suffering. Similarly, perpetrators had to relate a particular account of violations that worked within the overall teleology of the reconciliation narrative.[178]

Forgiveness as the emotional and spiritual substance of reconciliation emerges as a way back to this perfect South Africa that was created in God's image and lost to the poison of apartheid.[179] The narrative of the TRC adheres to this rewritten history and image of the future as restoration fueled by victim forgiveness.

Murphy contends that there is no justification for a state (or a state body like the TRC) to encourage victims to forgive in the name of reconciliation. She writes, "Citizens reasonably disagree about the justifiability of forgiving both in general and especially in transitional contexts. State policies designed to encourage victims to forgive fail to acknowledge such disagreement."[180] Ultimately, the question becomes whether a state can be in the business of mandating reactive emotions, such as promoting forgiveness as well as discouraging anger and resentment, which may have reasonable bases and play constructive roles in conflict transformation.

During the TRC, the promotion of forgiveness also served to stabilize the sometimes controversial grants of amnesty. If victims

---

178. Ibid., 136.
179. Ibid.
180. Murphy, *Moral Theory*, 13.

offered forgiveness to perpetrators, then the amnesty decisions were strengthened. Moon points out that the TRC's language of forgiveness was meant to make it seem like the amnesty decisions were supported by the victims. She writes, "Forgiveness worked retrospectively to legitimize the amnesty decision but was made to appear as if it had somehow been generated by popular will."[181] Thus the pressure on victims to forgive strengthens the overall narrative of forgiveness (including grants of amnesty) in service of the new South Africa, with all sides in agreement.

What gets lost in these narratives of forgiveness-as-reconciliation is the idea that reconciliation, or the restoration of a broken relationship, can take hold and thrive without interpersonal forgiveness. In the *TRC Report*, a section entitled "Reconciliation without Forgiveness" reluctantly acknowledges that "peaceful coexistence" may be the best South Africa can expect. It reports, "The emphasis on peaceful or non-violent co-existence suggests that a weak or limited form of reconciliation [or 'peaceful coexistence'] may often be the most realistic goal towards which to strive, at least at the beginning of the peacemaking process."[182] However, fewer than two pages of the seven-volume, more than 4,000-page report are given to exploring this topic. Given that the words "weak" and "limited" are used to describe it, "reconciliation without forgiveness" is far from the TRC's ideal.

Such a limited account of reconciliation might prove to be the most promising way forward. Ernesto Verdeja writes, "Many people calling for forgiveness are simply trying to articulate the need to avoid a return to violence. They are not necessarily apologists for dictators. But it is also clear that expecting a victim to overcome resentment and 'leave the past behind' for the sake of solidarity

---

181. Moon, *Narrating Political Reconciliation*, 122.
182. *TRC Report*, 5:400–401. See also Chapman, "Perspectives," esp. 88–89.

does little to convince survivors that society takes them seriously."[183] He proposes a "weaker" form of forgiveness that is "normatively defensible and practically attainable."[184] This "partial pardon" is distinct from forgiveness in that it allows victims to maintain negative emotions and retributive desires while also committing to peaceful coexistence with the perpetrator. Verdeja writes, "Here, forgiveness is not so much about moral transformation on the part of victims, perpetrators, and bystanders, but rather is about forswearing violence and coming to acknowledge the [humanity] of former enemies."[185]

This version of forgiveness is based on shared humanity and depends heavily on recognition of wrongdoing and victim harm on the part of the perpetrator. Verdeja argues, "[The partial pardon] is more robust than the thin coexistence because even to consider pardoning there must be some acknowledgment of past wrongs and recognition of victims. The pardon is premised on the belief that any stable and just future must focus on creating a common moral, political, and social space for former enemies."[186] In this proposal, victims contribute to reconciliation not with catharsis and moral transformation, but with the practical steps of accepting apology and forswearing retaliation. Central is the recognition of victim suffering and the expectation that perpetrators will make their own contribution by acknowledging and accepting responsibility for that suffering. The "partial pardon" stands in contrast to both amnesty, which "undermine[s] the rule of law and signal[s] that the interests of victims can be sacrificed for the common good of stability,"[187] and forgiveness, which claims an unreasonable moral superiority and burdens victims with a requirement for reconciliation.[188]

183. Verdeja, *Unchopping a Tree*, 168.
184. Ibid., 169.
185. Ibid.
186. Ibid., 172.
187. Ibid., 108.

The Lord's Prayer as a counterbalance

Any understanding of interpersonal forgiveness must attend to the bilateral nature of wrongdoing. Forgiveness becomes coercive in the South African context when victims are pressed to forgive unilaterally and unconditionally and in service not to restoring a specific ruptured relationship, but to an ideal of national reconciliation. The TRC pressured victims to forgive both implicitly through its religious imagery and language, lavish praise for forgiving responses, and linking forgiveness to the hope for reconciliation, and explicitly through direct requests from commissioners. By separating victims and perpetrators into separate committees and official processes, the TRC headed off potentially ugly exchanges. As a result, "The TRC did not provide the official forum through which victim-perpetrator encounters, which might seem to be the perfect exemplar of a reconciliation event, could be enacted."[189]

While the TRC's final report acknowledges a bilateral process of forgiveness, on the ground things were quite different.[190] Its reliance on unconditional, unilateral forgiveness as the source of reconciliation put the burden on victims to achieve internal, emotional changes and to create the reconciliation the new South Africa needed. A community that is reconciled in this way can only be imbalanced; victims must go forward to live alongside perpetrators they may have reason to fear. To be sure, while violence in South Africa is nowhere similar in terms of quantity or circumstance to what it was before the TRC, the post-reconciliation Eden is not a reality. "The post-apartheid crime figures in South Africa . . . suggest a society ill at ease with itself," write Roger Mac Ginty and Andrew

---

188. Ibid., 168.
189. Moon, *Narrating Political Reconciliation*, 55.
190. "The religious paradigm is tendered as a solution for our ills. There is a call for representative confession, repentance and forgiveness" (*TRC Report*, 443).

Williams. "So is this ["reconciled" South Africa] the 'lesser of two evils?'"[191]

In summary, this chapter argues that the TRC and specifically Tutu present a corrupted account of biblical forgiveness. By appealing to the Lord's Prayer and other biblical forgiveness texts, Tutu gives victims a mandate for unconditional, unilateral forgiveness. Instead, I argue that the biblical text consistently presents a bilateral process of forgiveness that must include repentance on the part of the perpetrator. The Lord's Prayer, which Tutu interprets as a command to forgive unconditionally under the threat of the loss of divine forgiveness,[192] in fact demonstrates the importance of this bilateral process and the connection between that process and right relationship with God.

The Lord's Prayer contains an acknowledgment that wrongdoing and forgiveness are ongoing, just like the need for food and the presence of temptation. The point of saying this prayer is not for sin to disappear and forgiveness to reign supreme. Rather, the point is to participate in the bilateral process of asking for forgiveness and giving forgiveness on a daily basis. The forgiveness petition is an acknowledgment that wrongdoing happens, and there is a mechanism for addressing it. Repentance and forgiveness are ongoing and intertwined, and they may often be connected to a community's wholeness and relationship to God. In order to be in right relation to God, human beings must be in right relation to each other, and this includes forgiving with repentance. Communities will necessarily have injury and estrangement, along with forgiveness and reconciliation. But forgiveness and repentance work together, and according to the prayer, human beings receive forgiveness from God

---

191. Roger Mac Ginty and Andrew Williams, *Conflict and Development*, Routledge Perspectives on Development (New York: Routledge, 2009), 115.

192. Tutu, *Rainbow People of God*, 224.

at least as far as they are willing to ask for it and give it to others. This daily prayer is a reminder: that being human is difficult work requiring daily maintenance, that conflict can be transformed, and that repentance and forgiveness both have a place.

Where the Lord's Prayer provides a prescription for community cohesion, Tutu's vision of unconditional, unilateral forgiveness leads to an uncomfortable integration of victims and offenders with varying commitments to communal harmony. The Promotion of National Unity and Reconciliation Act invokes *ubuntu* toward the end of a reconciled community, but *ubuntu* is an ethic of interdependence, not of solitary acts of victim forgiveness.

Such a vision of shared humanity suggests an exchange. Lives can only be bound up in each other by reciprocal design; one has *ubuntu* only as far as others also have *ubuntu*. Unilateral, unconditional forgiveness does not fit this form since it needs only the singular. *Ubuntu* is profoundly plural; it is more adequately represented by the bilateral process of admission and absolution given in the Lord's Prayer, which is another declaration of how human beings become persons: "Forgive us . . . as we forgive." There is repentance (forgive us), and there is the offer of forgiveness (we forgive). Neither happens independently. Thus the Lord's Prayer stands as a Christian correlate to *ubuntu*. Where Tutu says, "My humanity is inextricably bound up in yours," he could just as easily say, "My forgiveness is inextricably bound up in yours." Both victims and perpetrators must inhabit the new South Africa, and the work of reconciliation cannot fall only to the victims. So much emphasis on the astounding feats of unconditional forgiveness—indeed, declaring that there is "no future without forgiveness"—neglects to hold the perpetrators responsible for their fair share of the future.

4

Passionate Prayer, or Pastoral Pressure? Forgiveness in Luke 23:34a and the Pastoral Care of Victims of Domestic Violence

From Joy M. K. Bussert, "Letter from a Battered Wife":

> I am in my thirties and so is my husband. . . . We have four children and live in a middle-class home with all the comforts we could possibly want. I have everything, except life without fear. For most of my married life I have been periodically beaten by my husband. What do I mean by 'beaten'? I mean that parts of my body have been hit violently and repeatedly, and that painful bruises, swelling, bleeding wounds, unconsciousness, and combinations of these things have resulted.

> I have been kicked in the abdomen when I was visibly pregnant. I have been whipped, kicked and thrown, picked up again and thrown down again. I have been punched and kicked in the head, chest, face, and abdomen more times than I can count. . . . Few people have ever seen my black and blue face or swollen lips because I have always stayed

indoors afterwards, feeling ashamed. I was never able to drive following one of these beatings, so I could not get myself to a hospital for care.

Now, the first response to this story, which I myself think of, will be 'Why didn't you seek help?' I did. Early in our marriage I went to a clergyman who, after a few visits, told me that my husband meant no real harm, that he was just confused and felt insecure. I was encouraged to be more tolerant and understanding. Most important, I was told to forgive him the beatings just as Christ had forgiven from the cross. I did that, too.

Everyone I have gone to for help has somehow wanted to blame me and vindicate my husband. . . . I have learned that the doctors, the police, the clergy, and my friends will excuse my husband for distorting my face, but won't forgive me for looking bruised and broken. The greatest tragedy is that I am still praying and there is not a human person to listen.[1]

According to the National Institutes of Justice and the Centers for Disease Control, approximately 1.5 million women are raped and/or physically assaulted by an intimate partner annually in the United States.[2] Because many victims are assaulted more than once, approximately 4.8 million intimate partner assaults and rapes are perpetrated against U.S. women annually.[3] Since domestic violence ranks among the most underreported of all crimes, the actual number of annual victims is likely much larger.[4]

---

1. "Letter from a Battered Wife," in Joy M. K. Bussert, *Battered Women: From a Theology of Suffering to an Ethic of Empowerment* (New York: Division for Mission in North America, LCA, 1986), 81–85.

2. P. Tjaden and N. Thoennes, *Extent, Nature, and Consequences of Intimate Partner Violence: Findings from the National Violence against Women Survey*, Publication No. NCJ 181867 (Washington, DC: Department of Justice, 2000), iii. "Intimate partner" is defined here as current or former spouses or boyfriends. While domestic violence is also perpetrated by women and in same-sex relationships, the above study shows that women are far more likely than men to be assaulted by a male intimate partner (iv).

3. Tjaden and Thoennes, *Intimate Partner Violence*, iii.

4. "Approximately one-fifth of all rapes, one-quarter of all physical assaults, and one-half of all stalkings perpetrated against female respondents by intimates were reported to the police" (Tjaden and Thoennes, *Intimate Partner Violence*; see also U.S. Department of Justice, Bureau

While domestic violence crosses all demographic categories, this chapter focuses on the pastoral care of women who are victims of physical violence in heterosexual marriages. In one study of 350 victims of domestic abuse, 28 percent sought help from clergy members. The primary responses these women reported hearing were instructions to remember their marital duties, to "forgive and forget," and to avoid involving the church.[5] In another study of 5,700 Protestant clergy in the United States and Canada, 72 percent reported that they would not counsel a woman to leave an abusive husband and 92 percent stated that they would never tell a woman to divorce an abusive husband.[6]

As seen in the opening story, pastors often raise the topic of forgiveness in the pastoral care of victims of domestic abuse. Clergy and other pastoral caregivers frequently use Scripture to encourage women to forgive and endure patiently. In the above example, the pastor calls on Jesus's example by advising, "forgive him the beatings just as Christ had forgiven from the cross."[7] While not all pastoral-care providers advise women to stay in abusive marriages, many will discuss with victims the importance of forgiveness, either in the context of reconciling the marital relationship or in promoting the individual health and well-being of the victim. I examine how Christian women are sometimes encouraged to follow the model of Christ on the cross when he prays for the forgiveness of his

---

of Justice Statistics, "Criminal Victimization," 2011, v. http://bjs.ojp.usdoj.gov/index.cfm?ty=pbdetail&iid=4494).

5. Nancy Nason-Clark, *The Battered Wife: How Christians Confront Family Violence* (Louisville, KY: Westminster John Knox Press, 1997), 15.

6. The study was conducted in 1985. Mary Ann Douglas, "The Battered Woman Syndrome," in *Domestic Violence on Trial: Psychological and Legal Dimensions of Family Violence*, ed. Daniel J. Sonkin (New York: Springer, 1987), 41, cited in Judith A. Boss, "Throwing Pearls to the Swine: Women, Forgiveness, and the Unrepentant Abuser," in *Philosophical Perspectives on Power and Domination*, ed. Laura Duhan Kaplan and Laurence F. Bove, Value Inquiry Book Series 49, Philosophy of Peace (Amsterdam: Rodopi, 1997), 242.

7. Bussert, *Battered Women*, 83.

executioners (Luke 23:34a) and so, as their encouragers prompt, forgive without condition. Nancy Nason-Clark writes, "The famous cry of Jesus from the cross . . . is often portrayed as the exemplary pattern that abuse victims ought to imitate as they approach their aggressors."[8] I suggest that Jesus's dying words—"Father, forgive them; for they do not know what they are doing" (Luke 23:34a)—instead reflect an absence of forgiveness and an opening for victims to remain faithful to the biblical model without forgiving their abusers.

In this chapter, I first review the history of interpretation of Luke 23:34a. I show how this verse has been used in both ancient and contemporary contexts to promote unconditional forgiveness. In light of the other forgiveness texts in Luke's Gospel—including the healing of the paralyzed man (5:17–26), the sinful woman forgiven (7:36–50), the seven-times-seven instructions (17:3–4), and the instruction for reciprocal forgiveness (6:37–38)—Jesus might be expected to forgive his executioners or at least announce their forgiveness as he does with the paralyzed man and the sinful woman. However, he does not do so. Instead, he prays that God might forgive them. Such prayer is consistent with his teachings on enemy love ("Love your enemies, do good to those who hate you, bless those who curse you, pray for those who abuse you"; Luke 6:27–28), but it does not constitute a first-person act of forgiveness according to his earlier instructions (see esp. Luke 17:1–4).

Next, I show how Christian pastoral-care practices impose explicit or tacit pressure on victims of domestic abuse to forgive their abusers. Pastoral caregivers put women in danger when they counsel that forgiveness is the right response to an abusive spouse and suggest that forgiveness should lead to reconciliation. Further, the emphasis

---

8. Nancy Nason-Clark, "Christianity and Domestic Violence," in *Encyclopedia of Domestic Violence*, ed. Nicky Ali Jackson (New York: Routledge, 2007), 163.

on forgiveness—even in the context of separation and safety planning—implies that it is the victim's responsibility to respond to the abuse with unilateral or unconditional forgiveness. Such forgiveness is presented as the imitation of Christ, the moral duty of the victim, or the only way to heal from abuse.[9] Here I demonstrate how pastoral caregivers downplay the role of offender repentance and enlarge the biblical definition of forgiveness to include contemporary psychological understandings such as suggesting that forgiveness is required for the victim's mental health. In many pastoral-care settings, whether a woman is counseled to forgive and stay in her marriage or she is told that forgiveness is the only way for her to heal

---

9. Christian pastoral caregivers sometimes stress forgiveness in light of the New Testament household codes regarding wifely submission and obedience. These include Eph. 5:22–24 ("Wives, be subject to your husbands as you are to the Lord. For the husband is the head of the wife just as Christ is the head of the church, the body of which he is the Savior. Just as the church is subject to Christ, so also wives ought to be, in everything, to their husbands"); Col. 3:18 ("Wives, be subject to your husbands, as is fitting in the Lord"); 1 Pet. 3:1–2, 6a ("Wives, in the same way, accept the authority of your husbands, so that, even if some of them do not obey the word, they may be won over without a word by their wives' conduct, when they see the purity and reverence of your lives. . . . Thus Sarah obeyed Abraham and called him lord"). For careful treatment of these and other problematic texts, see Virginia Ramey Mollenkott, "Emancipative Elements in Ephesians 5:21–33: Why Feminist Scholarship Has (Often) Left Them Unmentioned, and Why They Should Be Emphasized," in *A Feminist Companion to the Deutero-Pauline Epistles*, ed. Amy-Jill Levine with Marianne Blickenstaff (London: T&T Clark International, 2003), 29–38; Angela Standhartinger, "The Epistle to the Congregation in Colossae and the Invention of the 'Household Code,'" in Levine and Blickenstaff, *Feminist Companion to the Deutero-Pauline Epistles*, 88–97; Betsy J. Bauman-Martin, "Feminist Theologies of Suffering and Current Interpretations of 1 Peter 2.18–3.9," in *A Feminist Companion to the Catholic Epistles and Hebrews*, ed. Amy-Jill Levine with Maria Mayo Robbins (London: T&T Clark International, 2004), 63–81; Catherine Clark Kroeger, "Toward a Pastoral Understanding of 1 Peter 3.1–6 and Related Texts," in Levine and Robbins, *Feminist Companion to the Catholic Epistles and Hebrews*, 82–88; Alan G. Padgett, *As Christ Submits to the Church: A Biblical Understanding of Leadership and Mutual Submission* (Grand Rapids, MI: Baker Academic, 2011); Teresa J. Hornsby, *Sex Texts from the Bible: Selections Annotated and Explained*, SkyLight Illumination Series (Woodstock, VT: SkyLight Paths Publishing, 2007); Dale B. Martin, *Sex and the Single Savior: Gender and Sexuality in Biblical Interpretation* (Louisville, KY: Westminster John Knox Press, 2006), 112–14 ("The Pro-family Paul"); Peter H. Davids, "A Silent Witness in Marriage: 1 Peter 3:1–7," in *Discovering Biblical Equality: Complementarity without Hierarchy*, ed. Ronald W. Pierce and Rebecca Merrill Groothuis (Downers Grove, IL: InterVarsity Press, 2005), 224–40; I. Howard Marshall, "Mutual Love and Submission in Marriage: Colossians 3:18–19 and Ephesians 5:21–33," in Pierce and Groothuis, *Discovering Biblical Equality*, 186–204.

apart from her abuser, forgiveness plays a role in subjugating women to abuse. Further, since expressions of repentance from the offender may prove to be insincere, forgiveness may set the victim up for more abuse. Thus forgiveness followed by abuse followed by repentance simply mimics the cycle of violence ("the tension-building phase, the acute battering incident phase, and the honeymoon phase"), only cloaked in religious language.[10]

Scripture provides an alternative. When Jesus prays, "Father, forgive them," he turns the matter of forgiveness over to God. He is shown as enduring violence to the point of death, a depiction that can be read by victims to indicate that forgiveness in the midst of suffering is not an obligation and maybe not even possible. We may reasonably take Jesus's prayer in place of forgiveness to provide an alternative model for responding to abuse, a model that relieves victims of abuse of the burden of forgiveness and restores moral agency to them.

A note on language

Domestic violence goes by a number of names, including domestic abuse, intimate partner abuse, intimate partner violence, wife battering, family abuse, family violence, intimate abuse, relationship abuse, and spouse abuse. The term favored by the Bureau of Justice Statistics (BJS) and the Centers for Disease Control and Prevention (CDC) is "intimate partner abuse," a broad category that includes physical or psychological violence committed in the context of heterosexual or same-sex dating or marriage relationships by current or former partners.[11] Since my subject is limited to female victims

10. Mary P. Brewster, "Domestic Violence: Theories, Research, and Practice," in *Handbook of Domestic Violence Intervention Strategies: Policies, Programs, and Legal Remedies*, ed. Albert R. Roberts (Oxford: Oxford University Press, 2002), 31.
11. The Centers for Disease Control and Prevention (CDC) define intimate partner violence as "physical, sexual, or psychological harm by a current or former partner or spouse. This type

of physical violence in the context of marriage, I employ the terms that are used most commonly in the literature and media to refer to this kind of offense: "domestic abuse" and "domestic violence." Both the BJS and the CDC use these terms interchangeably with "intimate partner violence."[12]

There is an ongoing debate about the use of the words "victim" and "survivor" in the context of domestic violence. Some authors define a trajectory of healing from abuse that includes moving "from victim to survivor."[13] In this chapter, I will refer to victims of domestic violence as "victims." This is not to suggest that they are weak, continue to be abused, or are somehow lacking in healing. Here, I intend the label "victim" to indicate only that a woman is or has been subjected to domestic abuse.[14]

of violence can occur among heterosexual or same-sex couples and does not require sexual intimacy" (http://www.cdc.gov/violenceprevention/intimatepartnerviolence/index.html). The Bureau of Justice Statistics (BJS) specifies, "Intimate partner violence includes victimization committed by spouses or ex-spouses, boyfriends or girlfriends, and ex-boyfriends or ex-girlfriends" (http://bjs.ojp.usdoj.gov/index.cfm?ty=tp&tid=971).

12. For examples of "domestic violence" as a default term interchangeable with other descriptors, see Stacy L. Mallicoat, *Women and Crime: A Text/Reader* (Los Angeles, CA: Sage Publications, 2012), 136; Nancy Berns, *Framing the Victim: Domestic Violence, Media, and Social Problems* (New Brunswick, NJ: Transaction Publishers, 2004), 20; Richard L. Davis, *Domestic Violence: Intervention, Prevention, Policies, and Solutions* (Boca Raton, FL: CRC Press, 2008), 1–12; Brewster, "Domestic Violence: Theories, Research, and Practice," 24.

13. Pamela Cooper-White, *The Cry of Tamar: Violence against Women and the Church's Response*, 2nd ed. (Minneapolis, MN: Fortress Press, 2012), 253; Nason-Clark, "Christianity and Domestic Violence," 164; Nancy Werking Poling and Marie M. Fortune, eds., *Victim to Survivor: Women Recovering from Clergy Sexual Abuse* (Eugene, OR: Wipf & Stock, 2009); Juliann Mitchell and Jill Morse, *From Victims to Survivors: Reclaimed Voices of Women Sexually Abused in Childhood by Females* (Washington, DC: Taylor & Francis, 1998); Cheryl L. Karp and Traci L. Butler, *Treatment Strategies for Abused Children: From Victim to Survivor*, Interpersonal Violence: The Practice Series 19 (Thousand Oaks, CA: Sage Publications, 1996); James Leehan, *Defiant Hope: Spirituality for Survivors of Family Abuse* (Louisville, KY: Westminster/John Knox Press, 1993), 123.

14. For a full discussion of the terms "victim" and "survivor" in the context of abuse, see Sharon Lamb, "Constructing the Victim: Popular Images and Lasting Labels," in *New Versions of Victims: Feminists Struggle with the Concept*, ed. Sharon Lamb (New York: New York University Press, 1999), 108–38. On the implications of using the word "victim" in the Christian context, see Jan van Dijk, "In the Shadow of Christ? On the Use of the Word 'Victim' for Those Affected by Crime," *Criminal Justice Ethics* 14 (2008): 13–24.

Forgiveness in Luke 23:34a

Jesus's cry from the cross in Luke—"Father, forgive them; for they do not know what they are doing" (23:34a)—is most commonly interpreted as an outpouring of unconditional forgiveness from a suffering man to his executioners.[15] This verse marks the only example in the Gospels in which Jesus speaks about forgiveness with regard to someone committing an offense against him directly. Elsewhere in Luke, he either instructs his followers on when and how to forgive or pronounces the sins of others to be forgiven. The forgiveness petition follows from his earlier instruction to "pray for those who abuse you" (Luke 6:28), but it raises questions in light of his teachings about unlimited forgiveness (Matt. 18:21–22; Luke 17:3–4).

15. For examples of this interpretation across several disciplines, see Anthony Bash, *Forgiveness and Christian Ethics* (Cambridge, UK: Cambridge University Press, 2007), 79; Célestin Musekura, *An Assessment of Contemporary Models of Forgiveness*, American University Studies VII; Theology and Religion 302 (New York: Peter Lang, 2010), 73; Geraldine Smyth, "Brokenness, Forgiveness, Healing, and Peace in Ireland" in *Forgiveness and Reconciliation: Religion, Public Policy, and Conflict Transformation*, ed. Raymond G. Helmick and Rodney L. Peterson (Philadelphia: Templeton Foundation, 2001), 319–50; William H. Willimon, "Following Jesus," *Christian Century* 102, no. 8 (March 3, 1985): 236–37; Brian Zahnd, *Unconditional? The Call of Jesus to Radical Forgiveness* (Lake Mary, FL: Charisma House, 2010),197; W. R. Domeris, "Biblical Perspectives on Forgiveness," *Journal of Theology for Southern Africa* 54, no. 1 (March 1986): 48–50; Miguel Rubio, "The Christian Virtue of Forgiveness" in *Forgiveness*, ed. Casiano Floristan and Christian Duquoc, Concilium (Edinburgh: T&T Clark, 1986), 80–84; Johann Christoph Arnold, *Seventy Times Seven: The Power of Forgiveness* (Farmington, PA: Plough Publishing House, 1997), 102; Stephen Cherry, *Healing Agony: Re-Imagining Forgiveness* (London and New York: Continuum International, 2012). 125; Chris Brauns, *Unpacking Forgiveness: Biblical Answers for Complex Questions and Deep Wounds* (Wheaton, IL: Crossway Books, 2008), 55; B. Bruce Cook, "Justice That Reconciles and Heals: Developing a Ministry for Crime Victims with a Restorative Justice Perspective" (DMin diss., Drew University, 2002); Cynthia Ransley and Terri Spy, *Forgiveness and the Healing Process: A Central Therapeutic Concern* (New York: Routledge, 2004), 14; Dan B. Allender, "'Forgive and Forget' and Other Myths of Forgiveness," in *God and the Victim: Theological Reflections on Evil, Victimization, Justice, and Forgiveness*, ed. Lisa Barnes Lampman and Michelle D. Shattuck (Grand Rapids, MI: Eerdmans, 1999), 212. For early examples, see St. John Chrysostom, "Homily LXXIX on Matthew" (*NPNF*[1] 10:478); St. Irenaeus of Lyons, *Against Heresies*, Book III, Ch. 18 (*ANF*, vol. 1); St. Jerome, "Letter 50: To Domnio" (*NPNF*[2], vol. 6).

Forgiving the soldiers, the Jews, and all humanity

The question of the prayer's object is the subject of much debate. The immediate context suggests that Jesus means to pray for the soldiers who are executing him.[16] However, the direct antecedent of "them" in this verse is the "chief priests, the leaders, and the people" (Luke 23:13). Later material in Acts such as Stephen's similar prayer for his tormentors (7:60) and Peter's speech—"Therefore let the entire house of Israel know with certainty that God has made him both Lord and Messiah, this *Jesus whom you crucified*" (2:36; emphasis mine)—indicate that Luke intends to hold the chief priests, leaders, and people responsible as well.[17] Other interpretations expand the object of the prayer to include not only the soldiers or the Jewish leaders, but also all humanity for all time.[18]

Whether the object of the prayer is the soldiers, the Jew opponents, or all of humanity, the important point is that Jesus prays for the forgiveness of whoever is responsible for his suffering. He also applies

16. Darrell L. Bock, *Luke*, IVP New Testament Commentary Series (Downers Grove, IL: InterVarsity Press, 1994), 373; Luke Timothy Johnson, *The Gospel of Luke*, SP (Collegeville, MN: The Liturgical Press, 1991), 381; Miroslav Volf, *Exclusion and Embrace: A Theological Exploration of Identity, Otherness, and Reconciliation* (Nashville, TN: Abingdon Press, 1996), 124–25.

17. Shelly Matthews, "Clemency as Cruelty: Forgiveness and Force in the Dying Prayers of Jesus and Stephen," *BibInt* 17 (2009), 126–27; Fred B. Craddock, *Luke*, IBC (Louisville, KY: John Knox Press, 1990), 273; Leon Morris, *Luke: An Introduction and Commentary*, TNTC (Grand Rapids, MI: Eerdmans, 2002), 357; Joel B. Green, *The Gospel of Luke*, NICNT (Grand Rapids, MI: Eerdmans, 1997), 819–20; I. Howard Marshall, *The Gospel of Luke: A Commentary on the Greek Text*, NIGTC (Grand Rapids, MI: Eerdmans, 1978), 867; Robert C. Tannehill, *The Narrative Unity of Luke-Acts: A Literary Interpretation*, vol. 1, *The Gospel of Luke*, FF (Minneapolis, MN: Fortress Press, 1986), 272–73; Robert H. Stein, *Luke*, NAC 24 (Nashville, TN: B & H Publishing Group, 1992), 589, 591.

18. Geiko Müller-Fahrenholz, *Vergebung macht frei: Vorschläge für eine Theologie der Versöhnung* (Frankfurt-am-Main: Lembeck Verlag, 1996), 155–56; David E. Garland, *Luke*, Zondervan Exegetical Commentary on the New Testament (Grand Rapids, MI: Zondervan, 2001), 923; Giovanni Paolo II (John Paul II), "Le ultime parole di Cristo sulla croce: «Padre, perdona loro...,»" Udienza Generale, 16 Novembre 1988, in *Catechesi sul Credo, parte II: Gesù Figlio e Salvatore* (Internet Office, Vatican 2002), http://www.vatican.va/holy_father/john_paul_ii/audiences/1988/documents/hf_jp-ii_aud_19881116_it.html.

the excuse of ignorance as a reason they should be forgiven. Ignorance as a basis for forgiveness coincides with Aristotle's "excuse of ignorance," which absolves the offender of the crime, but only insofar as the offender regrets what he has done.[19] But Luke gives no indication that the soldiers feel bad for having killed Jesus; on the contrary, in the same verse, just after Jesus's prayer that the Father forgive, Luke reports, "And they cast lots to divide his clothing" (23:34b). The soldiers likely did not have a choice in whether they killed Jesus that day, but they did voluntarily roll dice to divide up his belongings.

The prayer prefigures the motif of ignorance that is evident in Acts.[20] Peter indicts the Jewish audience for the crucifixion of Jesus, but offers the ignorance excuse: "And now, friends, I know that you acted in ignorance, as did also your rulers. . . . Repent therefore, and turn to God so that your sins may be wiped out" (3:17, 19). Later, Paul preaches, "While God has overlooked the times of human ignorance, now he commands all people everywhere to repent" (17:30). In these verses, it is clear that offenses committed in ignorance must be followed by repentance. As with Aristotle's instruction, sins committed in ignorance may be overlooked when there is remorse (or repentance, given here as μετανοεῖν).

Forgiveness in Luke-Acts

The first instance of forgiveness in the Gospel of Luke occurs when Jesus encounters the paralyzed man (5:17–26). Upon restoring the man's ability to walk, Jesus declares, "Friend [ἄνθρωπε (lit., "man");

---

19. D. S. Hutchison, "Ethics," in *The Cambridge Companion to Aristotle*, ed. Jonathan Barnes (Cambridge, UK: Cambridge University Press, 1995), 208; Aristotle, *Nichomachean Ethics*, Book III. See also David Konstan, *Before Forgiveness: The Origins of a Moral Idea* (New York: Cambridge University Press, 2010), 121.
20. See William S. Kurz, *Reading Luke-Acts: Dynamics of Biblical Narrative* (Louisville, KY: Westminster/John Knox Press, 1993), 149.

there is no prior relationship between Jesus and this man], your sins are forgiven you" (v. 20). Here, the passive voice (ἀφέωνται) suggests that Jesus is announcing forgiveness performed by God. However, when the scribes and Pharisees question Jesus's ability to forgive sins, Jesus counters, "The Son of Man has authority on earth to forgive sins" (v. 24). Later, when the woman identified as a sinner anoints Jesus (7:36–50), he offers identical words of forgiveness, first to Simon the Pharisee and then to the woman herself: "Therefore, I tell you, her sins, which were many, have been forgiven [ἀφέωνται]" (v. 47), and "Your sins are forgiven [ἀφέωνταί]" (v. 48). These pronouncements also arouse suspicion among those present who "began to say among themselves, 'Who is this who even forgives sins?'" (v. 49).

Both episodes use the passive voice to deflect the agency for forgiveness from Jesus to God.[21] Both consequently raise but do not explicitly answer the question of Jesus's own ability to forgive sins versus the ability of any person—any "son of man" or "human being"—to do so. Jesus heals the paralyzed man and declares that "the Son of Man has authority . . . to forgive sins" (5:24). However, this action proves only that Jesus has the ability to heal, something that was true for other miracle workers at the time.[22] It is Jesus's interlocutors who conclude that Jesus is claiming the ability to forgive on his own authority by asking, "Who can forgive sins but God alone?" (5:21) and "Who is this who even forgives sins?" (7:49).

---

21. On the use of the "divine passive" in the Gospels, see Joachim Jeremias, *New Testament Theology: The Proclamation of Jesus*, trans. J. Bowden (New York: Scribner's, 1971), 9–14; William R. Herzog, *Prophet and Teacher: An Introduction to the Historical Jesus* (Louisville, KY: Westminster John Knox, 2005), 84; David B. Wallace, *Greek Grammar beyond the Basics: An Exegetical Syntax of the New Testament* (Grand Rapids, MI: Zondervan, 1996), 437; Joseph F. Mali, *The Christian Gospel and Its Jewish Roots: A Redaction-Critical Study of Mark 2:21–22 in Context* (New York: Peter Lang, 2009), 48; Ben Witherington, *The Gospel of Mark: A Socio-rhetorical Commentary* (Grand Rapids, MI: Eerdmans, 2001), 115. On the divine passive as circumlocution in the Old Testament, see Christian Macholz, "Das Passivum divinum: Seine Anfänge im Alten Testament und der 'Hofstil,'" *ZNW* 81 (1990): 247–53.
22. R. Alan Culpepper, "Luke," *NIB*, 9:124.

It is clear from these passages that Jesus understands himself as having the authority to speak for God in matters of forgiveness.[23]

In the Sermon on the Plain (6:17–49), forgiveness and love of one's enemies are prominent themes. Jesus instructs, "Love your enemies, do good to those who hate you, bless those who curse you, pray for those who abuse you. . . . Forgive, and you will be forgiven" (6:27–29, 37). These words anticipate Jesus's prayer from the cross. Indeed, Jesus does offer a prayer for those who torment him (23:34a), but he does not forgive them even though he has both asserted his authority to do so (5:24) and instructed his listeners that it is possible and necessary for humans to forgive (6:37).

The Lord's Prayer reinforces the point that human beings have the ability and obligation to forgive one another: "When you pray, say . . . forgive us our sins, for we ourselves forgive everyone indebted to us" (11:2, 4). Jesus instructs the disciples further on forgiveness when he tells them, "If the same person sins against you seven times a day, and turns back to you seven times and says, 'I repent,' you must forgive" (17:4; see discussion of these texts in chapter 2). Jesus teaches his disciples to be forgiving of one another, although where Matthew leaves a similar instruction for unlimited forgiveness in vague terms (Matt. 18:21–22), Luke makes the condition explicit: the offender must repent.

These examples demonstrate that according to the Lukan program, forgiveness is not the exclusive province of God. They show that Jesus, and indeed everyone, also have the ability to forgive others. In light of this, we might expect Jesus to say from the cross, "I forgive you! You don't know what you're doing." Given Luke's emphasis on repentance, such forgiveness might not be in order. However, having already claimed the authority to speak on God's behalf ("the

---

23. On Jesus's authority to forgive sins, see esp. Tobias Hägerland, *Jesus and the Forgiveness of Sins: An Aspect of His Prophetic Mission* (Cambridge, UK: Cambridge University Press, 2011).

Son of Man has authority on earth to forgive sins"; Luke 5:24), he might say to his crucifiers as he did before to both the paralyzed man and the tearful woman at his feet (without any immediately obvious repentance on their part), "Your sins are forgiven you! You don't know what you're doing." Instead, in the midst of a violent death, Jesus pleads, "Father, forgive them; for they do not know what they are doing" (23:34a).[24]

Jesus's language in this prayer is identical to the words he uses to exhort his disciples to forgive one another. Speaking to the disciples about interpersonal forgiveness, Jesus uses the imperative, ἄφες αὐτῷ ("if there is repentance, you must forgive [him]"; 17:3). On the cross, Jesus utters the same words, ἄφες αὐτοῖς ("forgive them"; 23:34a), an imperative plea for God to forgive. But as he is dying, Jesus does not follow the instruction he issued to his disciples or exercise his own authority to forgive. His words from the cross raise the issue of forgiveness, but the prayer suggests that Jesus was unable or unwilling to offer forgiveness to his attackers.

Although Jesus does not directly forgive his executioners, he does pray for them in accordance with his earlier instruction: "Love your enemies, do good to those who hate you, bless those who curse you, pray for those who abuse you" (6:27–28). The point is not that enemies or persecutors will stop cursing and abusing. What should change is one's disposition to them. Jesus issues the instructions as an ethical challenge:

> If you love those who love you, what credit is that to you? For even sinners love those who love them. If you do good to those who do good to you, what credit is that to you? For even sinners do the same. If you lend to those from whom you hope to receive, what credit is that to you? Even sinners lend to sinners, to receive as much again. But love your enemies, do good, and lend, expecting nothing in return. Your

---

24. On the textual authenticity of Luke 23:34a, see the excursus, pp. 127-29.

reward will be great, and you will be children of the Most High; for he is kind to the ungrateful and the wicked. Be merciful, just as your Father is merciful. (6:32–36)

These words immediately precede the reciprocal forgiveness formula, "Forgive, and you will be forgiven" (6:37). Here it is clear that Jesus considers forgiveness to be a kind action on the order of loving and praying for one's enemies. He gives no precondition for that forgiveness, just as there is no precondition for enemy love or prayer. We should not extrapolate from this observation that women who are victims of abuse should stay in violent situations and love and pray for their abusers. On the contrary, each of these actions may be performed from a safe distance.

The martyrdom of Stephen provides a second example of substituting prayer for direct forgiveness during a violent act: "[Stephen] prayed, 'Lord Jesus, receive my spirit.' Then he knelt down and cried out in a loud voice, 'Lord, do not hold this sin against them [κύριε, μὴ στήσῃς αὐτοῖς ταύτην τὴν ἁμαρτίαν].' When he had said this, he died" (Acts 7:59–60). Stephen prays not to God, but to "Lord Jesus," whom he sees standing at the right hand of God (7:56), and while he does not use language of forgiveness, Stephen indicates that he wishes Jesus will deal mercifully with his attackers (there is no question here that the antecedent of "them" is the Jewish mob who is stoning him to death). Stephen does not call out, "I forgive you," although he might have done so given Jesus's teachings in the Gospel. Instead, he prays in imitation of his Lord, "Do not hold this sin against them" (7:60).[25] However, refraining from holding a sin against someone is not the same thing as forgiving that person. This becomes clear in Jesus's encounter with the adulterous woman in the Gospel of John. He does not hold her sin against her, but he does not

25. See the excursus for a discussion of the text-critical issues with this verse.

forgive her. He says simply, "Neither do I condemn you. Go your way, and from now on do not sin again [οὐδὲ ἐγώ σε κατακρίνω, πορεύου καὶ ἀπὸ τοῦ νῦν μηκέτι ἁμάρτανε]" (John 8:11). Stephen's model is potentially more useful to victims of domestic violence struggling with whether to forgive. As Jesus demonstrates in John, such passing over or not condemning does not require a continued relationship, but it does require a change in behavior. Jesus tells the woman, "Go your way, and from now on do not sin again" (8:11).

Early interpretations of Luke 23:34a

Many ante- and post-Nicene interpreters distinguished between Jesus's prayer for his executioners and a direct act of forgiveness. Augustine (354–430) understands the prayer in the context of the hypostatic union of human and divine in Christ, both simultaneously praying (and thus setting an example) and also hearing the prayer for the forgiveness.[26] The example of prayer is also central to Pseudo-Clement (writing ca. 140–160). He explains, "For the Teacher Himself, being nailed to the cross, prayed to the Father that the sin of those who slew Him might be forgiven. They also therefore, being imitators of the Teacher in their sufferings, pray for those who contrive them, as they have been taught."[27]

Like Pseudo-Clement, both Irenaeus (130–202) and John Chrysostom (347–407) connect Jesus's cry to his instructions to love enemies (Luke 6:27) and pray for persecutors (6:28). Chrysostom writes, "As therefore He commanded men to pray so does He Himself pray, instructing you to do so by his own unflagging utterances of prayer. Again He commanded us to do good to those who hate us,

---

26. Augustine of Hippo, Sermon 382.2, "Sermon on the Birthday of St. Stephen the First Martyr," in *The Works of St. Augustine: A Translation for the Twenty-First Century*, trans. Edmund Hill (Hyde Park, NY: New City Press, 1995), 376.
27. *Clementine Homilies*, Homily XI, ch. 20, *ANF*, vol. 8.

and to deal fairly with those who treat us despitefully."[28] Irenaeus echoes this sentiment: "The long-suffering, patience, compassion, and goodness of Christ are exhibited. For the Word of God, who said to us, Love your enemies, and pray for those that hate you, Himself did this very thing upon the cross."[29] In these interpretations, Jesus's prayer from the cross is consistent with his instructions on enemy love and an ideal for Christian piety, although the teachings on enemy love do not explicitly contain instructions to forgive.

Later interpreters also focus on Jesus's act of prayer. Martin Luther preaches that as he prays, Jesus is fulfilling the role of high priest: Jesus "prays for us and all men, who by our sins had furnished the cause for His crucifixion and death. For this reason we should not regard the gallows, or the cross, on which Christ suffered, as anything else than that altar, upon which He offers up His life and at which He discharges the priestly duty of prayer."[30] For Luther, Jesus's prayer for forgiveness is actually a prayer for all humanity. In that the crucifixion secures forgiveness for everyone, the prayer serves as a narration for the atonement that is enacted with his suffering and death.[31]

Luther stops short of claiming this verse as a mandate for human forgiveness. Rather, he aligns with earlier interpreters in citing it as an example of right prayer and enemy love. He explains, "Therefore if thou wilt be a Christian, thou shalt then imitate thy Lord, and have compassion on those who cause thee suffering, and even pray for them that God might not punish them."[32] For Luther, wrongdoing is more an occasion for pity and prayer than it is forgiveness, at least

28. John Chrysostom, Homily on "Father, if it be possible . . . ," section 4, http://www.newadvent.org/fathers/1910.htm. See also John Chrysostom, Homily 7 on Ephesians.
29. Irenaeus, *Against Heresies* 3.18, in *Ancient Christian Commentary on Scripture: New Testament III: Luke*, ed. Arthur A. Just (Downers Grove, IL: InterVarsity Press, 2003), 361.
30. Martin Luther, *Sermons on the Passion of Christ*, trans. J. T. Isensee (Rock Island, IL: Lutheran Augustana Book Concern, 1871), 180.
31. Ibid., 191.

in the context of this verse. Forgiveness is a foregone conclusion for Christians, secured by the death and resurrection of Jesus and embodied in this prayer on the cross. He writes, "Therefore you ought to be so pious as to rather pity [the ones who wrong you] … as Christ also himself has done toward us, when he prayed on the cross, 'Father forgive them.'"[33]

The prayer as lacking forgiveness

Contemporary interpreters note the absence of forgiveness in this verse. S. John Roth cites Jesus's earlier claim that "the Son of Man has authority on earth to forgive sins" (Luke 5:24), as well as his pronouncements of forgiveness for the paralyzed man (5:20) and sinful woman (7:47) and asks, "Why doesn't Jesus just forgive the offenders himself?"[34] Like earlier interpreters, Roth distinguishes between the prayer and forgiveness, and emphasizes consistency with the earlier teachings on enemy love.[35] Jesus is not forgiving them. Roth concludes that the primary reason Jesus does not directly forgive his executioners is that there is no display of repentance.[36] It is for this reason that the prayer may well represent a circumlocution for forgiveness.

In accounting for the lack of forgiveness in the prayer, Frederick W. Keene explains that the prayer is a reflection of how one in a weak position cannot forgive the stronger party.[37] He argues that had Jesus wanted to show that the weak should forgive the strong,

---

32. Martin Luther, in John Nicholas Lenker, ed., *Epistles of St. Peter and St. Jude Preached and Explained by Martin Luther, the Hero of the Reformation, the Greatest of the Teuton Church Fathers, and the Father of Protestant Church Literature* (Minneapolis, MN: Lutherans in All Lands Co., 1904), 269.

33. Martin Luther, "Commentary on the Lord's Prayer," in *Commentary on the Sermon on the Mount*, trans. Charles A. Hay (Philadelphia: Lutheran Publication Society, 1892), 240–269.

34. Roth, "Jesus the Pray-er," *Currents in Theology and Mission* 33, no. 6 (2006): 496.

35. Ibid., 497–98.

36. Ibid., 497.

this would have been a perfect opportunity. However, Jesus turns the matter over to the one who is more powerful than either the victim or the abuser. Keene explains, "Surely the idea of a forgiving Christ would tell us that if he could he would forgive. But he did not, and thus no one should be asked or expected to forgive those who retain the power in a relationship where forgiveness might be applicable."[38]

However, Jesus's forgiveness instructions in the Gospel of Luke suggest the contrary; any person may forgive another person regardless of his or her standing in the community. In both the Lord's Prayer ("forgive us . . . for we ourselves forgive"; 11:4) and the reciprocal formula ("Forgive, and you will be forgiven"; 6:37), Jesus speaks in terms general enough to imply that everyone has the ability to forgive. Even if Jesus intended his instructions for unlimited forgiveness for a particular community (suggested by the "brother" language in 17:3–4), there is no suggestion here or elsewhere that such forgiveness is governed by considerations of power. Therefore, Jesus's withholding of forgiveness from the cross may not be explained simply by out-of-balance power dynamics.

Jesus as Stoic or martyr

Jesus's forgiveness prayer fits both the Stoic and martyrological traditions of his time. Because the Stoic sage is considered to be invulnerable to injury, he would not feel resentment but neither would it be appropriate for him to forgive.[39] Moreover, the Stoic wise man "acts according to what is due, and so he will not remit the penalty for an intentional wrong."[40] In keeping with this, Jesus

---

37. Keene, "Structures of Forgiveness," 130; see also Andrea Lehner-Hartmann, "Familial Violence against Women as a Challenge for Theology and Ethics," in *When 'Love' Strikes: Social Sciences, Ethics and Theology on Family Violence*, ed. Annemie Dillen (Leuven: Peeters, 2009), 127.

38. Keene, "Structures of Forgiveness," 130.

39. Charles Griswold, *Forgiveness: A Philosophical Exploration* (New York: Cambridge University Press, 2007), 12–13.

provides the ignorance excuse ("for [γαρ, also "because"] they do not know what they are doing"; 23:34a) as a causative for God's forgiveness. For the Stoics, however, the issue of forgiveness is moot because the wise man cannot be harmed.[41] Thus there would be no reason to forgive. Friedrich Nietzsche reveals a similar understanding when he argues that the strong person will not allow wrongdoing to affect him in such a way that forgiveness is necessary. He writes, "To be incapable of taking one's enemies, one's accidents, even one's misdeeds seriously for very long—that is the sign of strong, full natures in whom there is an excess of the power to form, to mold, to recuperate and to forget."[42] Jesus may be seen as exemplifying this detachment by neither forgiving nor calling for vengeance for his persecutors.

At the time of Jesus, the martyrological tradition included the belief that God would emerge on the side of the righteous and judge those who tormented them.[43] The typical martyr's cry for vengeance reflects this idea.[44] This is seen in the murder of Abel, the prototypical martyr, whose spilled blood calls for vengeance. God speaks to Cain: "Listen; your brother's blood is crying out to me from the ground! And now you are cursed from the ground, which has opened its mouth to receive your brother's blood from your hand" (Gen. 4:10–11). However, Jesus's words as he is dying call for mercy rather than vengeance; this prayer becomes a model that Christian martyrs will follow, beginning with Stephen.

Regarding both Jesus's prayer from the cross and Stephen's plea as he is being stoned in Acts, Shelly Matthews argues, "The forgiveness

40. Konstan, *Before Forgiveness*, 32.
41. Griswold, *Forgiveness*, 13–15.
42. Nietzsche, *On the Genealogy of Morals and Ecce Homo*, ed. and trans. Walter Kaufmann (New York: Vintage, 1989), 39.
43. Matthews, "Clemency as Cruelty," 131.
44. Shelly Matthews, *Perfect Martyr: The Stoning of Stephen and the Construction of Christian Identity* (Oxford: Oxford University Press, 2010), 108–9.

prayer in itself is a dramatic overturning of the expected cry of the martyr for vengeance. As an expression of self-mastery and the ability to refrain from retaliating in the face of undeserved violence, it is an assertion of the ethical superiority of Christianity over Judaism."[45] However, the prayers may not represent such a stark reversal as Matthews suggests. Martyrs' prayers for the forgiveness of their killers may serve to amplify blame on their attackers. According to Irenaeus, the forgiveness prayer only postpones the vengeance God has in store.[46] Jennifer Wright Knust even suggests that the prayer may have an element of sarcasm; instead of an expression of mercy, Jesus's words contain a wish for the divine punishment of the executioners (who include both the Roman soldiers and also, as becomes clear in Acts, the Jewish authorities) and a proclamation of the superiority of Christianity over Judaism.[47]

Matthews demonstrates that Jesus's prayer models a new way of being in the world for his followers. She writes, "The prayer radically challenges both the stoic silence of the suffering righteous one, who is confident in God's ultimate vengeance, and the martyr whose dying cry to God is that vengeance be done. This unprecedented plea for mercy upon those tormentors is the assertion of a 'new testament' for a new social group."[48] Matthews suggests the prayer reflects the Marcionite concern for dividing the Jewish martyrdom tradition from the kinder, gentler Christianity expressed in Jesus's prayer.[49]

Jim Harrison also sees the prayer as countering popular notions of social relations. "Jesus' logion . . . radically undermined the ancient politics of hatred, irrespective of its religious and cultural context."[50]

---

45. Matthews, "Clemency as Cruelty," 120.
46. *Against Heresies* 3.18.5; quoted in Jennifer Wright Knust, "Jesus' Conditional Forgiveness," in *Ancient Forgiveness: Classical, Judaic, and Christian*, ed. Charles L. Griswold and David Konstan (Cambridge, UK: Cambridge University Press, 2011), 177.
47. Knust, "Jesus' Conditional Forgiveness," 192.
48. Matthews, *Perfect Martyr*, 128.
49. Matthews, "Clemency as Cruelty," 120.

Harrison also points out that Jesus's willingness to appeal on behalf of his attackers goes against the Greco-Roman ethic of "helping friends and harming enemies" and could have made Jesus appear weak.[51] He writes, "Above all, at the most basic level of ancient civil ethics, Jesus had not helped his friends at all by *loving* his enemy." With this prayer, Jesus overturns the prevailing ethic and, according to Harrison, institutes a "radical new ethic and paradigm of behavior."[52] Harrison interprets the prayer as running counter to a variety of social conventions, thus presenting Jesus on the cross as heralding social reform even as he prays in the moment of his death. Regardless of whether enemies are loved or hated, they are still enemies. Jesus's prayer presents a new way to approach those enemies—by interceding for forgiveness on their behalf—and is therefore consistent with his earlier teachings. While such analyses shed light on relationships of power in the time of Jesus, they do so by playing to popular ideas of Jesus as a revolutionary leader bent on overturning oppressive social attitudes. Thus Jesus's merciful prayer is cast as heroically undermining the vague "ancient politics of hatred."[53]

50. Jim Harrison, "Jesus and the Grace of the Cross: Luke 23.34a and the Politics of 'Forgiveness' in Antiquity" (paper presented at the Annual Meeting of the Society of Biblical Literature, New Orleans, 2009), 3.

51. Ibid., 3, 17. On the Greek ethical principle, see Mary Whitlock Blundell, *Helping Friends and Harming Enemies: A Study in Sophocles and Greek Ethics* (Cambridge, UK: Cambridge University Press, 1989).

52. Harrison, "Jesus and the Grace of the Cross," 16–17.

53. For contemporary scholars who portray Jesus as "radical," "countercultural," or "revolutionary," see, for example, Obery M. Hendricks, *The Politics of Jesus: Rediscovering the True Revolutionary Nature of the Teachings of Jesus and How They Have Been Corrupted* (New York: Three Leaves Press, 2006); John Dominic Crossan, *The Greatest Prayer: Rediscovering the Revolutionary Message of the Lord's Prayer* (New York: HarperCollins, 2010); John C. Hutchison, "Servanthood: Jesus' Countercultural Call to Christian Leaders," *Bibliotheca Sacra* 166 (2009): 53–69; Tom Wright, *The Original Jesus: The Life and Vision of a Revolutionary* (Oxford: Lion Publishing, 1996); R. T. France, *Jesus the Radical: A Portrait of the Man They Crucified* (Vancouver, BC: Regent Publishing, 1989); Robert Thornton Henderson, *Subversive Jesus, Radical Grace: Relating Christ to a New Generation* (Colorado Springs, CO: NavPress, 2001); Michael Ball, *The Radical Stories of Jesus: Interpreting the Parables Today*, Regent's Study Guide Series (Macon, GA: Smith and

Jesus suffers and struggles

Understanding Jesus as a Stoic or a martyr portrays him as in complete control of his actions and emotions as he is being crucified. However, there is no reason to believe that Luke intended to present Jesus as a martyr or Stoic figure.[54] Interpreting Jesus as a Stoic sage incapable of feeling pain is not useful for the pastoral care of victims of domestic violence. Calm forbearance of injury only permits injury to continue, and martyr-like cries for vengeance likely beget more severe abuse. Instead of reading Jesus in these ways, I suggest using Luke's account of Jesus's last words to construct a model of a suffering Christ who struggles with forgiveness as victims may also struggle.

In his passion narrative, Luke depicts Jesus's emotional conflict: "Father, if you are willing, remove this cup from me" (22:42). In some manuscripts, the next verses recount, "Then an angel from heaven appeared to him and gave him strength. In his anguish he prayed more earnestly, and his sweat became like great drops of blood falling down on the ground" (22:43–44).[55] Even after the angel strengthened him, Jesus was still "in agony" (ἐν ἀγωνίᾳ). The sweat that poured off his skin was so copious that it is said to be "like great drops of blood."[56] While some argue that Luke's Gospel portrays an

---

Helwys, 2000); Cameron Lee, *Unexpected Blessing: Living the Countercultural Reality of the Beatitudes* (Downers Grove, IL: InterVarsity Press, 2004).

54. G. N. Stanton, *Jesus of Nazareth in New Testament Preaching*, SNTSMS 27 (Cambridge, UK: Cambridge University Press, 1974), 36.

55. These verses are textually disputed, with some scholars arguing that the verses were interpolated later to protect Jesus's divinity in light of his suffering. Others find the verses thematically consistent with Luke. The manuscript evidence is split evenly; I err on the side of inclusion. See Johnson, *Luke*, 351; C. M. Tuckett, "Luke 22,43–44: The 'Agony' in the Garden and Luke's Gospel," in *New Testament Textual Criticism and Exegesis: Festschrift J. Delobel*, ed. A. Denaux, BETL 161 (Leuven: Leuven University Press, 2002), 140–44; Raymond E. Brown, "The Lucan Authorship of Luke 22:43–44," in *SBL 1992 Seminar Papers*, ed. E. H. Lovering (Atlanta, GA: Scholars Press, 1992), 154–64; Bart D. Ehrman and Mark A. Plunkett, "The Angel and the Agony: The Textual Problem of Luke 22:43–44," *CBQ* 45 (1983): 410–16.

56. Craig A. Evans, *Luke*, Understanding the Bible Commentary Series (Grand Rapids, MI: Baker Books, 1990), 329.

"imperturbable Jesus,"[57] these visceral physical descriptions suggest that he was already struggling to accept the fate that awaited him on the cross.

Moreover, death by crucifixion was remarkably painful and protracted, and it is fair to assume that Jesus was at least in physical distress during the hours he hung conscious on the cross in Luke's account. While Luke omits the cry of dereliction ("My God, my God, why have you forsaken me?"; Mark 15:34//Matt. 27:46), there is still copious evidence that Jesus suffered. For Luke, Jesus's suffering is an integral part of what gives meaning to his death and resurrection. Throughout the Gospel and Acts, Jesus's suffering is understood to be both necessary and a foregone conclusion—"The Son of Man must undergo great suffering" (Luke 9:22); "first he must endure much suffering" (17:25); "I have eagerly desired to eat this Passover with you before I suffer" (22:15); "Was it not necessary that the Messiah should suffer these things?" (24:26); "it is written, that the Messiah is to suffer" (24:46); "After his suffering he presented himself alive to them" (Acts 1:3); "God fulfilled what he had foretold through all the prophets, that his Messiah would suffer" (3:18); "it was necessary for the Messiah to suffer and to rise from the dead" (17:3).

The most convincing evidence that Jesus experienced pain and struggled on the cross comes in his final words. Luke reports that just after the forgiveness prayer, Jesus tells the thief beside him, "Truly I tell you, today you will be with me in Paradise" (Luke 23:43). Several hours later, the sky darkened and Jesus spoke his last words. "*Crying with a loud voice,* [he] said, 'Father, into your hands I commend my spirit.' Having said this, he breathed his last" (23:46; emphasis mine). This last request does not reflect a calm and composed Jesus. Instead, he is crying out (φωνήσας φωνῇ μεγάλῃ, "calling out in a loud

---

57. Bart D. Ehrman, *Misquoting Jesus: The Story behind Who Changed the Bible and Why* (New York: HarperCollins, 2005), 139–44. Ehrman judges the verses to be inauthentic.

voice"), and while he entrusts his spirit to God, the shouting portrays Jesus as pleading for rescue as much as it indicates acceptance of his fate. Understanding Jesus this way allows for an interpretation of the forgiveness prayer as another example of his struggle on the cross. While he has claimed the authority to forgive sins on earth (5:24), Jesus cannot bring himself to pronounce forgiveness for his executioners.

The prayer as a direct act of forgiveness

Other expositors read the prayer as a direct act of forgiveness. A few early interpreters hint at this exegesis,[58] but contemporary interpreters make it explicit. Forgiving one's abusers—not simply praying for them—is what should be imitated. Miroslav Volf writes, "Under the foot of the cross we learn that in a world of irreversible deeds and partisan judgments redemption from the passive suffering of victimization cannot happen without the active suffering of forgiveness."[59] Volf sees Jesus's prayer as the enactment of the possibility of human reconciliation and communion. Like many contemporary readers, he downplays the prayer's significance as a prayer per se (as opposed to an act of forgiveness) and presents it as an act of transformative forgiveness.

A great number of scholars and ministers regard the prayer as a model for Christian practice,[60] an example of the kind of

---

58. Jerome, "Letter 50: To Domnio," *NPNF*[2], vol. 6; Augustine, Sermon 382.2, in *Works of St. Augustine*.

59. Volf, *Exclusion and Embrace*, 125. Volf follows Dietrich Bonhoeffer in envisioning forgiveness as "costly," and thus a source of "active suffering." See Bonhoeffer, *The Cost of Discipleship*, trans. R. H. Fuller (1959; New York: Touchstone, 1995), 43–56.

60. For examples, see Johnson, *Luke*, 381; Donald Senior, *The Passion of Jesus in the Gospel of Luke* (Collegeville, MN: The Liturgical Press, 1989), 146; Jack Dean Kingsbury, *Conflict in Luke: Jesus, Authorities, Disciples* (Minneapolis, MN: Augsburg Fortress, 1991), 106–7; Scott Hahn and Curtis Mitch, *The Gospel of Luke: Commentary, Notes, and Study Questions*, Ignatius Catholic Study Bible (Nashville, TN: Thomas Nelson Publishers, 2001), 82; Thomas W. Walker, *Luke*, Interpretation Bible Studies (Louisville, KY: Westminster John Knox, 2001), 86–87;

unconditional forgiveness Christians should aspire to imitate.[61] Raymond E. Brown notes that Jesus's forgiveness models the right response to persecution for Christians.[62] And describing a mother whose son had been murdered, Michael Henderson recounts how she looked to the example of Jesus on the cross when choosing to forgive his killers. Henderson even allows the verse to stand misquoted: "At the point of death, Jesus said, 'I forgive them.'"[63] Henderson reports that the mother said "I forgive them" rather than "I forgive *you*." Holding on to the third-person plural pronoun (just as Jesus did) gives her some necessary distance in the midst of trying to forgive the men who killed her son.

Theologians and pastoral caregivers often import contemporary psychological categories such as self-forgiveness, insecurity, depression, and self-esteem into their interpretations of Luke's verse. "Jesus forgave his own murderers because he understood all to which they were enslaved—the social and religious prejudices of the day, their own insecurities, their ordinary, passive minds, and their self-centered motivations," writes Augusto Cury.[64] Ron Clark also cites Jesus's prayer as an example of the therapeutic value of forgiveness. He counsels, "Through forgiveness, victims choose not to be like the abuser who is full of fear, anger, confusion, and low self-esteem.

Willimon, "Following Jesus"; Domeris, "Biblical Perspectives," 48–50; Rubio, "Christian Virtue of Forgiveness," 80–84; Arnold, *Seventy Times Seven,* 102; Tannehill, *Narrative Unity,* 272–73; and Gonzalo Andrés Ruiz Freites, *El carácter salvífico de la muerte de Jesús en la narración de San Lucas: Estudio exegético de Lc 23,33–49 desde la perspective soteriológica Lucana* (Vatican City: Libereria Editrice Vaticana, 2010), 74, as summarized in Thomas E. Phillips's review, *CBQ* 74 (2012): 179–80.

61. Cherry, *Healing Agony,* 125.

62. Raymond E. Brown, *The Death of the Messiah: From Gethsemane to the Grave; Commentary on the Passion Narrative in the Four Gospels,* 2 vols., ABRL (New York: Doubleday, 1994), 1:31.

63. Michael Henderson, *No Enemy to Conquer: Forgiveness in an Unforgiving World* (Waco, TX: Baylor University Press, 2009), 100.

64. Augusto Cury, *Think and Make It Happen: The Breakthrough Program for Conquering Anxiety, Overcoming Negative Thoughts, and Discovering Your True Potential* (Nashville, TN: Thomas Nelson, 2008), 149.

THE LIMITS OF FORGIVENESS

Victims and families can face the future with hope and can choose not to let the abuser determine their happiness and spiritual choices."[65]

With regard to the crucifixion, though, there is no indication in the biblical text that the soldiers or Jewish leaders suffered from "fear, anger, confusion, and low self-esteem." Earlier in Luke, Jesus does not elaborate on any mitigating psychological factors (unless repentance might count as "psychological") that might prequalify an offender for forgiveness. Some interpreters suggest that the psychological benefit of forgiveness belongs to the forgiver.[66] Considering that crucifying Jesus was all in a day's work for these men, they were unlikely to consider their actions to have been wrong.

Such an emphasis on the therapeutic value of forgiveness is anachronistic, as interpreters import post-Enlightenment psychological categories into the story of the crucifixion, but it also asserts pressure as sacred texts are mobilized to advocate psychological or emotional responses from victims of domestic violence. Jesus does not say, "Father, forgive them because they are insecure and self-centered," or "Father, forgive them so I will not be locked into victimhood." In such readings, the prayer of Jesus is transformed into an act of unconditional forgiveness to fit current models of offense as psychologically understandable and forgiveness as the key therapeutic response. This is not to say that psychological categories did not exist at the time of Jesus, nor that the Bible is never a suitable source of direction for Christian readers.

My reading of Luke 23:34a is careful not to overinterpret the prayer for forgiveness as a direct act of forgiveness. Uttered in the midst of terrible violence and excruciating pain, the prayer is a cry, a

65. Ron Clark, *Freeing the Oppressed: A Call to Christians concerning Domestic Abuse* (Eugene, OR: Cascade Books, 2009), 100.
66. Desmond Tutu, *No Future without Forgiveness* (New York: Doubleday, 1999), 272.

demand, even, for God the Father to do what Jesus either cannot or is not willing to do in that moment. As Luke emphasizes throughout his Gospel, repentance is a precondition for forgiveness (see esp. 17:3–4, "if there is repentance, you must forgive'). The idea of unilateral, unconditional forgiveness for the sake of emotional health would have been foreign to both Jesus's context and Luke's readers.

Forgiveness and the pastoral care of victims of domestic violence

Many women who are victims of abuse seek help from the church because they see it as a safe place.[67] As a result, Christian clergy and pastoral caregivers play a crucial role in responding to domestic violence. Religious beliefs very often play a role in abusive relationships. Batterers sometimes cite Scripture to defend their actions (Eph. 5:22, "Wives, be subject to your husbands as you are to the Lord," taken as obedience, even to physical abuse), as well as to pressure victims to forgive and reconcile—Matt. 6:9–15 and Luke 11:2–4 (the Lord's Prayer); Matt. 18:21–22 and Luke 17:3–4 (forgive without bound); Luke 23:34a ("Father, forgive them").[68] As a result, pastoral caregivers must address issues of domestic violence, submission, and forgiveness not only in the private counsel of victims but also in the life of the church body through preaching, education, and social action against domestic violence.

---

67. United States Conference of Catholic Bishops (USCCB), "When I Call for Help: A Pastoral Response to Domestic Violence against Women" (2002), http://www.usccb.org/issues-and-action/marriage-and-family/marriage/domestic-violence/when-i-call-for-help.cfm.

68. On abusers using Scripture (esp. Eph. 5:22) to defend their actions, see John J. Pilch, "Family Violence in Cross-Cultural Perspective: An Approach for Feminist Interpreters of the Bible," in *A Feminist Companion to Reading the Bible*, ed. Athalya Brenner and Carole Rader Fontaine (Sheffield, UK: Sheffield Academic Press, 1997), 308; Carol Klose Smith and Darcy Davis-Gage, "The Quiet Storm: Explaining the Cultural Context of Violence against Women within a Feminist Perspective," in *A Cry instead of Justice: The Bible and Cultures of Violence in Psychological Perspective*, ed. Dereck Daschke and Andrew Kille, LHBOTS 499 (New York: T&T Clark International, 2010), 121; Mark-Peter Lundquist, "Beaten into Submission," *The Clergy Journal* 77, no. 8 (2001): 13.

This section focuses specifically on the question of forgiveness in the pastoral care of victims of domestic violence. I identify three main problems in pastoral writings about forgiveness. First, while most sources advise against pressing victims to forgive in the crisis moment, forgiveness remains the goal. Second, pastoral caregivers often conflate biblical forgiveness with contemporary therapeutic definitions of the term, which can result in pressure on victims to forgive without any repentant expression from their abusers. Finally, forgiveness is often presented as the only alternative to being consumed by anger, bitterness, and resentment. In the pastoral-care context, the prayer from the cross becomes the ultimate example of the unconditional forgiveness that victims should imitate.

Pastoral caregivers could better serve victims of domestic violence by more carefully interpreting the biblical material. Forgiveness in the teachings of Jesus is neither unconditional nor a matter of improving the victim's mental health. In the Gospel of Luke, Jesus insists that forgiveness requires repentance (17:3–4), and the Lord's Prayer also presents a model of forgiveness that is paired with an expression of repentance ("Forgive us"; 11:4). Moreover, the cry from the cross actually represents a *prayer*—an imperative that demands action—for forgiveness rather than a direct act of forgiveness. The image of Jesus struggling with forgiveness in the face of violence can be an empowering one for victims who also struggle. The prayer represents an alternate response for faithful Christians in accordance with Luke 6:28 ("Pray for those who abuse you"). Thus instead of an impossible example for victims to imitate, Jesus choosing to pray on the cross becomes a model for victims to reclaim their agency by choosing *not* to forgive their abusers. This is not to say that all victims of domestic violence must pray for their abusers in order to be faithful to the text. Adopting a prayerful stance at a distance is one response, but it is not the only one. As demonstrated in the introduction, nonforgiveness is consistent with Jesus's teachings in the Gospel of John, when he instructs the disciples and the community to use their own judgment in deciding which sins to forgive and which to retain (John 20:23).

Psychology and pastoral care

Drawing on the biblical image of the shepherd, "pastoral" care "refers to the solicitous concern expressed within the religious community for persons in trouble or distress."[69] Pastoral care may take the form of private counseling, but it should extend beyond this model. Liston Mills writes, "[Care] may refer to any pastoral act motivated by a sincere devotion to the well-being of the other(s). In this sense liturgical forms and ritual acts may reflect care as may education and various forms of social action."[70] Pastoral care became increasingly influenced by psychology around the turn of the twentieth century. Psychology has had such an impact on pastoral care that some have worried that it has supplanted theology as the basis of contemporary pastoral practice.[71] This chapter focuses specifically on pastoral care in the context of Christian practice (mostly Protestant), primarily in the United States.

In the context of domestic violence, pastoral caregivers often offer psychological solutions conflated with theological or biblical guidance. A primary example of this is seen in the emphasis on forgiveness. Where the forgiveness advocated by Jesus is conditional and closely related to repairing broken relationships within the community, pastoral caregivers often promote a kind of forgiveness that takes place only in the mind and heart of the victim. This kind

---

69. Liston Mills, "Pastoral Care," in *The Concise Dictionary of Pastoral Care and Counseling*, ed. Glenn H. Asquith (Nashville, TN: Abingdon Press, 2010), 836.
70. Mills, "Pastoral Care," 836.
71. McClure, "Pastoral Care," 272.

of forgiveness is touted as "healing" and the only way to avoid being eaten up by anger and resentment.

At its worst, such forgiveness can lead victims to forgive their abusers and return to dangerous home situations. Any return to a previously abusive relationship is fraught with danger, but urging victims to "forgive" before the abuser has made any change can be especially problematic. At its best, it provides victims with a way of thinking about forgiveness that lets them control its conditions and its timing, but it still holds them responsible for the so-called ideal Christian outcome—forgiving their abusers. Pastoral caregivers who present this account of forgiveness draw heavily on psychological explanations in place of biblical illustrations.

In the context of abuse, pastoral caregivers are called to a more complex vision of care. Bonnie Miller-McLemore writes, "Pastoral care disturbs as well as comforts, provokes as well as guides ... [it] calls for confession, and moves vigilantly toward forgiveness and reconciliation, knowing that both are more difficult to effect than people have hoped."[72] In other words, pastoral caregivers must challenge victims as well as console them by making "a space for difficult change."[73] The acknowledgment that forgiveness is difficult is an important one, but forgiveness as the way to repair the marriage still emerges as the goal.

I propose a further step. The Gospel account requires repentance from the offender (Luke 17:3–4) and accountability from the community (Matt. 18:15–20). Relying on these biblical instructions and examples, pastoral caregivers light the way for victims to assert their moral agency in the face of abuse and to refuse forgiveness where such conditions are not met. Instead, the refusal to forgive

72. Bonnie J. Miller-McLemore, *Christian Theology in Practice: Discovering a Discipline* (Grand Rapids, MI: Eerdmans, 2012), 309.
73. Ibid., 309.

may reflect strength and self-protection in the face of abuse. Even in cases where repentance is visible and sincere and the community is supportive, a victim may still choose not to forgive. Along with his instructions on forgiveness and repentance, Jesus commissions his followers to make their own decisions about what to forgive and God will follow suit (John 20:23). Repentance, then, is a necessary but not sufficient requirement for forgiveness.

Redemptive suffering

In the context of pastoral care, well-meaning advice from pastors about the redemptive value of suffering and the importance of forgiveness sometimes leads to women returning to dangerous situations only to be further abused. It is not uncommon for victims of domestic violence to be told they should endure their suffering patiently. Joanna Dewey observes, "Many a woman . . . has embraced or endured suffering that could be alleviated because she has come to believe that such a way of life is pleasing to God and an imitation of Christ."[74]

Indeed, for many Christians, the suffering of Jesus has a redeeming value for all humanity. Citing Isaiah's description of the "suffering servant" ("But he was wounded for our transgressions, crushed for our iniquities; upon him was the punishment that made us whole, and by his bruises we are healed"; Isa. 53:5) and reading these words as a prophecy of Christ, they understand his suffering as necessary for "healing" humankind.[75] It is likely that Jesus interpreted his own experience in this way, argues N. T. Wright: that the sufferings of

---

74. Joanna Dewey, "'Let Them Renounce Themselves and Take Up Their Cross': A Feminist Reading of Mark 8.34 in Mark's Social and Narrative World," in *A Feminist Companion to Mark*, ed. Amy-Jill Levine with Marianne Blickenstaff (Sheffield, UK: Sheffield Academic Press, 2001), 23.

75. Niels Christian Hvidt, *Christian Prophecy: The Post-Biblical Tradition* (Oxford: Oxford University Press, 2007), 106.

Israel would be focused on one person, that that suffering would have redemptive significance, and that this person would be Jesus himself.[76] Paul develops this theme of redemptive suffering, as in Rom. 5:3 ("we also boast in our sufferings, knowing that suffering produces endurance") and Phil. 1:29 ("For he has graciously granted you the privilege not only of believing in Christ, but of suffering for him as well"). Just as Christ's suffering on the cross served to redeem humanity, whether as atoning sacrifice or sign of righteousness or even as confrontation with Roman oppression, victims of domestic violence are sometimes advised that their own suffering may serve a greater purpose.

And finally, 1 Peter presents God as approving of righteously motivated human suffering: "If you endure when you do right and suffer for it, you have God's approval. For to this you have been called, because Christ also suffered for you, leaving you an example, so that you should follow in his steps" (2:20–21). Such an understanding of suffering as redemptive, morally good, and in imitation of Christ stands to trap women in abusive situations. That this interpretation of suffering may have comforted early Christian martyrs who suffered under persecution for their faith is of little help to twenty-first-century women who suffer at the hands of abusive spouses. As Betsy J. Bauman-Martin observes, "to use the text to encourage women to remain in abusive relationships is a blundering cross-cultural misapplication of the text."[77] Of course, not all women have the means or social support to escape from abusive relationships, and for these women, the idea that suffering is somehow redemptive may be all they have to hold onto. For these women, the vision of

---

76. N. T. Wright, *The Challenge of Jesus: Rediscovering Who Jesus Was and Is* (Downers Grove, IL: InterVarsity Press, 1999), 88–89.
77. Bauman-Martin, "Feminist Theologies of Suffering." 63–81.

Jesus on the cross—also struggling, also unable to escape—can give meaning to suffering that may continue indefinitely.[78]

Enduring suffering is not the only way women are instructed to follow Christ's example; pastoral caregivers often present forgiveness as a nonnegotiable Christian virtue. Pastoral counselors Robert W. Harvey and David G. Benner write, "It is obvious that pastors must make the understanding of forgiveness central to their care for the members of the body of Christ. The unforgiving cannot grow into the image of Christ when the most Christ-like virtue is resisted."[79] Speaking directly to victims of domestic violence, Patricia Diann Heathman emphasizes that forgiveness is necessary for victims both to follow Jesus's example and to secure their own salvation. She writes, "While He was still on the cross, enduring the shame, anguish and pain of the crucifixion, Jesus prayed that God would forgive his abuser. Christ-likeness requires that we do the same."[80] Along with patient suffering, forgiveness of one's abuser thus becomes the ultimate imitation of Christ.

Many pastoral theologians are critical of such approaches. Nancy Nienhuis writes, "If we encourage the belief that suffering should be accepted as a means of becoming like Christ, we are endorsing violence as a vehicle for Christian character development."[81] Many note the destructive results of such pastoral counsel to forgive and return to falsely repentant abusers.[82] Joy M. K. Bussert argues, "Although the cross as a symbol of comfort and hope does give

78. On making suffering meaningful in these situations, see ibid., 78–81.
79. Robert W. Harvey and David G. Benner, *Understanding and Facilitating Forgiveness: A Short-Term Structural Model*, Strategic Pastoral Counseling Resources (Grand Rapids, MI: Baker Books, 1996), 68. The authors do not offer a straightforward definition of forgiveness.
80. Patricia Diann Heathman, *Abused but Not Shaken: A Christian Response to Domestic Violence and Abuse* (Pontiac, MI: Voice of the Spirit, 2007), 53.
81. Nancy Nienhuis, "Thinking Theologically about Violence and Abuse," *Journal of Pastoral Care and Counseling* 59, nos. 1–2 (2005): 112.
82. See the discussion of whether victims are obligated to forgive offenders who are sincerely repentant in the first two chapters.

significant meaning and dignity to the suffering, it is not enough. I find in working with battered women that all too often the direct application of this theological perspective to a woman's life-experience actually serves to glorify suffering and reinforces her belief that it is 'Christ-like' to remain in a violent relationship."[83] While the cross may provide dignity and meaning, the symbol alone does not point to a way forward for women who suffer in abusive relationships.

Pastoral caregivers counter the notion of abuse as redemptive suffering in several ways. James Leehan writes, "Jesus' suffering and death on the cross was not redemptive because it was painful. Its redemptive value was made possible through the resurrection."[84] In the first century, suffering could be redemptive because it was one way of expiating sin. Such understandings do not hold in contemporary contexts. According to Leehan, the suffering is not what "redeems" humanity, but rather the resurrection and defeat of death. Abused women who are counseled to imitate Christ may do well to remember that they will not likely survive their own murders.

Marie M. Fortune counsels victims to focus on the transformation of Jesus's suffering through the resurrection instead of on the suffering itself. Just as the resurrection transforms the suffering of Christ, women are called to transform their own suffering into something better rather than remain patiently in an abusive relationship. Marie Fortune writes, "Transformation is [having faith] that the way things are is not the way things have to be . . . [it is] the means by which, refusing to accept injustice and refusing to assist its victims to endure suffering any longer, people act. By refusing to endure evil and by seeking to transform suffering, we

83. Bussert, *Battered Women*, 65.
84. Leehan, *Pastoral Care for Survivors of Family Abuse* (Louisville, KY: Westminster/John Knox Press, 1989), 111.

are about God's work of making justice and healing brokenness."[85] In this view, standing up against abuse becomes a way of following Christ's example in transforming suffering. Where Jesus's suffering is transformed, it follows that victims of abuse may accomplish their own transformations by protecting themselves or leaving their abusers. Jesus is resurrected *in spite of* his suffering, not *because* he suffered.

However, Jesus's suffering is very different from domestic abuse. There is a qualitative difference between being summarily executed by the state and being systematically abused in one's home. For this reason, Nienhuis calls for transformation rather than veneration of suffering. "In the Christian tradition, if we are told to imitate Christ, and Christ was crucified, and the story ends there, we are left to endure suffering," she writes.[86] However, Christ's suffering is different in two ways. First, Jesus went to the cross on his own volition. Second, the point of the cross was not Jesus' suffering, but his resurrection.[87] Calling attention to these differences allows victims of domestic violence to see the limits of the call to imitate Christ in either his suffering or forgiveness. Jesus made a choice to go forward into his own suffering and death; victims of domestic abuse have suffering imposed on them. The idea that the crucifixion is meaningless without the resurrection may help victims of domestic violence understand that the most exacting imitation of Christ is to release themselves from suffering into better futures for themselves and their children.

The crucifixion may serve as a model of empowerment for victims of domestic violence. Carol J. Adams suggests harnessing the image

---

85. Marie M. Fortune, "The Transformation of Suffering: A Biblical and Theological Perspective," in *Christianity, Patriarchy, and Abuse: A Feminist Critique*, ed. Joanne Carlson Brown and Carole R. Bohn (New York: The Pilgrim Press, 1989), 147.
86. Nienhuis, "Thinking Theologically," 122.
87. Ibid.

of Christ suffering on the cross in a way that encourages women to take action rather than pressures them to forgive their abusers. She urges ministers to say to victims, "Let Jesus off the cross. We are a resurrection people. Let yourself off the cross. Your suffering should be over, too. Because of Jesus you do not need to die to experience the meaning and power of resurrection [here understood as new life, an end to suffering, and a new beginning]. If you don't get off the cross, however, you very well may die."[88] Adams writes, "In the case of battering, the death of Jesus is the metaphor for the death of the marriage as it now exists. The resurrection is the new possibility of a relationship without violence, either with or without the man who batters."[89] Thus not only may the victim hope for new life, but also the abuser and the relationship may not be beyond repair. However, the metaphor of murder may not be helpful in cases of domestic abuse. If the marriage is dead, the implication is that someone killed it. There is no room in this analogy for that person to be held accountable. Moreover, Jesus does not rise as a new-and-improved version of his former self; he still bears the wounds that caused his death. While the hope for "new life" as seen in the resurrection may be a powerful image for victims, envisioning the marriage as murdered and resurrected may not get them there.

Forgiveness as a double bind

In the pastoral care of victims of domestic violence, authors identify "premature forgiveness"[90] and "cheap grace"[91] as problems. Pastoral

---

88. Adams, *Woman-Battering*, Creative Pastoral Care and Counseling Series (Minneapolis, MN: Augsburg Fortress, 1994), 111.

89. Ibid.

90. Cooper-White, *Cry of Tamar*, 247; Marie M. Fortune, "Forgiveness: The Last Step," in *Violence against Women and Children: A Christian Theological Sourcebook*, ed. Carol J. Adams and Marie M. Fortune (New York: Continuum, 1995), 205; Nason-Clark, *Battered Wife*, 54; James Newton Poling, *Understanding Male Violence: Pastoral Care Issues* (St. Louis, MO: Chalice Press, 2003), 191; Sue Atkinson, "On Forgiving Too Soon," *Third Way* 29, no. 9 (2006): 23; Carol L. Schnabl

caregivers often counsel victims to withhold forgiveness until there is genuine repentance (or repentance the victim judges to be genuine or sufficient for forgiveness),[92] or suggest that forgiveness is a process that may be difficult or take time.[93] Even so, an ideology of forgiveness persists and, whether tacit or explicit, a preference for forgiveness comes through.

Even though she leaves room for nonforgiveness, Pamela Cooper-White describes forgiveness in religiously appealing terms. She suggests pastors say to victims, "Do not blame yourself if you cannot forgive *yet*. Forgiveness is a gift of grace, and if it is right to happen, it will be given to you by God and in God's own time. In the meantime, don't worry, and let it go."[94] Such platitudes contain tacit pressure to forgive. What Christian victim doesn't want to receive such a "gift of grace" from God? The flip side of this is that such language relieves victims of the burden and psychological challenge to summon forgiveness on their own. Instead, they can wait for God's "gift of grace" just as Jesus waits on the cross.

Schweitzer, "Violence against Women and Children: How Churches Can Respond," *Word & World* 24, no. 1 (2004): 71.

91. Fortune, "The Last Step," 202; Nancy J. Ramsay, "Confronting Family Violence and Its Spiritual Damage," *Family Ministry* 20, no. 3 (2006): 37; Marie M. Fortune, "Preaching Forgiveness?" in *Telling the Truth: Preaching about Sexual and Domestic Violence*, ed. John S. McClure and Nancy J. Ramsay (Cleveland, OH: United Church Press, 1998), 57; Christie Cozad Neuger, "Narratives of Harm: Setting the Developmental Context for Intimate Violence," in *In Her Own Time: Women and Developmental Issues in Pastoral Care*, ed. Jeanne Stevenson-Moessner (Minneapolis, MN: Augsburg Fortress, 2000), 75.

92. James Leehan, *Defiant Hope*, 104–5, 123; Ramsay, "Confronting Family Violence," 37–38; Smith and Davis-Gage, "Quiet Storm," 127–28; Rita-Lou Clarke, *Pastoral Care of Battered Women* (Philadelphia, PA: Westminster Press, 1986), 79–80; Marie M. Fortune, *Keeping the Faith: Guidance for Christian Women Facing Abuse* (New York: HarperCollins, 1987), 53, 56; Poling, *Understanding Male Violence*, 185; Adams, *Woman-Battering*, 49; Lehner-Hartmann, "Familial Violence," 128; Catherine Clark Kroeger and Nancy Nason-Clark, *No Place for Abuse: Biblical and Practical Resources to Counteract* (Downers Grove, IL: InterVarsity Press, 2001), 70; Fortune, "The Last Step," 202; Boss, "Throwing Pearls," 242.

93. Miller-McLemore, *Christian Theology*, 309; Mary White, "Every Knee Shall Bow," in Lampman and Shattuck, *God and the Victim*, 187; Atkinson, "On Forgiving Too Soon," 23.

94. Cooper-White, *Cry of Tamar*, 259.

Rita-Lou Clarke warns against rushing women into forgiveness and cites the necessity of repentance and confession, and recognition from abusive men of the damage they have done to their wives.[95] With that condition, forgiveness can and should proceed. She writes, "Forgiveness means recognizing that the batterer is human and that both he and she are made in the image of God. Forgiveness does not mean condoning his behavior or excusing it, but it does mean being able to accept God's gift of the future possibilities [for a restored relationship] in spite of what has happened."[96] For many conservative Christian women, however, the "image of God" is a dominating male figure, and so not necessarily a helpful conceit in this instance. Here again, forgiveness comes as "God's gift," so there is no need for victims to rush to enact it. In this way, Clarke suggests that foregrounding theological ideas rather than psychological concepts allows victims to collaborate with God toward forgiveness rather than confronting the entire task by themselves.

Many pastoral counselors paint an attractive picture of forgiveness against the backdrop of the dark alternative of negative emotions. Ron Clark writes, "Through time, healing, and validation, victims can one day forgive those who abused them. They do not have to live the rest of their lives with anger, bitterness, and guilt. They are not forced to forgive, but they can one day make that choice."[97] No Christian victim would refuse the hope and opportunities provided by the resurrection, or choose to live with the other option: anger, bitterness, and guilt. In this context, forgiveness may be a choice, but for the faithful Christian there is only one option.

When a victim is faced with the implicit "choice" of forgiveness now or forgiveness later, she becomes alienated from the very faith

---

95. Clarke, *Pastoral Care of Battered Women*, 79.
96. Ibid.
97. Clark, *Freeing the Oppressed*, 126.

community that should be a source of support. Carol Klose Smith and Darcy Davis-Gage write, "The Christian tradition, with its emphasis on 'preserving the family' and 'forgiveness,' has placed the battered woman in a no-win situation. What choice does she really have?" When forgiveness is held out as a goal—immediate or eventual—a victim remains defined by her response to the abuser. If she chooses to forgive, that may mean reconciliation and a return to the cycle of violence. If she doesn't forgive, she could feel she is not being a good conservative Christian.[98]

Conflating biblical and therapeutic forgiveness

Pastoral-care authors conflate therapeutic forgiveness with biblical forgiveness in two ways. First, they advise victims that forgiveness need not involve the offender or the community and that it must be achieved for their own emotional and physical health. Second, they present victims with a false dichotomy, with forgiveness together with its concomitant categories of healing, freedom, and peace on the one side, and on the other side the dark world of negative emotions: anger, bitterness, indignation, vengeance, resentment, rage. Either a victim forgives or she is consumed by these negative emotions. Neither of these ideas has biblical warrant, and neither leaves room for a woman to feel either angry or particularly free, but rather simply a sense of self-preservation and restoration.

When biblical forgiveness is conflated with contemporary psychological quick fixes, the communal character of forgiveness gets lost. Peter Horsfield writes, "The practice of forgiveness is more than just the psychological action of an individual. . . . I believe that in our current [cultural and historical context], much of our thinking about what forgiveness is has become 'unethical,' i.e. separated from the

---

98. Smith and Davis-Gage, "Quiet Storm," 129.

ethos of its origins and from the communal context within which it has meaning."[99] Thus the presumption that the victim alone can (and should) forgive the offender neglects the basic structure presented in the teachings of Jesus; namely, that forgiveness involves the community holding the offender accountable for his actions (Matt. 18:15–17).

Reading the prayer from the cross as something other than forgiveness has two direct effects for victims of domestic violence. First, it discloses that there are circumstances in which forgiveness is morally wrong. Second, it restores the moral agency of victims by allowing them to choose a course that is not defined by their response to abuse. The question "Why doesn't she forgive him?" is closely related to another common question in situations of domestic abuse: "Why doesn't she leave?" Rather than having her responses to abuse questioned, I suggest the victim does not have any primary obligation to forgive or otherwise correct the violent situation. Rather, the question ought to be "Why doesn't he stop hitting her?" and pastoral caregivers and the church community should be the ones asking it. It is not the victim's responsibility to escape abuse—as though she is responsible for her own continued injury because she doesn't leave the home or the relationship—or to resolve the question of forgiveness—by forgiving an abuser who makes no effort to repent or change his behavior.

Imitatio Christi and the ideology of forgiveness

I propose a model of responding to domestic violence that takes into account Jesus's forgiveness instructions, the moral agency of the victim, and considerations of the impact of forgiveness on the future

---

99. Peter Horsfield, "Forgiving Abuse: An Ethical Critique," in *Forgiveness and Abuse: Jewish and Christian Reflections*, ed. Marie M. Fortune and Joretta Marshall (New York: The Haworth Press, 2002), 60 (emphasis in original).

as well as its effort to reconcile past wrongdoing. Where victims of domestic violence are often pressured to suffer in silence and to forgive their abusers in imitation of Christ on the cross, I say that there is more than one way to imitate Christ.

The ideology of forgiveness raises it to the level of an idol to be venerated. Forgiveness is a good thing simply because it is forgiveness. A reexamination of the biblical texts about forgiveness can counteract this overvaluing of the concept. What Jesus demonstrates in the Gospels is that forgiveness is not a good thing at all times and in all places. There is at least one sin that cannot be forgiven, by human beings or by God (Matt. 12:31; Mark. 3:29; Luke 12:10), and there are conditions for forgiveness that involve community rebuke (Matt. 18:15–17) and offender repentance (Luke 17:3–4). Individual disciples are charged to forgive and retain according to their own judgment, assured that God will follow suit (John 20:23). In light of this, Jesus's prayer from the cross is not surprising. It is possible that he determined that he simply could not forgive his attackers or the Jewish leaders at that time. At the very least, he is unable to forgive them in the absence of repentance. In either case, consistent with his own earlier instruction (Luke 6:28), he prays for them instead.

In doing so, Jesus becomes an empathetic partner in suffering rather than an impossible example for victims to imitate. In the midst of abuse, victims often see forgiveness as impossible or distant at best. On the cross, Jesus struggles, just as victims of domestic violence struggle. Even though he has chosen to accept this suffering, the fact remains that he is *suffering*. He is in excruciating pain. For Jesus in this moment, prayer is an option, but forgiveness is not.

There are occasions—and the crucifixion might be one of them—where forgiving is morally wrong. When abuse is ongoing and a woman's life is in danger, pastors agree that forgiveness (that leads to reconciliation) is not advisable.[100] However, in such cases forgiveness is usually deferred to some future time or circumstance, not canceled. On the other hand, reading Jesus's words on the cross as nonforgiveness offers victims a faithful alternative that is not primarily reactive. Peter Horsfield suspects this reading might reveal a faithful understanding. He asks, "What if, when women survivors of abuse say they are not able to forgive, they are not being weak, aberrant, or damaged, to be quarantined through prayer or counseling until they have recovered normality, but are reflecting a profound insight into the nature of Christian forgiveness?"[101] Indeed, the refusal to forgive is in exact imitation of Christ on the cross, and it suggests strength rather than weakness.

Further, the refusal to forgive allows victims to stand in defiance of the abuse that was perpetrated on them. "Holding wrongs 'unforgivable' is a way to mark the enormity of injury and the malignancy of wrongdoing as exceeding anything that could be made to fit back into a reliable framework of moral relations."[102] There are abusers who will never stop abusing, and there are acts of violence that may be beyond the reach of forgiveness. This does not mean that the unforgiving victim is morally deficient. Rather, it testifies to her agency in looking ahead to define the moral world and its boundaries. Jesus's prayer from the cross is consistent with this concern for the future. By praying that those responsible for his

100. Adams, *Woman-Battering*, 49–50; Leehan, *Pastoral Care for Survivors*, 104; Nason-Clark, "Christianity and Domestic Violence," 164; Nason-Clark, *Battered Wife*, 127–28; Poling, "Preaching to Perpetrators of Violence," in *Telling the Truth: Preaching about Sexual and Domestic Violence*, ed. John S. McClure and Nancy J. Ramsay (Cleveland, OH: United Church Press, 1998), 80; Neuger, "Narratives of Harm," 83–84.

101. Horsfield, "Forgiving Abuse," 57. Along with naming the sometimes impossible nature of forgiveness, this "insight" points to the patriarchal influence in the development of what forgiveness means in the church and questions whether it would look different if women had a greater role.

102. Margaret Urban Walker, *Moral Repair: Reconstructing Moral Relations after Wrongdoing* (New York: Cambridge University Press, 2006), 189–90.

execution might be forgiven, he accomplishes two things. First, he moves the responsibility for forgiveness from himself to God. Second, he looks to a future of restored moral relations. In order for the soldiers and Jewish leaders to be forgiven, they must repent for their actions. Given that they are ignorant of their own wrongdoing, this is unlikely, but Jesus's prayer contains the hope that they will do so.

Following Jesus's example is one way victims may communicate the seriousness of their suffering by refusing to forgive their abusers. For victims of domestic violence, the account of forgiveness as unconditional and unilateral holds little hope. Here I argue that a close reading of forgiveness in the Gospels reveals a more limited portrayal that requires repentance as a necessary but not always sufficient condition for forgiveness and makes room for individual discernment (as in John 20:23), with the decision not to forgive as a morally acceptable response. In imitating Christ by refusing to forgive their abusers, victims of domestic violence reclaim their moral agency and protect the life of the world to come.

Excursus: Luke 23:34a and the Question of Authenticity

The text-critical debate

There are four possibilities for the origin of Luke 23:34a ("Father, forgive them; for they do not know what they are doing"):

1) the verse was spoken by Jesus and recorded only by Luke, then removed by later copyists who found it unacceptable;

2) the verse was spoken by Jesus and not recorded by Luke, then inserted by later copyists who thought it fit with the Gospel's message;

3) it was not spoken by Jesus but was formulated by Luke, then removed by later copyists;

4) it was not spoken by Jesus but was invented in post-Gospel thought, inserted by a later copyist who thought it was appropriate to the context.[103]

The verse is absent in many of the oldest and most complete New Testament manuscripts (P75, B, ℵ^c, D*, W), but is included (with only minor variations) in other early witnesses (A, D^c, ℵ*). The verse is present in the earliest extant hand of Codex Sinaiticus (330–360), but is removed by later correctors of the same text (e.g., ℵ^c).

The fact that the verse is present in the original hand of Codex Sinaiticus suggests that anti-Judaism in the early church may account for the verse's later excision because Jesus appears to forgive the Jews for his execution. Robert Tannehill points out that Luke 23:28–31 (in which Jesus tells the daughters of Jerusalem, among other things, "Blessed are the barren, and the wombs that never bore, and the breasts that never nursed"; v. 29), if understood as an indication of God's final rejection of the Jews, would seem to conflict with 23:34.[104] Bruce Metzger considers the absence of the verse from some early manuscripts to be the result of copyists who viewed the fall of Jerusalem as evidence that God had not forgiven the Jews, so they removed the prayer that seemed to go unanswered.[105] Such arguments based on anti-Judaism and high Christology in the early church could account for the verse's absence in such major witnesses as later versions of the Codex Sinaiticus.

The presence of the Aristotelian "excuse of ignorance"[106] suggests that the verse was likely original and later excised. Instead of an addition, the verse was more likely excised by later scribes who

---

103. Brown, *Death of the Messiah*, 2: 975. For an overview of text-critical and theological perspectives on Luke 23:34a, see also Joshua Marshall Strahan, *The Limits of a Text: Luke 23:34a as a Case Study in Theological Interpretation*, JTISup 5 (Winona Lake, IN: Eisenbrauns, 2012).

104. Tannehill, *Narrative Unity*, 272n126.

105. Bruce Metzger, *A Textual Commentary on the Greek New Testament*, 2nd ed. (New York: United Bible Societies, 1994), 154.

106. See above for a discussion of the excuse of ignorance.

didn't like the suggestion that those responsible for Jesus's death were absolved of their crime. The ignorance motif here and in Acts also suggests the verse is original to Luke.[107]

Literary and theological analyses tend to judge Luke 23:34a as authentic based on its thematic coherence with the entire Lukan project.[108] The language and thought match Lukan theology, and the narrative unity of Luke-Acts shows that Luke 23:34a is connected to the overall themes of ignorance and prayer for adversaries, as seen in the martyrdom of Stephen ("Lord, do not hold this sin against them"; Acts 7:60). While Stephen's prayer is directed at Jesus rather than God, lacks the excuse of ignorance, and doesn't mention forgiveness, it is still considered to be in imitation of Jesus's prayer for his adversaries in Luke 23:34a.[109] Thus the cry from the cross prefigures this theme of ignorance that runs throughout Acts.

The "canonical argument" for the verse being added later suggests that the verse was ultimately included after the four Gospels were collected out of a desire for Jesus to speak seven rather than six "last words" from the cross.[110] Locating a four-Gospel tradition from the mid-second century, Whitlark and Parsons demonstrate that trends aimed at harmonizing these Gospels would have highlighted the group of six (an undesirable number; see Rev. 13:18; John 2:6; 19:14; Luke 23:44) last sayings of Jesus. Thus the verse (which likely was already in circulation as a "floating tradition")[111] was added by Gospel harmonizers to achieve the typologically significant number seven. The verse is found out of order in Tatian's *Diatesseron* (170), the

---

107. See above for a discussion of the ignorance motif in Luke-Acts.
108. I. Howard Marshall, *Luke: Historian and Theologian* (Downers Grove, IL: The Paternoster Press, 1970), 172n5; R. Alan Culpepper, "Luke," *NIB*, 9:455.
109. Matthews, "Clemency as Cruelty," 120.
110. Jason Whitlark and Mikeal Parsons, "The 'Seven' Last Words: A Numerical Motivation for the Insertion of Luke 23:34a," *NTS* 52 (2006): 188–204.
111. Ibid., 202.

earliest extant witness collecting the words of Jesus from the cross, suggesting that its position in the Gospel of Luke was not yet secure.

Some argue for the verse's authenticity based on purely aesthetic grounds.[112] Brown asks, "*Why would copyists have omitted this beautiful passage from mss. that contained it?*"[113] In the final analysis, he reveals his investment in the verse to be an aesthetic and emotional one. He writes, "It is ironical that perhaps the most beautiful sentence in the Passion Narrative should be textually dubious. The sentiment behind it is the essence of responding to hostility in what came to be thought of as a Christian manner."[114]

Questioning authenticity

For the purposes of this book, I leave the question of textual authenticity open. Those arguing against the authenticity of the verse cite the verse's thematic, stylistic, and theological consistency with the rest of Luke's Gospel as evidence for interpolation; supporters cite the same consistency as evidence for authenticity. The fact remains that the verse *is* present in the Byzantine text type (Textus Receptus) and thus it is in the King James Version. Therefore, it is printed in every modern version (although in double brackets). The modern church has always had this verse, and regardless of its textual authenticity, pastors, priests, scholars, and individual believers have to deal with it.

The important point for my project is not that the verse appears in double brackets with a microscopic text-critical apparatus in a footnote; the point is that the verse is there. In red-letter Bibles, the verse appears in red letters. The anguished cry, "Father, forgive

---

112. Nathan Eubank, "A Disconcerting Prayer: On the Originality of Luke 23:34a," *JBL* 129, no. 3 (2010): 536.
113. Brown, *Death of the Messiah*, 2:979 (emphasis in original).
114. Ibid., 2:980.

them; they don't know what they are doing" (uttered in Aramaic and subtitled in English) is the centerpiece of the bloody crucifixion scene in Mel Gibson's *The Passion of the Christ*.[115] The verse is considered by many to be an awe-inspiring and crucial instruction on how to live a perfect Christian life in the imitation of Christ. Textual authenticity has little bearing on the use of this verse in today's culture to encourage victims of violence or other offenses to forgive perpetrators without bound. For most contemporary readers, the model of unconditional forgiveness on the cross supersedes any text-critical concerns.

115. Timothy K. Beal and Tod Linafelt, *Mel Gibson's Bible: Religion, Popular Culture, and "The Passion of the Christ"* (Chicago, IL: University of Chicago Press, 2006), 202.

Conclusion: The Future of Forgiveness

In the United States, restorative justice is receiving new attention thanks in part to a recent feature in the *New York Times Magazine*, appearing under the headline "Can Forgiveness Play a Role in Criminal Justice?"[1] After Ann Grosmaire, 19, was shot and killed during an argument by her boyfriend, Conor McBride, also 19, her parents chose to engage in victim-offender mediation with McBride. The article embraces the restorative justice rhetoric of an idealized forgiveness, especially the notion of forgiveness-as-healing: "The [parents] said they didn't forgive Conor for his sake but for their own."[2] That forgiveness extended into influence over the prosecuting attorney and resulted in a somewhat lighter sentence for McBride. According to the article, restorative justice—packaged as forgiveness—gets the credit for allowing the girl's parents to move forward. While in this case McBride was repentant and expressed remorse, nowhere does the article indicate that this is a requirement for the restorative justice process or the parents' forgiveness.

In 2008 in South Africa's North West Province, Alex Ndlovu, a black squatter-camp resident, survived being shot in the shoulder while he was cleaning up his yard. Four other black South Africans

1. Paul Tullis, "Can Forgiveness Play a Role in Criminal Justice?," *New York Times Magazine*, January 4, 2013, 28–38.
2. Ibid.

were killed in the shooting spree, including a three-month-old child. Later, white South African teenager Johan Nel was sentenced to 169 years for the racially motivated attack.

Recently, reporters asked Ndlovu to respond to the call for forgiveness from the mayor of his community. "I find it very difficult to forgive someone who went out to kill us for no reason at all," Ndlovu responded. "Even during his court appearances, he would look at us and smirk. That made me very angry."[3]

Nearly twenty years after the end of apartheid and the opening of South Africa's Truth and Reconciliation Commission, racial violence and calls for forgiveness continue to make headlines. Forgiveness has not brought an end to all racial conflict in South Africa, nor does it come easy to victims of continued violence. Moreover, the systemic racism many South Africans hoped the TRC would address only continues. Millions of black and coloured South Africans continue to live in abject poverty in townships and improvised housing—including Ndlovu—even so many years after the TRC was declared a success and forgiveness heralded as a vehicle for change.

Another recent publication calls attention to the role of forgiveness in cases of domestic abuse.[4] Jill Filipovic warns against turning the focus to the victim to forgive the offender rather than to the offender to cease his abusive behavior. She writes, "While most people profess disgust at domestic violence, in reality, abuse victims are often pressured to work on the relationship or told they must have done something to provoke the abuse." Filipovic is critical of the article about McBride and especially of how the issue of domestic abuse—McBride had been physically abusive of his girlfriend leading

3. Mogomotsi Selebi, "It's Not Easy to Forgive," *Sowetan Live*, January 8, 2013, http://www.sowetanlive.co.za/news/2013/01/08/it-s-not-easy-to-forgive.
4. Jill Filipovic, "Restorative Justice in Domestic Violence Cases Is Justice Denied," *The Guardian*, January 12, 2013, http://www.guardian.co.uk/commentisfree/2013/jan/12/restorative-justice-domestic-violence.

up to the murder—is dwarfed by that story's celebration of forgiveness. She asks, "Does [the victim] have the support to get what she really needs—which is to get away from her abuser, and to have her community and her society take seriously acts of violence against her?" [5]

This book makes a constructive contribution to that discussion. Each of the three cases under consideration here reveals a preference for an idealized version of forgiveness presented as a biblical imperative. Restorative justice advocates claim biblical warrant but promote unilateral, unconditional forgiveness to victims engaging in VOM practices. In post-apartheid South Africa, Desmond Tutu and the TRC—often cited as a grand achievement of restorative justice—also promoted a brand of forgiveness that began and ended with a change in the victim's emotional disposition toward the crime. Such forgiveness is fastened to the future of the reconciled state, and victims are pressured to forgive and thus participate in the "new South Africa." Pastoral caregivers also posit a version of forgiveness that claims both biblical and psychological foundations. Victims are pressed to imitate Christ on the cross and forgive their abusers even in the absence of repentance.

As a result of these appropriations of forgiveness, victims may find themselves physically or emotionally vulnerable to those who injured them. Premature forgiveness (and reconciliation) can endanger victims. In restorative justice contexts, advocates claim to work on behalf of victims but neglect to consider the difficulty of promoting a particular emotional response to victims, especially victims of violence. Restorative justice advocates—who are often legal professionals in positions of authority—might succeed in coaxing a forgiving response from a victim using moral or religious pressure. However, such forgiveness might come at the expense of the victim,

5. Ibid.

whose emotional responses might change with the day or hour, and who may quickly regret succumbing to pressure to forgive.

In chapter 2, I present an alternative version of forgiveness that takes into account the seventy-times-seven instructions that advocates of restorative justice often cite as foundational. A more rigorous interpretation of these passages reveals a complex model of forgiveness that involves community rebuke and offender repentance before victims are expected to forgive. I challenge restorative justice proponents to consider the seventy-times-seven material in the fullness of its biblical context and to incorporate calls for offender repentance alongside their forgiveness imperatives. Moreover, I call for a scaled-back model that relies on a bilateral process rather than idealized notions of unilateral and unconditional forgiveness. Presenting victims with a forgiveness imperative that includes such emotional and psychological feats can serve to derail their ability to deal with their experience. Suggesting that a failure to achieve this kind of forgiveness represents a moral or religious failure only makes things worse.

Chapter 3 takes up similar questions in the context of post-apartheid South Africa. Through an analysis of the discourse around the end of apartheid and the TRC hearings, I show that Desmond Tutu and others also adopt an idealized version of forgiveness that, while claimed to come from biblical sources, actually has its roots in psychological understandings. Tutu and others demonize negative emotions such as anger and resentment, and victims are seduced with visions of unconditional forgiveness in which they contribute to the new, reconciled South Africa. By reading this discourse through the lens of the Lord's Prayer, I show that Tutu and other commissioners adopt the prayer's forgiveness imperative ("as we forgive"), but overlook the plea for forgiveness ("forgive us") that should be interpreted as an expression of repentance. Offenders are not expected to repent or apologize for their crimes in order to receive amnesty, but the pressure to forgive is immense. I suggest that a national ethic based on a more balanced approach stands to be more successful in the long term.

Finally, in chapter 4 I consider forgiveness in the context of the pastoral care of victims of domestic violence. Here again, psychological understandings of forgiveness as unilateral and unconditional become conflated with biblical teachings. In this case, I offer a close reading of Jesus's cry from the cross (Luke 23:34a) to demonstrate how the biblical understanding of forgiveness provides an opening for victims *not* to forgive their abusers. Where some pastors advise women to imitate Christ on the cross by patiently enduring their suffering and forgiving their abusers, I argue that this text provides the opposite message. Here, Jesus *prays* for his abusers; he does not forgive them himself. Indeed, his teachings up to that point are consistent: forgiveness requires repentance, and some crimes are unforgivable. On the cross, either case might hold. Imitation of Christ might involve praying for one's abuser, but need not require forgiving or reconciling with an unrepentant partner. This reading offers victims a way to remain faithful while also remaining safe.

Together, these case studies highlight the tendency to idealize forgiveness and the negative impact that might have on victims of violence and other offenses. I maintain that the biblical text offers strict guidelines for a kind of forgiveness that requires participation from both the victim and the offender. As such, forgiveness may flourish as a mode of community cohesion or relationship repair. In these pages I do not mean to suggest that forgiveness be abandoned. Quite the contrary; I challenge advocates to work toward a more thoroughgoing understanding of forgiveness, especially when they claim a biblical mandate. Forgiveness more accurately understood provides opportunities for victims and offenders to repair relationships, or for victims to move forward without guilt or pressure when the conditions for forgiveness are not forthcoming.

The concept of forgiveness, lifted from the biblical text and conflated with pop-psychological understandings, is often idealized and laden with emotional freight. When people ask what I am writing about, I give a simple answer: "Forgiveness." This usually elicits very positive, even awe-filled responses. "That's *amazing*," some say. Or, "Oh, that's wonderful! The world needs more forgiveness." These conversations may be my best evidence for how forgiveness has taken on a life of its own where general perceptions are concerned. On this point, David Konstan observes:

> That the demand to grant forgiveness may be coercive, the preconditions for eliciting it may be faked, its efficacy in assuaging rage may be overestimated, and, finally, the very concept may depend on assumptions that are philosophically incoherent—all this is reasonably well-known, and points to the possibility that we are dealing here with a notion that serves a particular ideological function in today's world.[6]

Biblical scholars in particular might take his words as a warning, as it is often the biblical account of forgiveness that is cited as the foundation of the most idealized versions.

Forgiveness, understood in religious or secular contexts, has enormous potential for binding communities and restoring relationships, but stands to be harmful when presented to victims as a moral or religious obligation. In everyday reality, forgiveness is an ongoing and even mundane process: I am late for lunch and you say it's okay; you step on my toe and I say, no problem; we trade harsh words but later resolve our differences. As the stakes get higher, though, forgiveness involves more effort and more risk. I present the

---

6. *Before Forgiveness: The Origins of a Moral Idea* (New York: Cambridge University Press, 2010), 170.

biblical text as a way of navigating this terrain. I do not dare to say when forgiveness is possible and when it is not.

The basic argument of this book is that forgiveness has limits, and our relationships are strengthened and guarded when we understand what those limits are. These boundaries are reflected in the biblical instructions, and victims may be morally and religiously correct in refusing to embrace forgiveness in some cases. Properly questioned and carefully negotiated, forgiveness stands to resolve differences and secure a better future than what came before. Imposed on victims who already suffer, however, it becomes but another burden with its emotional demands and promise to restore toxic—or even dangerous—relationships. It is the task of the community and those who suffer wrongdoing to determine the difference.

Bibliography

Acorn, Annalise E. *Compulsory Compassion: A Critique of Restorative Justice.* Law and Society Series. Vancouver: UBC Press, 2004.

Adams, Carol J. *Woman-Battering.* Creative Pastoral Care and Counseling Series. Minneapolis: Augsburg Fortress, 1994.

Allard, Pierre, and Wayne Northey. "Christianity: The Rediscovery of Restorative Justice." In *The Spiritual Roots of Restorative Justice*, edited by Michael L. Hadley, 119–42. Albany, NY: SUNY Press, 2001.

Allen, John. *Rabble-Rouser for Peace: The Authorized Biography of Desmond Tutu.* New York: Free Press, 2006.

Allender, Dan B. "'Forgive and Forget' and Other Myths of Forgiveness." In *God and the Victim: Theological Reflections on Evil, Victimization, Justice, and Forgiveness*, edited by Lisa Barnes Lampman and Michelle D. Shattuck, 199–216. Grand Rapids, MI: Eerdmans, 1999.

Allison, Dale C. "Matthew." In *The Oxford Bible Commentary*, edited by John Barton and John Muddiman, 844–86. New York: Oxford University Press, 2001.

Amstutz, Lorraine Stutzman, and Howard Zehr. *Victim Offender Conferencing in Pennsylvania's Juvenile Justice System* (1998). http://www.emu.edu/cjp/publications/faculty-staff/rjmanual.pdf.

Amstutz, Mark R. *The Healing of Nations: The Promise and Limits of Political Forgiveness.* Lanham, MD: Rowman and Littlefield Publishers, 2005.

Anderson, Gary A. *Sin: A History*. New Haven, CT: Yale University Press, 2009.

Arendt, Hannah. *Eichmann in Jerusalem: A Report on the Banality of Evil*. 1963. New York: Penguin Books, 2006.

———. *The Human Condition*. 1958. Chicago, IL: University of Chicago Press, 1998.

Arnold, Johann Christoph. *Seventy Times Seven: The Power of Forgiveness*. Farmington, PA: Plough Publishing House, 1997.

Atkinson, Sue. "On Forgiving Too Soon." *Third Way* 29, no. 9 (2006): 22–25.

Augsburger, David W. *Helping People Forgive*. Louisville, KY: Westminster John Knox Press, 1996.

———. *Seventy Times Seven: The Freedom of Forgiveness*. Chicago, IL: Moody Press, 1970.

Augustine. "Sermon 169." In *The Works of St. Augustine: A Translation for the Twenty-First Century*, translated by Edmund Hill, 222–34. Hyde Park, NY: New City Press, 1995.

———. *The Works of St. Augustine: A Translation for the Twenty-First Century*. Translated by Edmund Hill. Hyde Park, NY: New City Press, 1995.

Aune, David. *The Cultic Setting of Realized Eschatology in Early Christianity*. Supplements to Novum Testamentum 28. Leiden: Brill, 1972.

Ayo, Nicholas. *The Lord's Prayer: A Survey Theological and Literary*. Lanham, MD: Rowman & Littlefield, 1992.

Ball, Michael. *The Radical Stories of Jesus: Interpreting the Parables Today*. Regent's Study Guide Series. Macon, GA: Smith and Helwys, 2000.

Barker, James W. "John's Use of Matthew." PhD diss., Vanderbilt University, 2011.

Bash, Anthony. *Forgiveness and Christian Ethics*. Cambridge, UK: Cambridge University Press, 2007.

Battle, Michael. *Reconciliation: The Ubuntu Theology of Desmond Tutu.* Cleveland, OH: Pilgrim Press, 1997.

Bauer, Walter, William F. Arndt, F. Wilbur Gingrich, and Frederick W. Danker. *Greek-English Lexicon of the New Testament and Other Early Christian Literature.* 3rd ed. Chicago, IL: University of Chicago Press, 1999.

Bauman-Martin, Betsy J. "Feminist Theologies of Suffering and Current Interpretations of 1 Peter 2.18–3.9." In *A Feminist Companion to the Catholic Epistles and Hebrews,* edited by Amy-Jill Levine with Maria Mayo Robbins, 63–81. London: T & T Clark International, 2004.

Baumeister, Roy F., Julie Juola Exline, and Kristin L. Sommer. "The Victim Role, Grudge Theory, and Two Dimensions of Forgiveness." In *Dimensions of Forgiveness: A Research Approach,* edited by Everett L. Worthington, 79–104. Radnor, PA: Temple Foundation Press, 1998.

Beal, Timothy K., and Tod Linafelt. *Mel Gibson's Bible: Religion, Popular Culture, and "The Passion of the Christ."* Chicago, IL: University of Chicago Press, 2006.

Beck, Roger B. *The History of South Africa.* The Greenwood Histories of the Modern Nations. Westport, CT: Greenwood Press, 2000.

Bernauer, James, S.J. "The Faith of Hannah Arendt: Amor Mundi and its Critique—Assimilation of Religious Experience." In *Amor Mundi: Explorations in the Faith and Thought of Hannah Arendt,* edited by J. W. Bernauer, 1–28. Martinus Nijhoff Philosophy Library 26; Boston College Studies in Philosophy VII. Dordrecht, Netherlands: Martinus Nijhoff Publishers, 1987.

Berns, Nancy. *Framing the Victim: Domestic Violence, Media, and Social Problems.* New Brunswick, NJ: Transaction Publishers, 2004.

Bhargava, Rajeev. "Restoring Decency to Barbaric Stories." In *Truth v. Justice: The Morality of Truth Commissions,* edited by Robert I. Rotberg and

Dennis Thompson, 45–67. Princeton, NJ: Princeton University Press, 2000.

Blundell, Mary Whitlock. *Helping Friends and Harming Enemies: A Study in Sophocles and Greek Ethics.* Cambridge, UK: Cambridge University Press, 1989.

Bock, Darrell L. *Luke.* IVP New Testament Commentary Series. Downers Grove, IL: InterVarsity Press, 1994.

Boesak, Allan Aubrey. "'Just Another Jew in the Ditch': Incarnated Reconciliation." In *Radical Reconciliation: Beyond Political Pietism and Christian Quietism*, edited by Allan Aubrey Boesak and Curtiss Paul DeYoung, 57–74. Maryknoll, NY: Orbis Books, 2012.

Bonhoeffer, Dietrich. *The Cost of Discipleship.* Translated by R.H. Fuller. 1959. New York: Touchstone, 1995.

Book of Common Prayer. New York: Seabury Press, 1979.

Boraine, Alex. *A Country Unmasked: Inside South Africa's Truth and Reconciliation Commission.* Oxford: Oxford University Press, 2000.

Boss, Judith A. "Throwing Pearls to the Swine: Women, Forgiveness, and the Unrepentant Abuser." In *Philosophical Perspectives on Power and Domination*, edited by Laura Duhan Kaplan and Laurence F. Bove, 235–47. Value Inquiry Book Series 49; Philosophy of Peace. Amsterdam: Rodopi, 1997.

Bounds, Elizabeth M. "For Prisoners and Our Communities." In *To Do Justice: A Guide for Progressive Christians*, edited by Rebecca Todd Peters and Elizabeth Hinson-Hasty, 31–40. Louisville, KY: Westminster John Knox Press, 1989.

Braithwaite, John. "Principles of Restorative Justice." In *Restorative Justice and Criminal Justice: Competing or Reconcilable Paradigms?*, edited by Andrew von Hirsch, Julian V. Roberts, and Anthony Bottoms, 1–20. Oxford: Hart Publishing, 2003.

———. *Restorative Justice & Responsive Regulation.* Oxford: Oxford University Press, 2002.

Brauns, Chris. *Unpacking Forgiveness: Biblical Answers for Complex Questions and Deep Wounds.* Wheaton, IL: Crossway Books, 2008.

Brewster, Mary P. "Domestic Violence: Theories, Research, and Practice." In *Handbook of Domestic Violence Intervention Strategies: Policies, Programs, and Legal Remedies*, edited by Albert R. Roberts, 23–48. Oxford: Oxford University Press, 2002.

Brown, Jennifer Gerarda. "The Use of Mediation to Resolve Criminal Cases: A Procedural Critique." *Emory Law Journal* 43 (1994): 1247–1309.

Brown, Raymond E. *The Death of the Messiah: From Gethsemane to the Grave; Commentary on the Passion Narrative in the Four Gospels.* 2 vols. ABRL. New York: Doubleday, 1994.

———. "The Kerygma of the Gospel according to John." *Interpretation* 21 (1967): 387–400.

———. "The Lucan Authorship of Luke 22:43–44." In *SBL 1992 Seminar Papers*, edited by E. H. Lovering, 154–64. Atlanta, GA: Scholars Press, 1992.

Brudholm, Thomas. "On the Advocacy of Forgiveness after Mass Atrocities," in *The Religious in Responses to Mass Atrocity: Interdisciplinary Perspectives*, edited by Thomas Brudholm and Thomas Cushman, 124–53. New York: Cambridge University Press, 2009.

———. *Resentment's Virtue: Jean Améry and the Refusal to Forgive.* Philadelphia, PA: Temple University Press, 2008.

Brudholm, Thomas, and Arne Grøn. "Picturing Forgiveness after Atrocity." *Studies in Christian Ethics* 24 (2011): 159–70.

Bruner, Frederick Dale. *The Gospel of John: A Commentary.* Grand Rapids, MI: Eerdmans, 2012.

Brunk, Conrad G. "Restorative Justice and the Philosophical Theories of Criminal Justice." In *The Spiritual Roots of Restorative Justice*, edited by Michael L. Hadley, 31–56. Albany, NY: SUNY Press, 2001.

Buckley, Thomas W. *Seventy Times Seven: Sin, Judgment, and Forgiveness in Matthew.* Collegeville, MN: The Liturgical Press, 1991.

Bultmann, Rudolf. "ἀφίημι." In *Theological Dictionary of the New Testament*, edited by G. Kittel and G. Friedrich (eds.), 1:509. Grand Rapids, MI: Eerdmans, 1964.

Bussert, Joy M. K. *Battered Women: From a Theology of Suffering to an Ethic of Empowerment.* New York: Division for Mission in North America, LCA, 1986.

Butler, Joseph. "Sermon IX: Upon Forgiveness of Injuries." In *The Works of Bishop Butler*, edited by David E. White, 96–102. Rochester, NY: University of Rochester Press, 2006.

Calvin, John. *Calvin's Bible Commentaries: Matthew, Mark and Luke, Part II.* Translated by John King. Charleston, SC: Forgotten Books, 2007.

———. Vol. 2, *Institutes of the Christian Religion.* Translated and edited by John Allen. London: Thomas Tegg, 1844.

Carter, Warren. *Matthew and the Margins: A Sociopolitical and Religious Reading.* Maryknoll, NY: Orbis Books, 2000.

Cary, Phillip. *Inner Grace: Augustine in the Traditions of Plato and Paul.* Oxford: Oxford University Press, 2008.

Chapman, Audrey R. "Perspectives on the Role of Forgiveness in the Human Rights Violations Hearings." In *Truth and Reconciliation in South Africa: Did the TRC Deliver?*, edited by Audrey R. Chapman and Hugo van der Merwe, 66–89. Pennsylvania Studies in Human Rights. Philadelphia: University of Pennsylvania Press, 2008.

Cherry, Stephen. "Forgiveness and Reconciliation in South Africa." In *Forgiveness in Context: Theology and Psychology in Creative Dialogue*, edited by Fraser Watts and Liz Gulliford, 160–77. London: T&T Clark International, 2004.

———. *Healing Agony: Re-Imagining Forgiveness*. London and New York: Continuum International, 2012.

Clark, Ron. *Freeing the Oppressed: A Call to Christians concerning Domestic Abuse.* Eugene, OR: Cascade Books, 2009.

Clarke, Rita-Lou. *Pastoral Care of Battered Women*. Philadelphia, PA: Westminster Press, 1986.

Coates, Robert B. "Mediation Observations: Case Examples and Analysis." In *Victim Meets Offender: The Impact of Restorative Justice and Mediation,* by Mark S. Umbreit with Robert B. Coates and Boris Kalanj, 119–38. Criminal Justice Press. Monsey, NY: Willow Tree Press, 1994.

Cook, B. Bruce. "Justice That Reconciles and Heals: Developing a Ministry for Crime Victims with a Restorative Justice Perspective." DMin diss., Drew University, 2002.

Cooper-White, Pamela. *The Cry of Tamar: Violence against Women and the Church's Response*. 2nd ed. Minneapolis: Fortress Press, 2012.

Costin, Teodor. *Il Perdono di dio nel Vangelo di Matteo: Uno studio esegetico-teologico.* Tesi Gregoriana Serie Teologia 133. Roma: Editrice Pontificia Università Gregoriana, 2006.

Cowell, Alan. "Tutu Urges Israelis to Pray for and Forgive Nazis." *New York Times*, December 28, 1989. http://www.nytimes.com/1989/12/27/world/tutu-urges-israelis-to-pray-for-and-forgive-nazis.html.

Craddock, Fred B. *Luke.* IBC. Louisville, KY: John Knox Press, 1990.

Crossan, John Dominic. *The Greatest Prayer: Rediscovering the Revolutionary Message of the Lord's Prayer*. New York: HarperCollins, 2010.Cury, Augusto. *Think and Make It Happen: The Breakthrough Program for Conquering Anxiety, Overcoming Negative Thoughts, and Discovering Your True Potential*. Nashville, TN: Thomas Nelson, 2008.

Davids, Peter H. "A Silent Witness in Marriage: 1 Peter 3:1–7." In *Discovering Biblical Equality: Complementarity without Hierarchy*, edited by Ronald W. Pierce and Rebecca Merrill Groothuis, 224–40. Downers Grove, IL: InterVarsity Press, 2005.

Davies, W. D., and D. C. Allison. *Matthew 1–7*. ICC. London: T&T Clark International, 1988.

Davis, Richard L. *Domestic Violence: Intervention, Prevention, Policies, and Solutions*. Boca Raton, FL: CRC Press, 2008.

de Gruchy, John W. *Reconciliation: Restoring Justice*. Minneapolis: Fortress Press, 2002.

Derrida, Jacques. *On Cosmopolitanism and Forgiveness*. Translated by Mark Dooley and Michael Hughes. New York: Routledge, 2001. Originally published as *Cosmopolites de tous le pays, encore un effort!* (Paris: Editions Galilée, 1997).

Dewey, Joanna. "'Let Them Renounce Themselves and Take Up Their Cross': A Feminist Reading of Mark 8.34 in Mark's Social and Narrative World." In *A Feminist Companion to Mark*, edited by Amy-Jill Levine with Marianne Blickenstaff, 23–36. Sheffield, UK: Sheffield Academic Press, 2001.

Domeris, W. R. "Biblical Perspectives on Forgiveness." *Journal of Theology for Southern Africa* 54, no. 1 (March 1986): 48–50.

Donahue, John R., and Daniel J. Harrington. *Mark*. SP. Collegeville, MN: The Liturgical Press, 2002.

Donnelly, Doris. *Seventy Times Seven: Forgiveness and Peacemaking*. Erie, PA: Pax Christi USA, 1993.

Douglas, Mary Ann. "The Battered Woman Syndrome." In *Domestic Violence on Trial: Psychological and Legal Dimensions of Family Violence*, edited by Daniel J. Sonkin, 39–54. New York: Springer, 1987.

Dunn, James D. G. "The Tradition." In *The Historical Jesus in Recent Research*, edited by James D. G. Dunn and Scot McKnight, 167–84. Sources for Biblical and Theological Study 10. Winona Lake, IN: Eisenbrauns, 2005.

Ehrman, Bart D. *Misquoting Jesus: The Story behind Who Changed the Bible and Why*. New York: HarperCollins, 2005.

Ehrman, Bart D., and Mark A. Plunkett. "The Angel and the Agony: The Textual Problem of Luke 22:43–44." *CBQ* 45 (1983): 410–16.

Enright, Robert D. *Forgiveness Is a Choice: A Step-by-Step Process for Resolving Anger and Restoring Hope*. Washington, DC: American Psychological Association, 2001.

Enright, Robert D., Suzanne Freedman, and Julio Rique. "The Psychology of Interpersonal Forgiveness." In *Exploring Forgiveness*, edited by Robert D. Enright and Joanna North, 46–62. Madison: University of Wisconsin Press, 1998.

Eschholz, Sarah, Elizabeth Beck, Pamela Blume-Leonard, and Mark D. Reed. "Offenders' Family Members' Responses to Capital Crimes: The Need for Restorative Justice Initiatives." In *Current Perspectives in Forensic Psychology and Criminal Behavior*, edited by Curt R. Bartol and Anne M. Bartol, 220–29. 3rd ed. Los Angeles, CA: Sage Publications, 2012.

Eubank, Nathan. "A Disconcerting Prayer: On the Originality of Luke 23:34a." *JBL* 129, no. 3 (2010): 521–36.

Evans, Craig A. *Luke*. Understanding the Bible Commentary Series. Grand Rapids, MI: Baker Books, 1990.

Everts, Janet Meyer. "Unforgivable Sin." In *ABD* 6:745–46.

Exline, Julie Juola, and Roy F. Baumeister. "Expressing Forgiveness and Repentance: Benefits and Barriers." In *Forgiveness: Theory, Research, and Practice*, edited by Michael E. McCullough, Kenneth I. Pargament, and Carl E. Thoresen, 133–55. New York: Guilford Press, 2000.

Faulkner, John Alfred. *Cyprian the Churchman*. Cincinnati, OH: Jennings and Graham, 1906.

Fiadjoe, Albert. *Alternative Dispute Resolution: A Developing World Perspective.* New York: RoutledgeCavendish, 2004.

Filipovic, Jill. "Restorative Justice in Domestic Violence Cases Is Justice Denied." *The Guardian,* January 12, 2013. http://www.guardian.co.uk/commentisfree/2013/jan/12/restorative-justice-domestic-violence.

Forget, Marc. "Crime as Interpersonal Conflict: Reconciliation between Victim and Offender." In *Dilemmas of Reconciliation: Cases and Concepts,* edited by Carol Prager and Trudy Govier, 111–36. Waterloo, ON: Wilfrid Laurier University Press, 2003.

Fortune, Marie M. "Forgiveness: The Last Step." In *Violence against Women and Children: A Christian Theological Sourcebook,* edited by Carol J. Adams and Marie M. Fortune, 201–6. New York: Continuum, 1995.

———. *Keeping the Faith: Guidance for Christian Women Facing Abuse.* New York: HarperCollins, 1987.

———. "Preaching Forgiveness?" In *Telling the Truth: Preaching about Sexual and Domestic Violence,* edited by John S. McClure and Nancy J. Ramsay, 49–57. Cleveland, OH: United Church Press, 1998.

———. "The Transformation of Suffering: A Biblical and Theological Perspective." In *Christianity, Patriarchy, and Abuse: A Feminist Critique,* edited by Joanne Carlson Brown and Carole R. Bohn, 139–47. New York: The Pilgrim Press, 1989.

France, R. T. *The Gospel of Matthew.* NICNT. Grand Rapids, MI: Eerdmans, 2007.

———. *Jesus the Radical: A Portrait of the Man They Crucified.* Vancouver, BC: Regent Publishing, 1989.

Freites, Gonzalo Andrés Ruiz. *El carácter salvífico de la muerte de Jesús en la narración de San Lucas: Estudio exegético de Lc 23,33–49 desde la perspective soteriológica Lucana.* Vatican City: Libereria Editrice Vaticana, 2010.

Friedberg, Jennifer P., Sonia Suchday, and Danielle V. Shelov. "The Impact of Forgiveness on Cardiovascular Reactivity and Recovery." *International Journal of Psychophysiology* 65, no. 2 (2007): 87–94.

Garland, David E. *Luke*. Zondervan Exegetical Commentary on the New Testament. Grand Rapids, MI: Zondervan, 2001.

Garvey, Stephen P. "Punishment as Atonement." *UCLA Law Review* 46 (1999): 1801–58.

Giovanni Paolo II (John Paul II). "Le ultime parole di Cristo sulla croce: «Padre, perdona loro...»" Udienza Generale. 16 Novembre 1988. In *Catechesi sul Credo, parte II: Gesù Figlio e Salvatore*. Internet Office, Vatican 2002. http://www.vatican.va/holy_father/john_paul_ii/audiences/1988/documents/hf_jp-ii_aud_19881116_it.html.

Gobodo-Madikizela, Pumla. *A Human Being Died That Night: A South African Story of Forgiveness*. New York: Houghton Mifflin, 2003.

Graybill, Lyn S. *Truth and Reconciliation in South Africa: Miracle or Model?* Boulder, CO: Lunne Rienner Publishers, 2002.

Green, Joel B. *The Gospel of Luke*. NICNT. Grand Rapids, MI: Eerdmans, 1997.

Griswold, Charles. *Forgiveness: A Philosophical Exploration*. New York: Cambridge University Press, 2007.

Grunebaum, Heidi, and Yazir Henri. "Where the Mountain Meets Its Shadow: A Conversation of Memory and Identity and Fragmented Belonging in Present-Day South Africa." in *Homelands: The Politics of Space and the Poetics of Power*, edited by Bo Strath and Ron Robins, 267–83. Brussels: Peter Lang, 2003.

Gulliford, Liz. "Intrapersonal Forgiveness." In *Forgiveness in Context: Theology and Psychology in Creative Dialogue*, edited by Fraser Watts and Liz Gulliford, 83–97. London: T&T Clark International, 2004.

Hägerland, Tobias. *Jesus and the Forgiveness of Sins: An Aspect of His Prophetic Mission.* Cambridge, UK: Cambridge University Press, 2011.

Hahn, Scott, and Curtis Mitch. *The Gospel of Luke: Commentary, Notes, and Study Questions.* Ignatius Catholic Study Bible. Nashville, TN: Thomas Nelson Publishers, 2001.

Hallet, Brien. "To Forgive and Forget?" In *Fear of Persecution: Global Human Rights, International Law, and Human Well-Being*, edited by James D. White and Anthony J. Marsella, 279–86. Lanham, MD: Lexington Books, 2007.

Hamber, Brandon. *Transforming Societies after Political Violence: Truth, Reconciliation, and Mental Health.* Peace Psychology Book Series. London: Springer Science+Business Media, 2009.

Hanna, Edward. "The Sacrament of Penance." In *The Catholic Encyclopedia.* New York: Robert Appleton Company, 1911. http://www.new advent.org/cathen/11618c.htm.

Hansen, Steven E. "Forgiving and Retaining Sin: A Study of the Text and Context of John 20:23." *Horizons in Biblical Theology* 19 (1997): 24–32.

Hare, Douglas R. A. *Matthew.* Interpretation. Louisville, KY: John Knox Press, 1993.

Hargrave, Terry D. "Families and Forgiveness: A Theoretical and Therapeutic Framework." *The Family Journal* 2, no. 4 (1994): 339–48.

Harris, Alex H. S., and Carl E. Thoreson. "Forgiveness, Unforgiveness, Health, and Disease." In *Handbook of Forgiveness*, edited by Everett L. Worthington, 321–33. New York: Routledge, 2005.

Harrison, Jim. "Jesus and the Grace of the Cross: Luke 23.34a and the Politics of 'Forgiveness' in Antiquity." Paper presented at the Annual Meeting of the Society of Biblical Literature. New Orleans, 2009.

Harvey, Robert W., and David G. Benner. *Understanding and Facilitating Forgiveness: A Short-Term Structural Model.* Strategic Pastoral Counseling Resources. Grand Rapids, MI: Baker Books, 1996.

Hayner, Priscilla B. *Unspeakable Truths: Transitional Justice and the Challenge of Truth Commissions.* 2nd ed. New York: Routledge, 2011.

Heathman, Patricia Diann. *Abused but Not Shaken: A Christian Response to Domestic Violence and Abuse.* Pontiac, MI: Voice of the Spirit, 2007.

Henderson, Robert Thornton. *Subversive Jesus, Radical Grace: Relating Christ to a New Generation.* Colorado Springs, CO: NavPress, 2001.

Hendricks, Obery M. *The Politics of Jesus: Rediscovering the True Revolutionary Nature of the Teachings of Jesus and How They Have Been Corrupted.* New York: Three Leaves Press, 2006.

Herman, Judith Lewis. "Justice from the Victim's Perspective." *Violence against Women* 11 (2005): 571–602.

———. *Trauma and Recovery: The Aftermath of Violence—From Domestic Abuse to Political Terror.* New York: Basic Books, 1992.

Herzog, William R. *Prophet and Teacher: An Introduction to the Historical Jesus.* Louisville, KY: Westminster John Knox, 2005.

Holmgren, Margaret R. *Forgiveness and Retribution: Responding to Wrongdoing.* New York: Cambridge University Press, 2012.

Hornsby, Teresa J. *Sex Texts from the Bible: Selections Annotated and Explained.* SkyLight Illumination Series. Woodstock, VT: SkyLight Paths Publishing, 2007.

Horsfield, Peter. "Forgiving Abuse: An Ethical Critique." In *Forgiveness and Abuse: Jewish and Christian Reflections,* edited by Marie M. Fortune and Joretta Marshall, 51–70. New York: The Haworth Press, 2002.

Hull, Margaret Betz. *The Hidden Philosophy of Hannah Arendt.* London: RoutledgeCurzon, 2002.

Hutchison, D. S. "Ethics." In *The Cambridge Companion to Aristotle,* edited by Jonathan Barnes, 195–232. Cambridge, UK: Cambridge University Press, 1995.

Hutchison, John C. "Servanthood: Jesus' Countercultural Call to Christian Leaders." *Bibliotheca Sacra* 166 (2009): 53–69.

Hvidt, Niels Christian. *Christian Prophecy: The Post-Biblical Tradition.* Oxford: Oxford University Press, 2007.

Jacoby, Susan. *Wild Justice: The Evolution of Revenge*. New York: Harper and Row, 1988.

James, Kerrie. "The Interactional Process of Forgiveness and Responsibility: A Critical Assessment of the Family Therapy Literature." In *Hope and Despair in Narrative and Family Therapy: Adversity, Forgiveness, and Reconciliation*, edited by Carmel Flaskas, Imelda McCarthy, and Jim Sheehan, 127–38. New York: Routledge, 2007.

Jeremias, Joachim. *New Testament Theology: The Proclamation of Jesus*. Translated by J. Bowden. New York: Scribner's, 1971.

Johnson, Luke Timothy. *The Gospel of Luke*. SP. Collegeville, MN: The Liturgical Press, 1991.

Jones, L. Gregory. *Embodying Forgiveness: A Theological Analysis*. Grand Rapids, MI: Eerdmans, 1995.

Just, Arthur A., ed. *Ancient Christian Commentary on Scripture: New Testament III: Luke*. Downers Grove, IL: InterVarsity Press, 2003.

Kairos Theologians. *The Kairos Document: Challenge to the Church; A Theological Comment on the Political Crisis in South Africa*. Johannesburg: Skotaville Publishers, 1986.

Karp, Cheryl L., and Traci L. Butler. *Treatment Strategies for Abused Children: From Victim to Survivor*. Interpersonal Violence: The Practice Series 19. Thousand Oaks, CA: Sage Publications, 1996.

Keene, Frederick W. "Structures of Forgiveness in the New Testament." In *Violence against Women and Children: A Christian Theological Sourcebook*, edited by Carol J. Adams and Marie M. Fortune, 121–34. New York: Continuum, 1995.

Keener, Craig S. *The Gospel of John: A Commentary*. 2 vols. Peabody, MA: Hendrickson Publishers, 2003.

Kidder, Annemarie S. *Making Confession, Hearing Confession: A History of the Cure of Souls*. Collegeville, MN: The Liturgical Press, 2010.

Kingsbury, Jack Dean. *Conflict in Luke: Jesus, Authorities, Disciples.* Minneapolis: Augsburg Fortress, 1991.

Klein, Christoph. *Wenn Rache der Vergebung weicht: Theologische Grundlagen einer Kultur der Versöhnung.* Forschungen zur systematischen und ökumenischen Theologie 93. Göttingen: Vandenhoeck & Ruprecht, 1999.

Kluger, Ruth. *Still Alive: A Holocaust Girlhood Remembered.* New York: The Feminist Press, 2001.

Knust, Jennifer Wright. "Jesus' Conditional Forgiveness." In *Ancient Forgiveness: Classical, Judaic, and Christian,* edited by Charles L. Griswold and David Konstan, 176–94. Cambridge, UK: Cambridge University Press, 2011.

Kohen, Ari. "The Personal and the Political: Forgiveness and Reconciliation in Restorative Justice." In *Faculty Publications: Political Science.* Paper 34 (University of Nebraska-Lincoln, 2009): 399–423. http://digital commons.unl.edu/poliscifacpub/34.

Konstan, David. *Before Forgiveness: The Origins of a Moral Idea.* New York: Cambridge University Press, 2010.

Kroeger, Catherine Clark. "Toward a Pastoral Understanding of 1 Peter 3.1–6 and Related Texts." In *A Feminist Companion to the Catholic Epistles and Hebrews,* edited by Amy-Jill Levine with Maria Mayo Robbins, 82–88. London: T&T Clark International, 2004.

Kroeger, Catherine Clark, and Nancy Nason-Clark. *No Place for Abuse: Biblical and Practical Resources to Counteract.* Downers Grove, IL: InterVarsity Press, 2001.

Krog, Antjie. *Country of My Skull: Guilt, Sorrow, and the Limits of Forgiveness in the New South Africa.* New York: Three Rivers Press, 1999.

Kurz, William S. *Reading Luke-Acts: Dynamics of Biblical Narrative.* Louisville, KY: Westminster/John Knox Press, 1993.

Lamb, Sharon. "Constructing the Victim: Popular Images and Lasting Labels." In *New Versions of Victims: Feminists Struggle with the Concept*, edited by Sharon Lamb, 108–38. New York: New York University Press, 1999.

———. "Women, Abuse, and Forgiveness: A Special Case." In *Before Forgiving: Cautionary Views of Forgiveness in Psychotherapy*, edited by Sharon Lamb and Jeffrie G. Murphy, 155–71. Oxford: Oxford University Press, 2002.

Lee, Cameron. *Unexpected Blessing: Living the Countercultural Reality of the Beatitudes*. Downers Grove, IL: InterVarsity Press, 2004.

Leehan, James. *Defiant Hope: Spirituality for Survivors of Family Abuse*. Louisville, KY: Westminster/John Knox Press, 1993.

———. *Pastoral Care for Survivors of Family Abuse*. Louisville, KY: Westminster/John Knox Press, 1989.

Lehner-Hartmann, Andrea. "Familial Violence against Women as a Challenge for Theology and Ethics." in *When 'Love' Strikes: Social Sciences, Ethics and Theology on Family Violence*, edited by Annemie Dillen, 109–30. Leuven: Peeters, 2009.

Lenker, John Nicholas, ed. *Epistles of St. Peter and St. Jude Preached and Explained by Martin Luther, the Hero of the Reformation, the Greatest of the Teuton Church Fathers, and the Father of Protestant Church Literature*. Minneapolis: Lutherans in All Lands Co., 1904.

Lévinas, Emmanuel. *Difficult Freedom: Essays on Judaism*. Translated by Sean Hand. Baltimore, MD: Johns Hopkins University, 1990.

Liebmann, Marian. *Restorative Justice: How It Works*. London: Jessica Kingsley Publishers, 2007.

Lippman, Matthew. *Contemporary Criminal Law: Concepts, Cases, and Controversies*. 2nd ed. Thousand Oaks, CA: Sage Publications, 2010.

Llewellyn, Jennifer. "Restorative Justice and Truth Commissions." In *Handbook of Restorative Justice*, edited by Gerry Johnstone and Daniel W. Van Ness, 351–71. Portland, OR: Willan Publishing, 2007.

Long, Thomas G. *Matthew*. Westminster Bible Companion. Louisville, KY: Westminster John Knox Press, 1997.

Lundquist, Mark-Peter. "Beaten into Submission." *The Clergy Journal* 77, no. 8 (2001): 13–14.

Luter, A. Boyd. "Repentance (New Testament)." In *ABD* 5:672–74.

Luther, Martin. *Commentary on the Sermon on the Mount*. Translated by Charles A. Hay. Philadelphia: Lutheran Publication Society, 1892.

———. *Luther's Works: Church and Ministry II*. Luther's Works 40. Translated and edited by Conrad Bergendoff. Philadelphia: Muhlenberg Press, 1958.

———. *Sermons on the Most Interesting Doctrines of the Gospel*. Translated by J. Thornton. London: Paternoster-Row, 1830.

———. *Sermons on the Passion of Christ*. Translated by J. T. Isensee. Rock Island, IL: Lutheran Augustana Book Concern, 1871.

Mac Ginty, Roger, and Andrew Williams. *Conflict and Development*. Routledge Perspectives on Development. New York: Routledge, 2009.

Macholz, Christian. "Das Passivum divinum: Seine Anfänge im Alten Testament und der 'Hofstil.'" *ZNW* 81 (1990): 247–53.

Mali, Joseph F. *The Christian Gospel and Its Jewish Roots: A Redaction-Critical Study of Mark 2:21–22 in Context*. New York: Peter Lang, 2009.

Mallicoat, Stacy L. *Women and Crime: A Text/Reader*. Los Angeles, CA: Sage Publications, 2012.

Manemann, Juergen. "Anthropological Remarks on Reconciliation after Auschwitz (Response)." In *After-words: Post-Holocaust Struggles with Forgiveness, Reconciliation, Justice*, edited by David Patterson and John K. Roth, 128–31. The Pastora Goldner Series in Post-Holocaust Studies. Seattle: University of Washington Press, 2004.

Marshall, Christopher D. *Beyond Retribution: A New Testament Vision for Justice, Crime, and Punishment.* Studies in Peace and Scripture. Grand Rapids, MI: Eerdmans, 2001.

———. *Compassionate Justice: An Interdisciplinary Dialogue with Two Gospel Parables on Law, Crime, and Restorative Justice.* Theopolitical Visions 15. Eugene, OR: Cascade Books, 2012.

Marshall, I. Howard. *The Gospel of Luke: A Commentary on the Greek Text.* NIGTC. Grand Rapids, MI: Eerdmans, 1978.

———. *Luke: Historian and Theologian.* Downers Grove, IL: The Paternoster Press, 1970.

———. "Mutual Love and Submission in Marriage: Colossians 3:18–19 and Ephesians 5:21–33." In *Discovering Biblical Equality: Complementarity without Hierarchy*, edited by Ronald W. Pierce and Rebecca Merrill Groothuis, 186–204. Downers Grove, IL: InterVarsity Press, 2005.

Martin, Dale B. *Sex and the Single Savior: Gender and Sexuality in Biblical Interpretation.* Louisville, KY: Westminster John Knox Press, 2006.

Matthews, Shelly. "Clemency as Cruelty: Forgiveness and Force in the Dying Prayers of Jesus and Stephen." *BibInt* 17 (2009): 118–46.

———. *Perfect Martyr: The Stoning of Stephen and the Construction of Christian Identity.* Oxford: Oxford University Press, 2010.

Mayo, Maria. "Seventy Times Seven." In *The Dictionary of the Bible and Western Culture: A Handbook for Students*, edited by Michael Gilmour and Mary Ann Beavis, 482–83. Sheffield, UK: Sheffield Phoenix Press, 2012.

McClure, Barbara. "Pastoral Care." *The Wiley-Blackwell Companion to Practical Theology*, edited by Bonnie Miller-McLemore, 269–78. Malden, MA: Blackwell, 2012.

McCullough, Michael E., Kenneth I. Pargament, and Carl E. Thoresen. "The Psychology of Forgiveness: History, Conceptual Issues, and Overview." In *Forgiveness: Theory, Research, and Practice*, edited by M. E. McCullough,

K. I. Pargament, and C. E. Thoresen, 1–14. New York: Guilford Press, 2000.

Meiring, Piet. "The *Baruti* versus the Lawyers: The Role of Religion in the TRC Process." In *Looking Back Reaching Forward: Reflections on the Truth and Reconciliation Commission of South Africa*, edited by Charles Villa-Vicencio and Wilhelm Verwoerd, 123–31. Cape Town: University of Cape Town Press, 2000.

———. "Truth and Reconciliation in South Africa: The Role of the Faith Communities." *Verbum et Ecclesia* 26, no. 1 (2005): 146–173.

Merry, Sally Engle. "Mennonite Peacebuilding and Conflict Transformation." In *From the Ground Up: Mennonite Contributions to International Peacebuilding*, edited by Cynthia Sampson and John Paul Lederach, 203–17. Oxford: Oxford University Press, 2000.

Metzger, Bruce. *A Textual Commentary on the Greek New Testament.* 2nd ed. New York: United Bible Societies, 1994.

Milavec, Aaron. *The Didache: Text, Translation, Analysis, and Commentary.* Collegeville, MN: The Liturgical Press, 2003.

Miller-McLemore, Bonnie J. *Christian Theology in Practice: Discovering a Discipline.* Grand Rapids, MI: Eerdmans, 2012.

Mills, Liston. "Pastoral Care." In *The Concise Dictionary of Pastoral Care and Counseling*, edited by Glenn H. Asquith, 836–44. Nashville, TN: Abingdon Press, 2010.

Minow, Martha. *Between Vengeance and Forgiveness: Facing History after Genocide and Mass Violence.* Boston, MA: Beacon Press, 1998.

Mitchell, Juliann, and Jill Morse. *From Victims to Survivors: Reclaimed Voices of Women Sexually Abused in Childhood by Females.* Washington, DC: Taylor & Francis, 1998.

Mollenkott, Virginia Ramey. "Emancipative Elements in Ephesians 5:21–33: Why Feminist Scholarship Has (Often) Left Them Unmentioned, and Why They Should Be Emphasized." In *A Feminist Companion to the*

Deutero-Pauline Epistles, edited by Amy-Jill Levine with Marianne Blickenstaff, 29–38. (London: T&T Clark International, 2003.

Moloney, Francis J. *The Gospel of John*. Sacra Pagina. Collegeville, MN: The Liturgical Press, 1998.

Moon, Claire. *Narrating Political Reconciliation: South Africa's Truth and Reconciliation Commission*. Lanham, MD: Lexington Books, 2008.

Morris, Leon. *The Gospel according to John*. The New International Critical Commentary on the New Testament. Grand Rapids, MI: Eerdmans, 1995.

———. *Luke: An Introduction and Commentary*. TNTC. Grand Rapids, MI: Eerdmans, 2002.

Morton, Adam. "What Is Forgiveness?" In *Ancient Forgiveness: Classical, Judaic, and Christian*, edited by Charles L. Griswold and David Konstan, 1–14. Cambridge, UK: Cambridge University Press, 2011.

Mueller, E., ed. *Luther's Explanatory Notes on the Gospels*. Translated by P. Anstadt. York, PA: P. Anstadt & Sons, 1899.

Müller-Fahrenholz, Geiko. *Vergebung macht frei: Vorschläge für eine Theologie der Versöhnung*. Frankfurt-am-Main: Lembeck Verlag, 1996.

Murphy, Colleen. *A Moral Theory of Political Reconciliation*. Cambridge, UK: Cambridge University Press, 2010.

Murphy, Jeffrie G. "Forgiveness and Resentment." In Jeffrie G. Murphy and Jean Hampton, *Forgiveness and Mercy*, 14–34. Cambridge Studies in Philosophy and Law. Cambridge, UK: Cambridge University Press, 1998.

———. *Punishment and the Moral Emotions: Essays in Law, Morality, and Religion*. Oxford: Oxford University Press, 2012.

Musekura, Célestin. *An Assessment of Contemporary Models of Forgiveness*. American University Studies VII; Theology and Religion 302. New York: Peter Lang, 2010.

Nason-Clark, Nancy. *The Battered Wife: How Christians Confront Family Violence*. Louisville, KY: Westminster John Knox Press, 1997.

———. "Christianity and Domestic Violence." In *Encyclopedia of Domestic Violence*, edited by Nicky Ali Jackson, 161–66. New York: Routledge, 2007.

Nave, Guy D. *The Role and Function of Repentance in Luke-Acts*. Atlanta, GA: Society of Biblical Literature, 2002.

Neuger, Christie Cozad. "Narratives of Harm: Setting the Developmental Context for Intimate Violence." In *In Her Own Time: Women and Developmental Issues in Pastoral Care*, edited by Jeanne Stevenson-Moessner, 65–86. Minneapolis: Augsburg Fortress, 2000.

Nienhuis, Nancy. "Thinking Theologically about Violence and Abuse." *Journal of Pastoral Care and Counseling* 59, nos. 1–2 (2005): 109–23.

Nietzsche, Friedrich. *On the Genealogy of Morals and Ecce Homo*. Edited and translated by Walter Kaufmann. New York: Vintage, 1989.

Noll, Jennie C. "Forgiveness in People Experiencing Trauma." In *Handbook of Forgiveness*, edited by Everett L. Worthington, 363–75. New York: Routledge, 2005.

Nolland, John S. *The Gospel of Matthew: A Commentary on the Greek Text*. NIGCT. Grand Rapids, MI: Eerdmans, 2005.

Norlock, Kathryn. *Forgiveness from a Feminist Perspective*. Lanham, MD: Lexington Books, 2009.

North, Joanna. "Wrongdoing and Forgiveness." *Philosophy* 62 (1987): 499–508.

O'Hara, Erin, and Maria Mayo Robbins. "Using Criminal Punishment to Serve Both Victim and Social Needs." *Law and Contemporary Problems* 72, no. 2 (Fall 2009): 199–218.

Padgett, Alan G. *As Christ Submits to the Church: A Biblical Understanding of Leadership and Mutual Submission*. Grand Rapids, MI: Baker Academic, 2011.

Pavlich, George. *Governing Paradoxes of Restorative Justice*. London: GlassHouse Press, 2005.

Phatathi, Timothy Sizwe, and Hugo van der Merwe. "The Impact of the TRC's Amnesty Process on Survivors of Human Rights Violations." In *Truth and Reconciliation in South Africa: Did the TRC Deliver?*, edited by Audrey R. Chapman and Hugo van der Merwe, 116–42. Pennsylvania Studies in Human Rights. Philadelphia: University of Pennsylvania Press, 2008.

Philpott, Daniel. *Just and Unjust Peace: An Ethic of Political Reconciliation*. Oxford: Oxford University Press, 2012.

Pilch, John J. "Family Violence in Cross-Cultural Perspective: An Approach for Feminist Interpreters of the Bible." In *A Feminist Companion to Reading the Bible*, edited by Athalya Brenner and Carole Rader Fontaine, 306–25. Sheffield, UK: Sheffield Academic Press, 1997.

Pink, Arthur W. *The Beatitudes and the Lord's Prayer*. Grand Rapids, MI: Baker Books, 1979.

Poling, James Newton. "Preaching to Perpetrators of Violence." In *Telling the Truth: Preaching about Sexual and Domestic Violence*, edited by John S. McClure and Nancy J. Ramsay, 71–82. Cleveland, OH: United Church Press, 1998.

———. *Understanding Male Violence: Pastoral Care Issues*. St. Louis, MO: Chalice Press, 2003.

Poling, Nancy Werking, and Marie M. Fortune, eds. *Victim to Survivor: Women Recovering from Clergy Sexual Abuse*. Eugene, OR: Wipf & Stock, 2009.

Price, Marty. "Personalizing Crime: Mediation Produces Restorative Justice for Victims and Offenders." *Dispute Resolution Magazine*, Fall 2001. http://www.vorp.com/articles/justice.html.

Price, Marty D. "Victim-Offender Mediation: The State of the Art." *VOMA Quarterly* 7, no. 3 (1996): 1.

Ptacek, James. "Resisting Co-optation: Three Feminist Challenges to Antiviolence Work." In *Restorative Justice and Violence against Women*, edited by James Ptacek, 5–38. Interpersonal Violence. Oxford: Oxford University Press, 2010.

Radzik, Linda. *Making Amends: Atonement in Morality, Law, and Politics.* Oxford: Oxford University Press, 2009.

Ramsay, Nancy J. "Confronting Family Violence and Its Spiritual Damage." *Family Ministry* 20, no. 3 (2006): 28–40.

Ransley, Cynthia, and Terri Spy. *Forgiveness and the Healing Process: A Central Therapeutic Concern.* New York: Routledge, 2004.

Regehr, Keith Allen. "Judgment and Forgiveness: Restorative Justice Practice and the Recovery of Theological Memory." PhD diss., University of Waterloo, 2007.

Roche, Declan. *Accountability in Restorative Justice.* Clarendon Studies in Criminology. Oxford: Oxford University Press, 2003.

Ross, Robert. *A Concise History of South Africa.* 2nd ed. Cambridge Concise Histories. Cambridge, UK: Cambridge University Press, 2008.

Roth, S. John. "Jesus the Pray-er." *Currents in Theology and Mission* 33, no. 6 (2006): 488–500.

Rubio, Miguel. "The Christian Virtue of Forgiveness." In *Forgiveness*, edited by Casiano Floristan and Christian Duquoc, 80–84. Concilium. Edinburgh: T&T Clark, 1986.

Sadler, Gregory. "Forgiveness, Anger, and Virtue in an Aristotelian Perspective." *Proceedings of the American Catholic Philosophical Association* 82 (2008): 229–47.

Sampson, Anthony. *Mandela: The Authorized Biography.* New York: Random House, 1999.

Sanders, Benjamin E., and Mary B. Meinig. "Immediate Issues Affecting Long-term Family Resolution in Cases of Parent-Child Sexual Abuse." In *Treatment of Child Abuse: Common Ground for Mental Health, Medical, and Legal Practitioners*, edited by Robert M. Reece, 36–53. Baltimore, MD: The Johns Hopkins University Press, 2000.

Sanford, Peter. "Out of Africa." *Catholic Herald*, January 30, 2004. http://archive.catholicherald.co.uk/article/30th-january-2004/7/ut-of-frica.

Scheiber, Karin. *Vergebung: Eine systematisch-theologische Untersuchung.* Religion in Philosophy and Theology 21. Tübingen: Mohr Siebeck, 2006.

Scherer-Emunds, Meinrad. "No Forgiveness, No Future: An Interview with Archbishop Desmond Tutu." *U.S. Catholic* 65, no. 8 (2000): 24–28.

Schmidt, Janet P. "The Offender's Journey." In *Victim Offender Conferencing in Pennsylvania's Juvenile Justice System*, by Lorraine Stutzman Amstutz and Howard Zehr, 17–20. 1998. http://www.emu.edu/cjp/publications/faculty-staff/rjmanual.pdf.

Schweitzer, Carol L. Schnabl. "Violence against Women and Children: How Churches Can Respond." *Word & World* 24, no. 1 (2004): 66–73.

Selebi, Mogomotsi. "It's Not Easy to Forgive." *Sowetan Live*, January 8, 2013, http://www.sowetanlive.co.za/news/2013/01/08/it-s-not-easy-to-forgive.

Senior, Donald. *The Passion of Jesus in the Gospel of Luke.* Collegeville, MN: The Liturgical Press, 1989.

Shogren, Gary S. "Forgiveness (NT)." In *ABD* 2:835–38.

Shore, Megan. *Religion and Conflict Resolution: Christianity and South Africa's Truth and Reconciliation Commission.* Burlington, VT: Ashgate Publishing, 2009.

Simpson, Graeme, "'Tell No Lies, Claim No Easy Victories': A Brief Evaluation of South Africa's Truth and Reconciliation Commission." In *Commissioning the Past: Understanding South Africa's Truth and Reconciliation Commission*, edited by Deborah Posel and Graeme Simpson, 220–51. Johannesburg: Witwatersrand University Press, 2002.

Smedes, Lewis B. *The Art of Forgiving: When You Need to Forgive and Don't Know How.* New York: Random House, 1996.

———. *Forgive and Forget: Healing the Hurts We Don't Deserve.* New York: HarperCollins, 1984.

Smith, Carol Klose, and Darcy Davis-Gage. "The Quiet Storm: Explaining the Cultural Context of Violence against Women within a Feminist Perspective." In *A Cry instead of Justice: The Bible and Cultures of Violence in Psychological Perspective*, edited by Dereck Daschke and Andrew Kille, 107–30. LHBOTS 499. New York: T&T Clark International, 2010.

Smith, David. "Desmond Tutu Attacks South African Government over Dalai Lama Ban." *The Guardian*, October 4, 2011. http://www.guardian.co.uk/world/2011/oct/04/tutu-attacks-anc-dalai-lama-visa.

Smith, Nick. *I Was Wrong: The Meanings of Apologies.* New York: Cambridge University Press, 2008.

Smock, David. "The Process of Forgiveness." In *No Enemy to Conquer: Forgiveness in an Unforgiving World*, by Michael Henderson, 24–30. Waco, TX: Baylor University Press, 2009.

Smyth, Geraldine. "Brokenness, Forgiveness, Healing, and Peace in Ireland." In *Forgiveness and Reconciliation: Religion, Public Policy, and Conflict Transformation*, edited by Raymond G. Helmick and Rodney L. Peterson, 319–50. Philadelphia: Templeton Foundation, 2001.

Sparks, Allister, and Mpho Tutu. *Tutu: Authorized.* New York: HarperOne, 2011.

Standhartinger, Angela. "The Epistle to the Congregation in Colossae and the Invention of the 'Household Code.'" In *A Feminist Companion to the Deutero-Pauline Epistles*, edited by Amy-Jill Levine with Marianne Blickenstaff, 88–97. London: T&T Clark International, 2003.

Stanton, G. N. *Jesus of Nazareth in New Testament Preaching.* SNTSMS 27. Cambridge, UK: Cambridge University Press, 1974.

Stein, Robert H. *Luke.* NAC 24. Nashville, TN: B & H Publishing Group, 1992.

Strahan, Joshua Marshall. *The Limits of a Text: Luke 23:34a as a Case Study in Theological Interpretation.* JTISup 5. Winona Lake, IN: Eisenbrauns, 2012.

Strang, Heather. "Is Restorative Justice Imposing Its Agenda on Victims?" In *Critical Issues in Restorative Justice,* Howard Zehr and Barb Toew, 95–106. Monsey, NY: Criminal Justice Press, 2004.

———. "Justice for Victims of Young Offenders: The Centrality of Emotional Harm and Restoration." In *Restorative Justice for Juveniles: Conferencing, Mediation and Circles,* edited by A. Morris and G. Maxwell, 184–93. Oxford: Hart Publishing, 2001.

———. *Repair or Revenge? Victims and Restorative Justice* Oxford: Clarendon Press, 2002.

Szmania, Susan Jennnifer. "Beginning Difficult Conversations: An Analysis of Opening Statements in Victim Offender Mediation/Dialogue." PhD diss., University of Texas at Austin, 2004.

Tannehill, Robert C. *The Narrative Unity of Luke-Acts: A Literary Interpretation.* Vol. 1, *The Gospel of Luke.* Minneapolis: Fortress Press, 1986.

Thompson, W. G. *Matthew's Advice to a Divided Community.* Rome: Biblical Institute Press, 1970.

Tjaden, P., and N. Thoennes. *Extent, Nature, and Consequences of Intimate Partner Violence: Findings from the National Violence against Women Survey.* Publication No. NCJ 181867. Washington, DC: Department of Justice, 2000. https://www.ncjrs.gov/pdffiles1/nij/181867.pdf.

Toussaint, Loren, and Jon R. Webb. "Theoretical and Empirical Connections between Forgiveness, Mental Health, and Well-Being." In *Handbook of Forgiveness,* edited by Everett L. Worthington, 349–62. New York: Routledge, 2005.

Truth and Reconciliation Commission of South Africa Report. 7 vols. Cape Town: Juta, 1998. http://www.justice.gov.za/trc/report/index.htm.

Tuckett, C. M. "Luke 22,43–44: The 'Agony' in the Garden and Luke's Gospel." In *New Testament Textual Criticism and Exegesis: Festschrift J. Delobel*, edited by A. Denaux, 97–130. BETL 161. Leuven: Leuven University Press, 2002.

Tullis, Paul. "Can Forgiveness Play a Role in Criminal Justice?" *New York Times Magazine*, January 4, 2013, 28–38.

Tutu, Desmond. "Black South African Perspectives and the Reagan Administration." In *Hope and Suffering: Sermons and Speeches*, 103–17. Grand Rapids, MI: Eerdmans, 1984.

———. "Faith and the Problem of Evil and Suffering." In *Belief: Readings on the Reason for Faith*, edited by Francis S. Collins, 148–56. New York: HarperOne, 2010.

———. "The Divine Intention (1982)." In *Hope and Suffering: Sermons and Speeches*, 153–89. Grand Rapids, MI: Eerdmans, 1984.

———. "Foreword." In *Forgiveness and Reconciliation: Religion, Public Policy, and Conflict Transformation*, edited by Raymond G. Helmick and Rodney L. Peterson, ix–xiv. Philadelphia: Templeton Foundation, 2001.

———. "Foreword by Chairperson." In *Truth and Reconciliation Commission of South Africa Report*. Vol. 1, 1–23. Cape Town: Juta, 1998.

———. *God Has a Dream: A Vision of Hope for Our Time.* New York: Doubleday, 2004.

———. *God Is Not a Christian: And Other Provocations.* New York: HarperOne, 2011.

———. Interview by Marina Cantacuzino for The Forgiveness Project, London, UK, June 1, 2003. http://theforgivenessproject.com/stories/desmond-tutu-south-africa/.

————. "Nobel Lecture, December 11, 1984." In *Nobel Lectures, Peace 1981–1990*, edited by Tore Frängsmyr and Irwin Abrams, 115–21. Singapore: World Scientific Publishing Co., Singapore, 1997.

————. *No Future without Forgiveness*. New York: Doubleday, 1999.

————. *The Rainbow People of God: The Making of a Peaceful Revolution*. Edited by John Allen. New York: Doubleday, 1994.

————. "The Role of the Church in South Africa (1981)." In *Hope and Suffering: Sermons and Speeches*, 74–87. Grand Rapids, MI: Eerdmans, 1984.

————. "The Role of White Opposition in South Africa." In *Hope and Suffering: Sermons and Speeches*, 118–24. Grand Rapids, MI: Eerdmans, 1984.

————. "The Story of Exodus 2 (1978)." In *Hope and Suffering: Sermons and Speeches*, 48–87. Grand Rapids, MI: Eerdmans, 1984.

————. Symposium contribution in *The Sunflower: On the Possibilities and Limits of Forgiveness*, by Simon Wiesenthal, 266–68. Rev. and exp. ed. New York: Schocken Books, 1998.

————. "Without Forgiveness There Is No Future." in *Exploring Forgiveness*, edited by Robert D. Enright and Joanna North, xiii–xiv. Madison: University of Wisconsin Press, 1998.

Umbreit, Mark S. *The Handbook of Victim-Offender Mediation*. San Francisco: Jossey-Bass, 2001.

————. *National Survey of Victim-Offender Mediation Programs in the United States*. Office for Victims of Crime, NCJ 176350. St. Paul, MN: Center for Restorative Justice & Peacemaking, 2000.

————. *Victim Meets Offender: The Impact of Restorative Justice and Mediation*. Criminal Justice Press. Monsey, NY: Willow Tree Press, 1994.

Umbreit, Mark S., Betty Vos, Robert B. Coates, and Katherine A. Brown. *Facing Violence: The Path of Restorative Justice and Dialogue*. Monsey, NY: Criminal Justice Press, 2003.

———. "Victim-Offender Dialogue in Violent Cases: A Multi-Site Study in the United States." In *Restorative Justice: Politics, Policies and Prospects*, edited by E. van der Spuy, S. Parmentier, and A. Dissel, 22–39. Cape Town: Juta, 2008.

Umbreit, Mark S., and Jean Greenwood. *Guidelines for Victim-Sensitive Victim-Offender Mediation: Restorative Justice through Dialogue*. U.S. Dept. of Justice, Office for Victims of Crime, NCJ 176346. St. Paul, MN: Center for Restorative Justice and Peacemaking, 2000.

Umbreit, Mark S., William Bradshaw, and Robert B. Coates. "Victims of Severe Violence in Dialogue with the Offender: Key Principles, Practices, Outcomes and Implications." In *Restorative Justice in Context: International Practice and Directions*, edited by Elmar G. M. Weitekamp and Hans-Jürgen Kerner, 123–44. Portland, OR: Willan Publishing, 2003.

Umbreit, Mark S., and Marilyn Armour. "The Paradox of Forgiveness in Restorative Justice." In *The Handbook of Forgiveness*, edited by Everett L. Worthington, 491–502. New York: Routledge, 2005.

———. *Restorative Justice Dialogue: An Essential Guide for Research and Practice*. New York: Springer Publishing Company, 2011.

United Nations General Assembly. "The Policies of Apartheid of the Government of South Africa." December 2, 1968, A/RES/2396. http://www.unhcr.org/refworld/docid/3b00f1d74.html.

United States Conference of Catholic Bishops (USCCB). "When I Call for Help: A Pastoral Response to Domestic Violence against Women." 2002. http://www.usccb.org/issues-and-action/marriage-and-family/marriage/domestic-violence/when-i-call-for-help.cfm.

Van de Loo, Stephanie. *Versöhnungsarbeit: Kriterien—theologischer Rahmen—Praxisperspektiven*. Theologie und Frieden. Stuttgart: W. Kolhammer, 2009.

Van Dijk, Jan. "In the Shadow of Christ? On the Use of the Word 'Victim' for Those Affected by Crime." *Criminal Justice Ethics* 14 (2008): 13–24.

Van Ness, Daniel W. *Crime and Its Victims*. Downers Grove, IL: InterVarsity Press, 1986.

Verdeja, Ernesto. *Unchopping a Tree: Reconciliation in the Aftermath of Political Violence*. Philadelphia, PA: Temple University Press, 2009.

Verdoolaege, Annelies. "The Human Rights Violations Hearings of the South African TRC: A Bridge between Individual Narratives of Suffering and a Contextualizing Master-Story of Reconciliation." Ghent University, Belgium, 2002. http://cas1.elis.ugent.be/avrug/trc/02_08.htm.

———. *Reconciliation Discourse: The Case of the Truth and Reconciliation Commission*. Discourse Approaches to Politics, Society and Culture. Amsterdam: John Benjamins Publishing Company, 2008.

———. "Reconciliation: The South African Truth and Reconciliation Commission; Deconstruction of a Multilayered Archive." PhD diss., Universiteit Gent, 2005.

Vogel, Howard J. "The Restorative Justice Wager: The Promise and Hope of a Value-Based, Dialogue-Driven Approach to Conflict Resolution for Social Healing." *Cardozo Journal of Conflict Resolution* 8 (2007): 565–609.

Volf, Miroslav. *Exclusion and Embrace: A Theological Exploration of Identity, Otherness, and Reconciliation*. Nashville, TN: Abingdon Press, 1996.

———. *Free of Charge: Giving and Forgiving in a Culture Stripped of Grace*. Grand Rapids, MI: Zondervan, 2005.

Waldmeir, Patty. *Anatomy of a Miracle: The End of Apartheid and the Birth of the New South Africa*. New York: W. W. Norton & Co., 1997.

Walgrave, Lode. *Restorative Justice, Self-Interest, and Responsible Citizenship*. Cullompton, UK: Willan Publishing, 2008.

Walker, Margaret Urban. *Moral Repair: Reconstructing Moral Relations after Wrongdoing*. New York: Cambridge University Press, 2006.

Walker, Thomas W. *Luke*. Interpretation Bible Studies. Louisville, KY: Westminster John Knox, 2001.

Wallace, David B. *Greek Grammar beyond the Basics: An Exegetical Syntax of the New Testament.* Grand Rapids, MI: Zondervan, 1996.

Waltman, Martina Antonia. "The Psychological and Physiological Effects of Forgiveness Education in Male Patients with Coronary Artery Disease." PhD diss., University of Wisconsin-Madison, 2002.

Wenger, Andrea Schrock. "How Does a Congregation Deal with a Triple Murder?" *Gospel Herald*, February 9, 1993, 6–8.

White, Mary. "Every Knee Shall Bow." In *God and the Victim: Theological Reflections on Evil, Victimization, Justice, and Forgiveness*, edited by Lisa Barnes Lampman and Michelle D. Shattuck, 183–98. Grand Rapids, MI: Eerdsman, 1999.

Whitlark, Jason, and Mikeal Parsons. "The 'Seven' Last Words: A Numerical Motivation for the Insertion of Luke 23:34a." *NTS* 52 (2006): 188–204.

Williamson, Lamar. *Mark.* IBC. Louisville, KY: John Knox Press, 1983.

Willimon, William H. "Following Jesus." *Christian Century* 102, no. 8 (March 3, 1985): 236–37.

Wilson, Richard A. *The Politics of Truth and Reconciliation in South Africa: Legitimizing the Post-Apartheid State.* Cambridge Studies in Law and Society. Cambridge: Cambridge University Press, 2001.

Wilson, Stuart. "The Myth of Restorative Justice: Truth, Reconciliation and the Ethics of Amnesty." *South African Journal of Human Rights* 17 (2001): 531–62.

Witherington, Ben. *The Gospel of Mark: A Socio-rhetorical Commentary.* Grand Rapids, MI: Eerdmans, 2001.

Witvliet, Charlotte Vanoyen. "Forgiveness and Health: Review and Reflections on a Matter of Faith, Feelings, and Physiology." *Journal of Psychology and Theology* 29 (2001): 212–24.

Worthington, Everett L. "Initial Questions about the Art and Science of Forgiving." In *Handbook of Forgiveness*, edited by Everett L. Worthington, 1–14. New York: Routledge, 2005.

———. "The Pyramid Model of Forgiveness: Some Interdisciplinary Speculations about Unforgiveness and the Promotion of Forgiveness." In *Dimensions of Forgiveness: A Research Approach*, 107–38. Radnor, PA: Temple Foundation Press, 1998.

Wright, Martin. "Victim-Offender Mediation as a Step towards a Restorative System of Justice." In *Restorative Justice on Trial: Pitfalls and Potentials of Victim-Offender Mediation—International Research Perspectives*, edited by Heinz Messmer and Hans-Uwe Otto, 525–40. Dordrecht, The Netherlands: Kluwer Academic Publishers, 1992.

Wright, N. T. *The Challenge of Jesus: Rediscovering Who Jesus Was and Is.* Downers Grove, IL: InterVarsity Press, 1999.

Wright, Oliver. "Desmond Tutu Quits Summit with Tony Blair over Invasion of Iraq." *The Independent*, August 29, 2012. http://www.independent.co.uk/news/world/politics/desmond-tutu-quits-summit-with-tony-blair-over-invasion-of-iraq-8084805.html.

Wright, Tom. *The Original Jesus: The Life and Vision of a Revolutionary.* Oxford: Lion Publishing, 1996.

Zahnd, Brian. *Unconditional? The Call of Jesus to Radical Forgiveness.* Lake Mary, FL: Charisma House, 2010.

Zehr, Howard. *Changing Lenses: A New Focus for Crime and Justice.* Christian Peace Shelf. Scottsdale, PA: Herald Press, 1990.

———. *The Little Book of Restorative Justice.* The Little Books of Justice and Peacemaking. Intercourse, PA: Good Books, 2002.

———. "Restoring Justice." In *God and the Victim: Theological Reflections on Evil, Victimization, Justice, and Forgiveness*, edited by Lisa Barnes Lampman and Michelle D. Shattuck, 131–59. Grand Rapids, MI: Eerdmans, 1999.

Zerbe, Gordon M. *Non-Retaliation in Early Jewish and New Testament Texts: Ethical Themes in Social Contexts.* Sheffield, UK: Sheffield Academic Press, 1993.

Index of Authors

Acorn, Annalise, 82, 89, 92, 95, 134

Adams, Carol J., 194

Alexandria, Cyril of, 115, 117

Amstutz, Mark R., 100

Anderson, Gary, 11–12

Arendt, Hannah, 17–21

Armour, Marilyn Peterson, 77–78, 84

Arnold, Johann Christoph, 59

Augsburger, David W., 58

Augustine, 115, 118–19, 173

Ayo, Nicholas, 117–18

Barker, James W., 34

Battle, Michael, 123

Bauman-Martin, Betsy J., 190

Baumeister, Roy F., 37

Benner, David G., 191

Bhargava, Rejeev, 149

Bock, Darrell, 108

Boesak, Allan Aubrey, 122

Bonhoeffer, Dietrich, 120

Boraine, Alex, 133

Braithwaite, John, 76, 80

Brown, Raymond E., 183, 204

Brudholm, Thomas, 129, 132, 146

Brunk, Conrad G., 71

Bussert, Joy M.K., 191

Butler, Joseph, 21–22

Calvin, John, 57, 116–17

Carter, Warren, 11

Chapman, Audrey R., 127

Chrysostom, John, 55–56, 173

Clark, Ron, 183, 196

Clement, 173

Cooper-White, Pamela, 195

Costin, Teodor, 60

Crossan, John Dominic, 118

Cury, Augusto, 183

Cyprian, 109

Davies and Allison, 55

Davis-Gage, Darcy, 197

Dewey, Joanna, 189

DeYoung, Curtiss Paul, 122

Enright, Robert D., 23

Esack, Farid, 122

Exline, Julie Juloa, 37

Fortune, Marie M., 192

Garvey, Stephen P., 78–79

Ginty, Roger Mac, 155–56

Graybil, Lyn, 124, 134

Greenwood, Jean, 63

Griswold, Charles L., 24–25

Grøe, Arne, 132

Hanna, Edward, 111

Harrison, Jim, 179

Harvey, Robert W., 191

Heathman, Patricia Dianna, 191

Henderson, Michael, 183

Herman, Judith Lewis, 4, 91–92

Holmgren, Margaret, 71–72, 93

Horsfield, Peter, 197, 200

Irenaeus, 173–74

Jacoby, Susan, 91

Jones, L. Gregory, 17–18, 20–22, 29

Keene, Frederick W., 175–76

Kidder, Annemarie S., 111

Klein, Christoph, 52–53

Kluger, Ruth, 139

Knust, 178

Konstan, David, 3, 11–12, 211

Leehan, James, 192

Lou-Clarke, Rita, 196

Luther, Martin, 56–57, 116–17, 174

Marshall, Christopher D., 66, 68, 74–75

Matthews, Shelly, 178

Metzger, Bruce, 202

Miller-McLemore, Bonnie, 188

Mills, Liston, 187

Minow, Martha, 92

Moon, Claire, 151–53

Murphy, Colleen, 150–52

Murphy, Jeffrie, 133, 146

Nason-Clark, Nancy, 162

Nienhuis, Nancy, 191, 193

Nietzsche, Friedrich, 72, 177

North, Joanna, 24

Pavlich, George, 86–88

Pink, Arthur W., 117

Ptacek, James, 70

Ransley, Cynthia, 37
Regehr, Keith Allen, 83
Roche, Declan, 71, 89
Roth, S. John, 175

Sadler, Gregory, 73
Savage, Beth, 125
Schmidt, Janet P., 80
Simpson, Graeme, 146
Smedes, Lewis B., 26–29, 58
Smith, Carol Klose, 197
Spy, Terri, 37
Strang, Heather, 78

Tannehill, Robert, 202
Tertullian, 115
Thomas Aquinas (St.), 109–10
Tutu, Desmond, 5, 40, 42, 76, 99,
    101–7, 118–19, 121–22,
    124–25, 128, 131–32, 134,

136–37, 139–45, 147–48,
    150–51, 157

Umbreit, Mark, 49, 63, 77–78,
    81–85

van de Loo, Stephanie, 68–69,
    72–73
Verdeia, Ernesto, 149, 153–54
Volf, Miroslav, 22, 36, 182

Walgrave, Lode, 74
Walker, Margaret Urban, 45–46,
    91
Wenger, Andrea Schrock, 48
Williams, Andrew, 155–56
Worthington, Everett L., 29

Zehr, Howard, 48, 63–65, 68, 76,
    90

Index of Scripture References

Genesis
4:24......52

Leviticus
19:17......55
19:18......64
24:16......64
24:19-20......64

Isaiah
53:5......189

Matthew
4:20......15
6:9-13......2, 6–8, 40, 108, 185
6:12......10, 12, 32–33, 104, 112
6:14-15......7–8, 14, 16, 112
6:37-38......14
9:2-8......7, 52
12:31......199
12:32......8, 12, 16, 35
18:6......19

18:15-20......9, 32, 34, 50, 53–55, 188, 198–99
18:21......2, 6–9, 16, 33, 37, 49, 51, 53, 66, 145, 166, 170, 185
18:22......6, 16, 110, 185
18:23-35......7–8, 10, 16, 27, 33–34, 57, 60, 114
21:12-17......147
23:13-15......147
23:33......147
27:46......28, 181

Mark
2:2-12......52
3:29......12, 16, 35, 199
4:36......15
10:13-15......147
11:13-19......147
11:25......7–8, 113
15:11-32......22–23, 27
15:34......181

Luke
3:8......32
3:10-14......32
3:29......8
4:18-19......136
5:17-26......2, 162, 168
5:20......175
5:21......169
5:24......169, 171, 175, 182
5:30-32......31
6:17-49......170
6:27-28......43, 162, 171, 186, 199
6:37......7–8, 113–14, 162, 172, 176
7:36-50......7, 52, 169
7:49......169
9:22......181
11:2-4......6–8, 40, 108, 185
11:4......2, 10, 32, 104, 112–13, 176, 186
12:10......12, 16, 35, 199
13:8......15
15:7......31, 66
15:11-32......75
15:28-30......76
17:2......111
17:3-4......2, 6–9, 16, 31–33, 37, 43, 49, 51, 53, 55–57, 79, 145 162, 166, 176, 185–86, 188, 199

17:25......181
19:45-48......147
22:15......181
22:42......180
23:13......167
23:24......131, 141
23:28-31......202
23:34a......2, 6, 36, 43, 162, 166, 171, 177, 185, 201, 203, 211
23:34b......168
23:43-44......180–81
23:44......204
24:26......181
24:27......31, 56

John
2:6 203
2:13-22......147
8:1-11......27, 173
12:10......8
19:14......203
20:23......8, 34, 43, 189, 199, 201
23:44......8

Acts
1:3......181
2:36......167
3:17, 19......168
3:18......181
7:56......172
7:59-60......172

7:60......167, 172, 203

17:3......181

17:30......168

Romans

5:1 64

5:3 190

1 Corinthians

7:11......15

Ephesians

4:32......115

5:22......185

Philippians

1:29......190

Colossians

3:13......115

1 Peter

2:20-21......190

Revelation

13:18......203